THE MAN FROM COOLIBAH

James Knight, a country boy who was raised in the New South Wales town of Gunnedah, is an award-winning television reporter and bestselling author of biographies, whose career over the last decade has spanned Sydney metropolitan radio, press and television.

James lives in Sydney with his wife and son.

www.knightwriter.com.au

Also by James Knight

Lee²: Lee to the Power of Two

Mark Waugh: The Biography

The Dragon's Journey

Just Doing My Job

A Theory of Moments

Brett Lee: My Life

THE MAN FROM COOLIBAH

The extraordinary outback life of a Northern Territory cattleman

MILTON JONES
AND
JAMES KNIGHT

People of Aboriginal or Torres Strait Islander heritage are advised that this book contains names, descriptions and images of people who are deceased or may be deceased.

Published in Australia and New Zealand in 2012
by Hachette Australia
(an imprint of Hachette Australia Pty Limited)
Level 17, 207 Kent Street, Sydney NSW 2000
www.hachette.com.au

10 9 8 7 6 5 4 3 2 1

National Library of Australia
Cataloguing-in-Publication data

Knight, James.

The man from Coolibah / James Knight.

978 0 7336 2957 0 (pbk.)

Jones, Milton.

Ranch Life – Northern Territory.
Bush pilots – Northern Territory – Biography.
Frontier and pioneer life – Northern Territory.
Cattle – Northern Territory.
Coolibah Station (N.T.)

Northern Territory – Social life and customs.

626.201092

Cover and internal picture sections design by Christabella Designs
Front cover photograph courtesy of Tarsha Hosking Photography
Back cover and inside cover photographs courtesy WTFN Entertainment
Internal photographs: Jones family private collection; WTFN Entertainment; Jenny Jones; James Knight
Map by MAPgraphics
Text design by Bookhouse
Typeset in 12.2/18.6 pt Sabon LT Std by Bookhouse

Printed in Australia by Griffin Press, Adelaide, an Accredited ISO AS/NZS 4001:2004 Environmental Management Systems printer

The paper this book is printed on is certified against the Forest Stewardship Council® Standards. Griffin Press holds FSC chain of custody certification SGS-COC-005088. FSC promotes environmentally responsible, socially beneficial and economically viable management of the world's forests.

To the Northern Territory and its people

THE TOP END

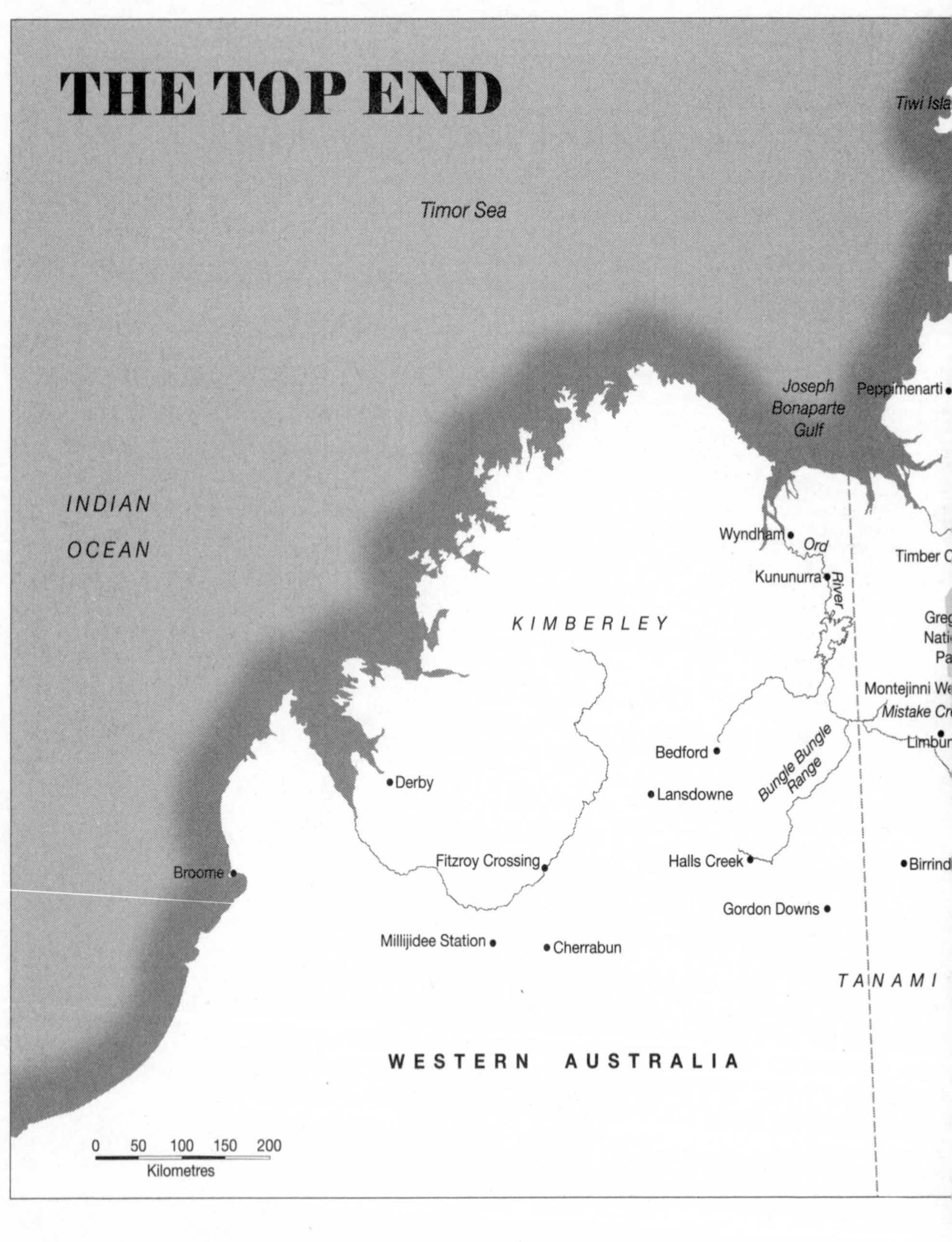
Tiwi Isla
Timor Sea
INDIAN
OCEAN
Joseph
Bonaparte
Gulf
Peppimenarti
Wyndham
Ord
River
Kununurra
Timber C
KIMBERLEY
Greg
Nati
Pa
Montejinni We
Mistake Cr
Limbur
Bedford
Bungle Bungle
Range
Derby
Lansdowne
Fitzroy Crossing
Halls Creek
Birrind
Broome
Gordon Downs
Millijidee Station
Cherrabun
TANAMI
WESTERN AUSTRALIA
0 50 100 150 200
Kilometres

Arafura Sea
Ramingining
Arafura Swamp
Darwin
ARNHEM LAND
Groote Eylandt
Gulf of Carpentaria
Phelp River
Katherine
Moroak
Goondooloo
Roper River
Limmen Bight
Mataranka
Mountain Valley
Menngen Aboriginal Land Trust
libah
ation
Willeroo Station
Larrimah
Maryfield
Limmen Bight River
Delamere
Victoria River Roadhouse
River
Wanimiyn Aboriginal Land Trust
Bauhinia Downs
Victoria River Downs
Hidden Valley
Top Springs
McArthur
Borroloola
Iontejinni East
Victoria River
Camfield Station
NORTHERN TERRITORY
ESERT
Tennant Creek
QUEENSLAND
Kurundi Station
Epenarra Station
Mt Isa
Elkedra Station
Willowra Station

CONTENTS

PREFACE

Australia's most unwanted gatecrashers were the first things I noticed when I got out of the LandCruiser. Cane toads: vomit-yellow, wart-riddled, bony-headed slabs of utter ugliness. There were 30 or more squatting on the grass around a lamppost, waiting for any luckless moth to plummet from the light. Nearby, a generator thump-thump-thumped, and the smell of diesel and dust thickened the air.

'You better meet the boss then,' said Trevor Easton who'd picked me up two hours – or 200 kilometres – earlier in Katherine. Trevor was the station cook who'd already revealed an intriguing concoction: his accent was a mix of slight Geordie sing-song and flat Australian vowels. A story to investigate at a later time.

The boss was sitting in a reclining chair in a slate-floored open area at the rear of his homestead. His bare feet were planted like clock-hands stuck at ten minutes to two. He wore blue Rugger shorts and a clean white short-sleeved shirt that was unbuttoned at the neck to reveal a vee of sun-reddened skin, grey chest hair, and an ample stomach. He put down a glass of white wine, stood up, and we shook hands. Firm grips are a signature of the bush.

I'd initially met Milton Jones about eight months earlier in Darwin. It was the dry season, and the first round of mustering had finished. In the cloudless warmth of a Top End afternoon, well away from the isolation of their usual life, the Jones family settled in for a long lunch. Hours after the first drink was downed I arrived at a restaurant courtyard to find Milton and his wife Cristina in conversation with comers, goers and stayers, including TV executive Daryl Talbot. Five-year-old 'Little' Milton stood leaning against his father. He wore a cowboy hat that dwarfed his head, and he fidgeted with a drinking straw while talking to himself in the daydreaming way a child does. On the other side of the bottle-strewn table, four-and-a-half-month-old Jack, clad only in a nappy, sat on his mum's lap and quietly watched the strange faces.

I sat next to Milton, who was dressed in his town best: jeans, boots, long-sleeved shirt rolled up to just above the wrists. His brown hat with its curling brim rested on the table. In this age of vicarious living and fascination with media-made celebrities, Milton had become well known. He'd shot out of the scrub and into the public spotlight in the reality television program *Keeping Up with the Joneses*, a portrayal of life on Coolibah, the 700 square kilometre cattle station Milton owns about 550 kilometres south of Darwin. From what I'd seen on the TV, Milton was a tough man who didn't suffer fools. I felt a little intimidated by him. After we shook hands, he ignored me while he chatted with a bloke who had a belt buckle the size of a fist. Occasionally Milton glanced at me; at my footwear in particular. I was glad I'd worn my nineteen-year-old RM Williams boots. Although originally a country boy from north-western New South Wales, I had lived most of the last twenty years in Sydney, and was thus more a suburbanite than someone who knew to look at the hinges on a post to determine which way a gate would swing.

I made polite conversation with Cristina about babies, and at one stage overheard Milton say to someone: 'This bloke has come from down south. He wants to write a book about me.' The conversation quickly changed to another topic. Later on, after I'd returned from the Gents, Milton finally spoke to me.

'You haven't ridden a horse for a while,' he said.

We swapped a few words – nothing much, but at least it was a start. He told me he'd been born in 1963 'in the old hospital, before the wind took it.' That wind was Cyclone Tracy, which destroyed much of Darwin and killed 71 people on Christmas Day, 1974. For a moment,

Milton switched his attention to Little Milton and pointed at Darwin Harbour.

'That's a big billabong, that one. You don't get them like that at Coolibah,' said senior to junior.

The lunch meandered into dinner at a cafe. Milton, with barrel chest and rounded shoulders, tucked Jack under his arm as though he were carrying a football. More hours passed. The booze bill mounted.

Next morning, headaches.

And then, over a hotel breakfast we talked about the book proposal which was the idea of Australian publisher, Hachette. Daryl Talbot and Cristina each gave their opinion. After a few 'Watchya reckon?'s Milton said, 'We'll do it, eh.'

I encouraged him to take his time, but he shook his head. The decision was made.

And so I came to be at Coolibah in January 2012 to begin the project. On that first night, with cane toads occasionally banging into the wall behind us, Milton and I made a loose plan for interviews. We'd spend a few hours every day in an air-conditioned demountable that had been constructed for the *Keeping Up with the Joneses* production crew. Apart from these structured sessions, we'd chat wherever else was possible: at the kitchen table; in the front of a LandCruiser; 1000 feet up in a helicopter; in a creek bed freckled with puddles while curling wire around star pickets for a floodgate.

Next morning, the shrill cries of plovers pierced the dawn. Pink smudged the sky, and a pale golden light spilled across ripening pastures of buffel grass. In the distance, steep, red escarpments stood watch, the guardians of the area for untold millennia. Not a bad office.

Milton was heading for a Robinson 44 helicopter when I caught sight of him. 'We'll talk when I get back, eh.'

The rumble of an engine followed. Frogs in the water pipes of the station hands' quarters broke into a chorus of croaks, leaves twirled upwards, demountables trembled, and the R-44 hovered as though collecting a final thought before it turned away with its pilot casting an eye over the day ahead.

When Milton returned a few hours later, a cuppa and a few slices of Trevor-the-cook's beef jerky fuelled him up for our first session. By the end of it, one thing was glaringly apparent: Milton didn't polish his p's and q's with political correctness. Aborigines were 'blackfellas', whites were 'whitefellas' and anyone in between was a 'yellafella'. At various points representatives of each or any of the designated colours might be labelled a 'useless bastard', more a catch-all description than an offensive one. After all, Milton's stable of the vernacular included a truck stuck in mud ('the bogged bastard'); a charging bull ('angry bastard'); slow racehorses ('worst bastards'); American immigration officials ('bastards in uniform');

buffalos in the Top End ('thousands of the bastards'); a helicopter bubble ('tough bastard'), and so on . . .

Some of the comments that Milton makes in this book may trouble people, but it could also be argued that most of those who take offence are looking at his life from the outside in. It's probable they never would have experienced anything at all like remote outback life. Indeed, with the majority of Australia's population crowded into its coastal fringes, few can truthfully say they know much about life in the heart of this country. Milton does. He frequently ended his sentences with, 'You know what I mean?' So often, I didn't.

As a general rule, cattle station people are products of their environment with attitudes and observations that don't genuflect to popular public convention. A tiny example: one day I was being driven back from a floodgate by Lurch, Milton's perennially barefooted, scruffy-bearded gardener. We passed some wallabies that stood their ground just metres from our LandCruiser. I immediately thought to myself how quiet they were.

Lurch had a different assessment. Keeping his lips close together to avoid any chance of dropping his rollie cigarette, he muttered, 'Them bastards haven't been shot at for a while.'

In 1974, author Frank Stevens, who'd conducted extensive research and interviews in the Top End, published a book called *Aborigines in the Northern Territory Cattle*

Industry. An insightful observation from that book is worth quoting:

> *From the castrating of bulls through to the dispatch of beasts to the meatworks for dismembering, the cattle industry might be considered a more brutal pursuit than those followed on the rolling green hills of the dairying country, or by the occupants of suburban villas throughout Australia. Consequently one does not expect the same standards of social decorum to operate in two such widely different areas of society. However, it has been noted by some authors that the needs of the frontier, historically, have produced individuals with distinct personality traits. These have been variously a strong sense of independence and individualism; a preference for the immediate and pragmatic resolution of problems and a bias towards practical adjustment to conflict rather than the use of theory.*

The same holds true today.

The cattle country of the Northern Territory is its own world, and Coolibah is another world within it. Strolling around the Joneses' station on any given day, the casual observer may discover: a vehicle with a .308 rifle resting across the dashboard and a box of soft-point bullets on the seat; a fenced-in swamp with crocodiles; a red-dust road that is also an airstrip; a mother who yells, 'Watch out for snakes,' to her son playing in the garden; an old truckie with skin cancers eroding his face; a meat-shop; a sawn-off cow horn; shark's jaws above a fridge; a shed containing a menagerie of spanners, fan belts and tyres; another with four helicopters, a tinnie, a surf ski, and a rusting LandCruiser whose owner had been known to yank crook teeth out with pliers.

There are stories at every turn. One of my favourite times was when I sat against the outside wall of the station hands' kitchen and listened to Milton roll out the yarns and advice for Beau, his broad-shouldered teenage son from his first marriage. They, together with Little Milton, had just returned from raiding some honeycomb from a 'bloody huge hive' in a gum tree that Milton had bulldozed earlier in the week. As expected, the bees had been 'angry bastards', which rekindled memories for father to pass down to eldest son.

'If you get worked over by itchy grubs get into mud, roll yourself in it, best way to calm your skin . . . There was another time there that I was climbin' up this slope with a .303 slung over me shoulder and I put me hand right on this hornets' nest. Jeeeeesus!'

The memories rolled on while Milton and Beau sucked honey from the combs they'd wrapped and squeezed in a cloth.

'Bloody beautiful, eh.'

During our sessions Milton told many such stories. He brushed over some tough times and tragedies with understatements, but relished other recollections with a mischievous smile that crinkled his dark eyes. He laughed in syllables: one to three chuckles was the general range, four to five after a cracking yarn. At those times he tapped the outside of his left thigh with his left hand. That same hefty mitt, in combination with the right, earned him a reputation for being 'good on the knuckle.' Milton had been a fighter ever since he was a boy. Apparently this wasn't unusual, and as I spoke with more people, I heard the well-worn line: 'If you haven't been in a blue in the Territory you haven't lived in the Territory.' Some of Milton's dust-ups were more serious than others. To this day, he has enemies, and it's likely he always will have. Of all the people I asked about this, the answer from self-confessed 'yellafella', neighbour and long-time family associate, Yidumduma Bill Harney, had the strongest resonance. 'Milton's a tough bugger,' I said.

'Oh well, that's the only way you can make anything happen,' replied Bill.

On the final day of my stay, Milton flew me over Coolibah, a palette of bauhinias, snappy gums, buffel grass, couch, urochloa, red soils, black soils . . . mostly 'marginal country'. The Northern Territory's longest river (some argue it's only the second-longest), the Victoria, runs through the station. Twice we saw the 'chewed-out' carcasses of calves at the water's edge. Near one of the dinner spots we hovered over a 4-metre, maybe longer, saltwater crocodile.

'Biggest bastard I've seen for a while,' said Milton.

It was the wet season. A peculiar one. Some rain had come a few months earlier, and the grass was 'short and sweet.' But now was the time for follow-up. Each day I was there, the temperature nudged 40 degrees Celsius and I could almost drink the air. But despite the brooding skies, only once did I hear rain drumming on a tin roof.

'I've never been able to drive across the river in January,' said Milton. 'But I reckon within a week she'll be comin'. You can always tell because the blood finches start nestin'.'

We eventually saw the rain, but not where we expected. A few weeks later, we met again in Tamworth, New South Wales. The Jones family had driven about 3500 kilometres from Coolibah to attend a stock horse sale. 'Hughie' sent it down for days. Floods spread across southern Queensland and northern New South Wales, and Milton, Cristina and their two boys stayed put in a spanking new gooseneck trailer that had its own bed and kitchen.

It was there that Milton and I had our final formal interview. As much as I may have learnt more about him during that chat, the most valuable time was spent when I took him to Gunnedah, 40 or so minutes' drive away. This was where I grew up. We went to a cattle sale where top prices touched a healthy $2.30 a kilo, food for thought for a bloke caught in the uncertainty over the future of the Territory's live cattle trade. We also visited a farmer who'd embraced technology with the use of computer-controlled boom sprays, heated silos and wide caterpillar tracks on harvesters to reduce soil compaction.

'Bloody interestin',' said Milton. It was a short statement but I could see he was deep in thought afterwards.

On our way back, we stopped for lunch. The beef man was keen to taste the area's produce. Lamb cutlets were on the menu.

'You've gotta eat what's local,' he declared.

On the road to Tamworth Milton stared out the window. This was a vastly different landscape from his backyard. On one ridge we looked towards the black soil sweeps of the Liverpool Plains, some of the richest farmland in Australia. Such a picture is said to have inspired Dorothea Mackellar's famous poem, 'My Country'. Its depiction of sunburnt land, ragged mountains and far horizons could all be applied to Coolibah, but to my mind, two lines in particular stand out:

All you who have not loved her,
You will not understand

* * *

Some of the stories Milton told me for this book involved people who are no longer part of his life. A few have drifted away, and others have turned on their heels and vowed never to look back. Then there are those who can't return; an all-too-frequent line I heard during our interviews was: 'He's dead now too. Geez, we've lost a few.'

Where possible, the stories throughout this book have been corroborated, but not all. Furthermore, some of the events in these pages may not be in their correct chronological order; Milton, and others interviewed have had so many experiences – some of which happened 60 or more years ago – it's understandable that their memories aren't always clear on times and places.

Mention must also be made of the particular speech patterns to be found in the Top End. In addition to the ubiquitous use of 'bastards', in interviews consonants were dropped off the ends of words, and there was never a need to worry about the trivialities of grammar. These features, together with some unique turns of phrase – 'Man didn't know much about horse, and horse didn't know much about man' – and some regional uses of words – 'that fella was a bit myall' (meaning slow or stupid) – help make Milton who he is, and what he represents: an authentic Australian bush character. For ease of reading, I have reinstated some of the missing consonants in longer quoted passages; shorter ones I have generally transcribed untouched. Readers can use their own imaginations as to how many great Australian adjectives (expletives) have been deleted.

The Man from Coolibah is not a definitive biography, nor an exposé. Rather, it is a whistle through the life and times of a bloke who has taken many a tumble to land on his feet. He is a self-made man who has undoubtedly been helped by others along the way, but as his wife Cristina told me: 'He always would have succeeded no matter who was there. Milton knows how to succeed. He is a smart man.' And a man who, when described in the language of his environment, has had a big life.

PART ONE

THE EARLY YEARS

CHAPTER 1
THE JONESES

When passing down stories from one generation to the next, memory can be an unreliable log book, and the life of Milton's father, the grandly named Stanley Knight Jones, is a case in point. Too many years have faded to know precisely all the bumps and turns of Stanley's life; nevertheless, the tales about him that have survived have become both treasured family heirlooms and poignant statements of a bygone age.

Stan, as he became known, was born in 1919 in Thargomindah, a speck of a place in south-west Queensland which despite its diminutive size had reason to be mentioned in the same breath as Paris and London: it was acknowledged as being only the third settlement in the world to power its streetlights using hydro-electricity. Aside from an artesian bore, a generator and a glimmer of international recognition, its character was defined by its location in the Channel Country, an arid region with a vast web of waterways which big rains could transform into a virtual inland sea. The Aborigines had lived in and traversed the region for thousands of years, and in the mid-nineteenth century it became a popular thoroughfare for explorers, including the ill-fated Burke and Wills expedition. Their reports helped encourage pastoralists to seek opportunities; at first sheep dominated, but by the early 1900s cattle had taken over. Among the opportunists was Sidney Kidman, later known as 'The Cattle King', who recognised the Channel Country as an integral link in his 'chain of supply' where his stock could be fattened and spelled on their way to southern markets.

Stan's father, John Josiah Jones, worked for the Kidman empire in some capacity; again the years have corroded knowledge of what exactly he did. Nevertheless, his job and the outback environment undoubtedly had a strong influence on young Stan.

As Australia moved out of the era of the Great War and into that of the Great Depression, Stan battled hardships of his own after he was kicked in the head by a horse. He was nursed for days by his mother in the back of a sulky while the family travelled to seek treatment. Stan never fully recovered his hearing. The accident was the introduction to a series of tangles with bad health and physical peculiarities. During his childhood he suffered from lead poisoning, believed to have been caused by ingesting lead-based house-paint, and in his teenage years his first job as a striker for a blacksmith earned him a small wage and a large calcified lump on his right shoulder that would stay with him for life. By that stage, the young man, who'd been a good wrestler at school, yearned for adventure.

So, in the best bush traditions of the day, and probably helped by his father's Kidman connections, he went droving. It's not known if this was before or after he and his brother, Llawrence, were rejected for military service in World War II. One had a bung ear and the other a shortage of fingers after a shooting mishap.

Adversity continued to mould Stan. One of his matter-of-fact hand-me-down stories to his family was about the fall he had off a camp-horse in the Channel Country. He'd been walking a mob of cattle by himself, and with no help within cooee he had to get on with the job. This was no small ask for someone – perhaps only in his teenage years – who thought he'd broken both his legs. He continued for weeks. Each morning he'd whistle up his horse, which would come alongside him and stand quietly while Stan pulled himself up into the saddle. At night he climbed down, weary and in pain. The result was a bowed left leg, a legacy every bit as permanent as his lumpy shoulder.

Despite such ill fortune, Stan was at home in the long paddock. He spent a dozen or more years working mobs through Queensland, the Northern Territory and South

Australia. At one time he said he did fourteen straight months in the saddle. Every single day: walking cattle one way, then bringing the horses back, picking up another mob and going again. His only complaint: boils on the backside.

As the family story goes, Stan still found time to kick up his Cuban heels. Brisbane and the Gold Coast were his favourite spots, but Sydney shaped his destiny. In the early 1950s while in a bar, he met a slender brown-haired 'stunner' from Mount Morgan, just south of Rockhampton, Queensland. Beef country. She was already married, but new love enticed her away, and in late February 1952, Mary Dawson walked down the aisle to become a Jones. Twelve days later, she and Stan had their first child, Jenny.

When the relationship initially became serious Stan knew he had a decision to make: follow his heart or the stock routes? Irony answered emphatically: in choosing to settle down, the man who so cherished the endless space of the outback became a prison guard in Sydney. As time went on, not only the inmates felt trapped. Stan found the call of his upbringing irresistible, so he applied for jobs on the other side of the Great Divide, and weeks after Jenny's birth he accepted an offer that would flip his life again. The giant British-owned company, Vestey, whose international portfolio included powerful meat and pastoral operations in Australia, needed a manager for one of its stations, Gordon Downs, and its outlying property, Birrindudu; in all, more than two million acres that straddled the Northern Territory–Western Australia border. To the west, the land reached into the Kimberley region, and to the east, it was on the fringes of the Tanami Desert, a haunting land of spinifex, termite mounds, rocks, sand and salt lakes. Stan the drover was on the move again, this time with the responsibility of raising a young family whose numbers quickly grew; by 1958 there were three more children: Randall, Llawrence and their little sister, Terry. It was another five years before the last, Milton Stanley Knight Jones, arrived on 30 September 1963. The nurses at Darwin Hospital christened him 'Prince Charming'; he was a healthy, fat baby.

Milton was cared for by his mother at Gordon Downs, and, as was the way with each Jones child, he had an Aboriginal nursemaid. Much of his time was also spent with sister Jenny whenever she returned for holidays from boarding school in Brisbane. She was eleven years older than her baby brother, and enjoyed her responsibilities, yet she could never have foreseen how those early days would establish a relationship that would challenge her maturity and sense of devotion in the future.

Milton himself has no first-hand memories of Gordon Downs or his father at that time. Instead, he has turned to Stan's recollections and those of others. Some stories are tragic; none more so than the one about the Aboriginal woman who went missing in the area with her baby. She was found dead a few days later with her child still alive and sucking on a breast, or as Milton explained, 'swingin' off the milk.' Other stories beggar belief, including the strapping of a dead man to the axle of a plane, and then flying him to the nearest town, Halls Creek, 110 kilometres away. As macabre as these recollections may be, they underline a critical point about Milton: he has lived an altogether different life.

Thankfully, there are many happier yarns. Among them was the day a 'yellafella' came looking for work at Gordon Downs from another Vestey station. The new man proved his worth by breaking the spirit of a chestnut stallion that had already hurled a few would-be riders into the dust. Now, nearly 60 years later, Yidumduma Bill Harney still has vivid memories of the day.

'I put me foot on the side iron and he bucked like hell and I said: "Open the gate." They opened the gate, the horse was buckin' and I was screamin' and yellin', swingin' me hat, bashin' him to go faster. And after a while I brought this horse back, he was puffin' and snortin', and Stan said: "Bill, you're my man!" That's what he said to me: "You're my man!"'

Bill now lives on the Menngen Aboriginal Land Trust which borders Coolibah station. Skin sags under his eyes, and beneath his small-brimmed hat dark reddish hair flows to his shoulders. He says he is in his eighties. That is neither the truth nor a lie because he doesn't actually know when he was born; it was only when he'd needed to apply for a driver's licence as a young man that a policeman gave him an official date of birth. (In some books, including his own, Bill's birth year is acknowledged as 1936.) Bill was born the son of a Wardaman woman, Ludi Yibuluyma, and a white man, Bill Harney, whose deeds forged a Territory legend; Bill senior was a drover, a World War I soldier who fought on the Western Front, a road-builder, cattle stealer, welfare officer, story-teller and a popular author.

At a time when co-habitation between white and black was illegal, Bill senior moved on, leaving his son to be raised on Willeroo station, about 100 kilometres east of Coolibah. His mother rubbed him with charcoal to make him look blacker in the hope he would avoid being recognised as a 'half-caste' by government authorities; this was the age of the Stolen Generations, when paler Aboriginal children were at high risk of being taken from their parents by government agencies as part of the then-current policy of assimilation. Bill avoided such a fate, and was 'grown up' by his Aboriginal stepfather, Joe Jormorji, who taught him the traditions of his people.

As he grew older Bill was linked with 'whitefella ways'. A Scotsman, 'Old Peter Hogg', in a stock camp taught him how to read by using the labels of a tomato sauce bottle and fruit tin. Bill then practised writing with pieces of charcoal on flat rocks. And every night, he reckoned,

'I was teachin' meself in me own brains.' While having these abilities pleased him, nothing excited him as much as developing station skills. He learnt how to spay cows, build fences and yards, fix windmills, make saddles, ride and break in horses. All the learning hours inevitably led to his becoming a stockman. For many Wardaman men, and indeed many Aboriginal men in the cattle-growing areas of the Northern Territory and beyond, each year was divided between droving and mustering usually under the direction of whites, then returning to go 'walkabout' – looking after country – during the wet season.

Bill reckoned he became 'cattle mad; they were my dream.' This self-described 'passion' took him beyond Willeroo and eventually to Gordon Downs, where he went on to become head stockman for a while at Birrindudu. He developed a strong bond with Milton's father, who was known by the Aborigines as 'Hard and Fast', a reference to the first time they saw him heaving a two-man cross-cut saw while building a stockyard.

'Stan would say: "Come on, you gotta work hard and fast. You pull, I push, you pull, I push, hard and fast,"' said Bill.

Apart from a two-storey homestead, there was little infrastructure when Stan arrived at Gordon Downs. He took to changing this with his 'hard and fast' philosophy. Of only moderate height, but strong through the chest and shoulders, he cut a distinctive figure with his trousers hitched up by braces, shirt sleeves rolled neatly up to the elbows and frequently a cigarette clinging to his lips. He bent his back from the earliest hours, and he expected nothing less from his staff, the majority of whom were Aboriginal. A vegetable garden, yards, stables and several other buildings all sprang up, but it was the construction of a fence around the homestead that became station legend. Bill remembered it 'was a magnificent wall with all flat rock on top of one another. You know them Aborigines thought it was great fun buildin' it.' Fun or not, the fence was a stark example of a different time and place. According to Jenny Jones, 'It was to segregate the blackfellas from our homestead area.'

Jenny now lives in Cairns, far north Queensland. In a life that has included farming, truck driving, race-horse training, nursing, and working with asylum-seekers, she says her biggest achievement was her close bond with her father. The stories Stan told her, and the vivid memories she has of her childhood evoke images that today's world might struggle to comprehend.

'There were about 250 Aborigines on the station. The blackfella camp was the other side of the wall. There was a lot of syphilis and gonorrhoea, so Dad had to "shortarm" them [inspect the men's penises]. Then he built a shower, and he had to supervise showers daily, they were so filthy. He did it for the wellbeing of everybody. Mum and Dad had a full medical kit, morphine, everything. Remember, there were no telephones, no ringing the doctor up. When you were in trouble you were a long way to Halls Creek by dirt road in a truck or a weapon carrier [old army vehicle, similar to a jeep], and it wasn't only an hour or two, it was *hours*. One night Dad was away in the stock camp and we [the Jones children] were in bed with the old girl [their mother Mary] and of course the generator is off and it's very dim light. This old gin [Aboriginal woman] came up, head wide open and blood dripping from fighting. Got hit with a nulla-nulla [club].'

Jenny Jones is writing her own book, so only a glimpse of her recollections can be revealed here. Importantly though, she said Stan taught all his children to be 'firm but kind' with the Aborigines. At the time, those designated 'full-bloods' and 'half-castes' who worked received a type of keep for themselves and their families. On Friday afternoons they went to the station store to be given a variety of goods including flour, tea, sugar and clothes. Then they went to the yards for beef. Some workers were paid small amounts of money, which was normally used to purchase 'nicki-nicki' (tobacco). Alcohol wasn't allowed.

Keep and payment varied from station to station. It was just one example of the feudal-like relationship between white Australian pastoralists and Aborigines, a history that includes many dark episodes. Coolibah had its share, but as for Gordon Downs under Stan and Mary Jones . . .

'Stan was very good and polite to people,' said Bill Harney. 'You know, he give them [the Aborigines] the right directions, he took the lead and he showed them what to do. They liked him so much. His missus used to go to the Salvation Army place collectin' clothes. The men and the women, they reckoned it was ideal.'

Mary, with a treadle sewing machine, added to the collection by making her own dresses for the Aboriginal women. This was when she wasn't working in the kitchen or cleaning; she was a meticulous housekeeper who was also fastidious about her own appearance.

The Joneses were fond of social occasions, and none were livelier than the Gordon Downs Christmas parties. Everyone, black and white, on the station was invited. There were numerous races along a rock-strewn road: 100-yard sprints, three-legged events, and Bill recalled 'jumpin' like a kangaroo' in empty chaff sacks. Jockeys of all shapes and sizes steered camels and donkeys over a dirt racetrack; there were boxing bouts, spear and boomerang throwing contests, and painful tugs-of-war where men would stand toe-to-toe with a belt or bull-strap tied over their heads, and the winner would be the one who, using only his neck strength, pulled the other across a line drawn on the ground. Bill's favourite event was the bull-fighting, a memory that prompted him to imitate the snorts and bellows of an angry beast while he recalled the scene.

'It was two fellas head to head chargin' like bulls. You'd try to hit him down or to lift him. You couldn't get up – you only had hands and knees, that's all. You'd have a time limit and the fella who tipped the other over was the winner. It was great to see. If anyone had a long nose, he'd have scratches all over his nose because he'd have to get down underneath his belly to lift anyone, and then anyone with a flat nose would have scratches all over his forehead from tryin' to do the same thing. It was great.'

The other main events on the social calendar were race meetings. One of the biggest in the Kimberley region was the 'Negri Picnics' where for four days every August the trails of dust led only to the Linacre Course at Nicholson station, the northern neighbour of Gordon Downs. People would come from hundreds of kilometres away for the carnival that had 'grass fed' horseraces, a rodeo and campdrafting competitions. It was there that Stan, wearing a smart pork-pie hat that he reserved for only the best occasions – and always tipped when being introduced to a woman – basked in every moment. Although riding stock horses with cattle was in his blood, training thoroughbreds to pin their ears back and gather up country in a blur was when he truly felt alive.

'He told me he bred and trained a lot of horses at Gordon Downs for Vestey's; they imported blood horses there,' said Milton. 'He was a smart trainer. He used to get the gins and give them an extra stick of nicki-nicki if they brought in a sugar bag full of spinifex seed. He'd feed the horses that to give 'em a bit of sting. He won a lot of races that way because his horses had a bit of guts in 'em. He had trophies, lots of trophies. He was also one of the first to ever put a horse on a truck and take it to the races. Before that, they used to send blackfellas in the lead and they would trot the horses to the track a few days before the races.'

Stan was so devoted to his horses that, when his other jobs allowed, he headed out well before sunrise for track-work along stretches of road on Gordon Downs. His jockeys were Aborigines, probably in their teenage years.

'There was Jock Mosquito,' remembered Bill Harney. 'Old Stan would say, "Jock, come on you mosquito, you can fly like a mosquito." There was another young one, Tomato, yeah Tomato Gordon. Stan was a trainer for the human and he was trainer for the horse.'

It's worth further noting the names of Stan's riders. While 'Jock' was simply short for jockey, 'Gordon' was a term of identification. It was common in those days for white station owners or managers to give their Aboriginal workers the same surname as the property where they worked; to this day some of their descendants continue to carry those names.

Racing gave Stan an outlet from his work. Bill reckoned his boss delighted in the combination of horses and speed.

'One day I went with Stan to have a look at a stock camp. And I stood at the side of this buggy and we had swags and everything on top. We were drivin' along and all these camels were lyin' down and these horses [pulling the buggy] had never seen a camel before and God almighty they took off, and Stan said: "Hang on, Bill, hang on." There were swags flyin' off and billies have gone and buckets have gone. And I'm hangin' on pretty tight. It was scary. And Stan says: "Isn't this good fun?" And I say: "No!" And he has put a whip on the horses to make 'em go faster. Oh God almighty!'

Gordon Downs was established in the 1860s. It was initially a sheep station. But by Stan's time, Shorthorn beef cattle had taken over. In the pragmatic terms dictated by the balance sheet, stock was money. However, this wasn't a business protected by a lock and key. Instead, the land itself was the cash register upon which the pounds and pence were free to wander for months at a time. When it came time to collect and count numbers, even the very best cattlemen were challenged, for no two musters were ever alike. Gordon Downs had a mix of country, from spinifex plains to lignum and turpentine scrub that could rip the shirt off an unwary rider's back. Deviant gullies that had a tendency to appear when horses were at full stride added further obstacles for the stockmen. From Bill's experience there were few tougher places to pull cattle in from. One moment small mobs could be seen on the flats, the next 'the tricky little mongrels' would be rushing into the gullies and out of sight after hearing the horses or voices. It was there that Bill passed onto Stan a valuable practice he'd learnt from another stockman. It concerned the use of a 'killer', a beast that was shot to provide meat for the station or a stock camp.

'You take a killer's blood in a bucket, and you spread all his blood all around here, and you take all these coachers [quiet cattle] and you let 'em go there. And they'd be cryin' for the blood. God, they make a lot of noise: *oh, oh, oh, ohhhhhh!*' said Bill, producing a sound that could best be described as a blend of a pig's grunt and a foghorn. 'Everyone was just goin' *ohh, ohh, oohhh!* That would encourage all the other ones comin' in from the scrub, and they all put on a turn then. And anyway, then we'd bring this blood all the way down to where we were with another lot of herd and the other mob would come cryin' all the way. And we'd come in behind 'em and push 'em over. Bulls and everything. All cryin', everybody cryin'. That's the only way we could get 'em out of the scrub, cryin' for the blood. You'd see them lopsided with their heads to their side puttin' on a different show. Then, after the blood run out they'd be lookin' round and you'd see 'em thinkin', Oh, the men got us. Too late! Some of them old bulls were really fiery then.'

Jenny Jones says her father delivered 6000 head each year to the meatworks, the most 'fats' of any Vestey station in the area. This required walking various numbers at different times to the Western Australian port town of Wyndham, about 550 kilometres to the north. It's believed the journey sometimes took several weeks. On other occasions walking could be a dramatically different proposition that revealed how savage the country and its climate could be. During one desperately dry year on Gordon Downs, Stan and about 50 stockmen took 14 000 head – or thereabouts – off the station and went in search of adequate water and feed. They passed through Birrindudu, and other Vestey stations, Limbunya and Waterloo. They were on the move for months, a relentless grind of setting up camps and assigning 'watches' to keep an eye on the cattle every hour of the day. There was one directive above all others: if the situation demanded it, shoot the calves and weaners, but keep the cows (breeders) alive. The memories have faded too much to know how many times a .303 bullet cut the numbers.

Although witnessing life and death on a daily basis is often the reality for those on a remote station, a brush with both had unexpectedly dramatic consequences for the Jones family. It happened so quickly: a horse that was tied to the children's slippery slide pulled back without warning, and in the crash that followed, Terry, who was about five or six, was crushed across the stomach. The Royal Flying Doctor Service was called, and when the emergency plane approached, Stan had to light flares on the airstrip. The pilot, doctor and nurse stayed that night, and flew out the next morning with their patient who'd been vomiting blood. Stan began a day-long drive to the hospital at Derby not knowing whether his youngest daughter would survive.

She did. But as Terry recovered, a decision was made: after twelve years at Gordon Downs, Stan knew it was time to take his wife and children away. It was 1964. Unbeknownst to the family, the decision marked the beginning of a period that was to have longstanding consequences for everyone, especially baby Milton.

CHAPTER 2
YOUNG MILTON

After leaving Gordon Downs, Stan took to droving a mob that was never allowed to settle down for too long: it was his own family. As time passed, the numbers dwindled as each member went their separate way; being the youngest, Milton had to stay with his parents for the longest in a relationship that was frequently on the move. In the first twelve or so years of his life, Milton was to have no fewer than eight homes.

The first stop was Rockhampton, but when a job opportunity for Stan fell through, the Joneses headed west to Longreach, central Queensland, where Stan returned to droving cattle and sheep. Later, he accepted the manager position at El Rita station about 450 kilometres to the north. His family stayed behind, but joined him when they could, usually in school holidays.

During this period Milton grew from being a white-haired baby – the neighbours called him 'Snowflakes' – to a little boy with a penchant for creating mischief. One day Mary couldn't find her three-year-old, but discovered where he'd been when flames leapt from a mattress and bedspread in an outdoor area at the back of the weatherboard house. A frantic search located the culprit striking matches under Jenny's bed. The incident gave rise to a favourite family saying: 'Where there's smoke, there's a Jones.'

In pursuit of adventure, Milton found a willing partner in Terry, five years older, but closest in age to him of all the siblings. Their lively spirits prompted Mary to develop a unique strategy at El Rita.

'Because the house was so big and Mum was always scared we'd run off, she used to lock us in a meat safe when we had our afternoon sleeps,' said Terry who now lives in Katherine. 'I was on the bottom shelf and Milton on the top. We each had a little pillow and a rug. It was quite a big meat safe, would have been a couple of metres high. That's where Mum would cool down all the beef and bread.'

The Joneses settled for just a few years before Stan seemingly showed signs of setting deeper foundations when he bought a service station at Ranges Bridge in Queensland's south-east, just a matter of hours from Brisbane and minutes from the rural service town of Dalby. It was 1967, and Milton was nearly four, old enough to begin collecting his own memories. One of his earliest concerned his introduction to a formal education.

'Mum and Dad drove me into town [Dalby] and dropped me off. The next day they tried to put me on the bus, and I didn't want to go. I thought you only had to do one day of school. That was it. Right from the first day I'd barred it.'

Milton battled through the three R's, while reserving most of his energies for home life. There was a paddock to run in; stables for hide-and-seek; horses, dogs and a pet calf named Burri to play with. He also had brothers and sisters to annoy in the 'little shit' manner that the youngest of any family is duty-bound to inherit.

As soon as any Jones child was able to keep their balance well enough, Stan would put them on a bareback horse and begin their equine education. They were taught to stand up, jump old tyre tubes, bring their mounts to a gallop and race each other. Terry became 'horsey mad' but at times Milton needed some encouragement to join her. 'Not unless we play cowboys and itchy bums,' he'd say. Then they'd be off, chasing each other around trees and through the creeks. Milton had come to believe all these things were usual for a boy his age, but there was one alluring pastime that surely made him the luckiest kid in the district: the raiding of lollies from the service station. Jellies, caramels, chocolates, all-day-suckers. The successful theft of a jar was followed by a locked bedroom door, and a will – and also often a willing accomplice, Terry – to keep eating until there was no need to put the lid back on. Such behaviour not only prompted a heady spike in blood sugar, but raised the ire of Stan, an old-fashioned disciplinarian.

'Milton and I used to get a few floggings,' said Terry. 'We were always up to something. Just trying to test the limits, I suppose. Dad was very strict with our manners. We weren't able to have our hands on the dinner table. He used to say, "Are you an uncle or an aunt yet? If you are, you're allowed to put your elbows on the table, but if you're not . . ." He'd whack our knuckles with a jockey whip.'

Revenge comes in myriad ways. To this day Terry wonders if anyone has ever found three whips hidden in a wall cavity at the diner of the Ranges Ridge service station.

Stan was a hard man. Just *how* hard he was on each of his children is open to their individual interpretation. Jenny's view is perhaps an apt overall reflection: 'When Dad spoke it was: How high do you want us to jump?' Jenny believes she came in for the toughest treatment. Because of the demands of running a 24-hour business, Stan pulled his eldest child out of school. She was fifteen. By that stage she'd met a local grain farmer, Gavin Dempsey, and was in the early stages of courting; initially she'd turned down any offers to go out because she'd been too afraid to ask her father for permission. The relationship was eventually allowed to develop, albeit with the considerable involvement, and undoubted interference, of a third party.

'When we started going out we had to take Milton,' said Jenny. 'We only had a ute so Milton would sit between us, and sometimes I used to get quite shitty because I might want to kiss my new boyfriend, but couldn't because there was this little kid in the car! Milton was a part of us; he was glued to us really.'

Despite his edict that no daughter of his would marry before she turned 21, Stan softened his views when Gavin formally asked for Jenny's hand. After being summoned to the fuel pump to hear her father's decision, Jenny was told: 'He's a good hard worker. He'll look after you.' She was just sixteen and married a year later. At the wedding reception, Milton the page boy ignored the usual etiquette for the occasion and had to be whisked away during the speeches after he'd been caught sneaking mouthfuls of beer from any glass he could find.

The marriage further developed a three-way bond: husband, wife and an 'instant son'. While Jenny's influence was obvious, Milton acknowledges Gavin also played 'a big part in my childhood.' This was no ordinary relationship between a young man and a boy. Instead, it was partly built on the ethic that Stan so admired: hard work. Milton wasn't only someone to have fun with, he was an extra set of hands that could be put to good use. One time Gavin needed to get his tractor and ute from the service station to the farm, a distance down the back roads of about 10 kilometres. To avoid an extra trip, he stood Milton up in the driver's seat in the ute, knocked the automatic into first gear, and told his novice driver to follow him. The only instructions were: 'If anything goes wrong, just turn it off.' So, a seven-year-old, barely able to see over the dashboard, began an occupation that would see him graduate to wheeling tractors and trucks as well. Although it was easy for a boy to consider these experiences as an adventure, hindsight tells Milton he did his share of work, at times with some risk.

'I remember this old Chamberlain tractor. You'd pull this handle back on the old clutch and pull her into gear. I was ploughin', went to sleep and went through a few fences. I found out where I was by followin' the plough tracks all the way back. It was night-time, black soil plains. You don't know where you are.'

While he assumed adult responsibilities, Milton was still very much a child discovering who he was, *and* what he could get away with.

'He was a little rogue,' said his brother Randall, who remembers taking seven-year-old Milton to the Dalby show. 'The showies had a monkey on a chain tied to a peg in the ground. The kids were crowded around, looking at it and feeding it. Milton started teasing it. The monkey sat still, pulled in the chain, and sat near the peg as Milton kept teasing it. Then suddenly the monkey jumped out onto Milton's head and started pulling his hair, and scratching him and biting him and Milton's screaming till they pulled it off him. He had teeth marks.'

As with the 'showies' who lived their lives on the move, Stan eventually decided to roll on again; he'd learnt that pumping petrol didn't fit in with who he was, so he sold up and returned to Longreach for more stock work. The family, minus Jenny, went with him. Milton was about eight, perhaps a little older. Randall and Llawrence, well into their teenage years and students of Stan's spit-on-your-hands-and-get the-job-done teaching, were keen to enter the adult world, once again leaving Milton and Terry to amuse themselves. Not all went smoothly, especially when Terry began dating. Stan allowed her to go to the movies with a boyfriend once, on the proviso they came straight home afterwards. Milton and a friend also went, but long before the final credits rolled they slipped out and returned to Stan, telling him the session had finished. When Terry came back half an hour later she received a grilling from the 'old fella', much to Milton's glee.

With his trouble-making trait well established, it seemed inevitable that Milton would run into a clenched fist. On a Sunday afternoon at the Longreach pool, Terry was chatting with a 'cornfed' – the name given to boys who attended a particular school – when she heard a ruckus nearby. She rushed over to find her little brother threshing against a bigger, older opponent. Terry stepped in, threw a haymaker and the fight was over. Milton was impressed: 'That was really good, Tair!' But Terry was so shaken she began to cry, petrified about what Stan would do if he found out. She made Milton promise not to say anything, but the moment they were home the words rushed out: 'Dad you shoulda seen Terry knock this fella out!'

After hearing the story, the Jones patriarch declared: 'I'm glad you stuck up for your brother.' Nothing else needed to be said.

Before long, it was time for the Joneses to move again. The destination: Katherine, nearly 2000 kilometres away, where contract mustering was a suitable lure for Stan. He didn't have to be in a hurry because he'd saved up a healthy swag of dollars; this was a man who preferred money on the hip to money in the bank, which had led him to stashing his hard-earned in some unlikely places – including among the chaff in the horse's feed drums at Ranges Bridge. He reckoned having a ready supply of capital gave him choices. A Chevrolet Pontiac was testament to that. He saw it, he liked it, he bought it. Deal done.

As the Joneses began the haul west, the Chev and a caravan were towed behind a Bedford truck carrying the kids, who mostly lay on swinging wire beds that were tied to the crate with hobble chains. There was also room for a few horses.

While Randall went ahead in another truck, the rest of the family bumped along dirt roads until they neared Min Min, a remote spot in the Channel Country named after the mystical lights that unpredictably came and went, often dancing across the horizon, at times even giving the impression of following travellers. Milton doesn't recall seeing any illusions. Instead he saw an outback curse: relentless rain, a flood, and a family literally stuck in the mud. Accounts vary as to how long the Joneses, with their vehicles bogged, were forced to camp near a swollen waterway. Ten days, a fortnight, a month, maybe more. Milton remembers it was long enough for a plane to 'drop off some tucker', although the marooned family seemed self-sufficient during the long days of waiting.

'We had our ponies, so we used to trot along the creek and run these sheep down, cut a throat and bring one back,' Milton recalled. 'Terry, Llawrence and me; we just used to move around on our ponies a lot of the time. We spent hours up at the old Min Min pub pokin' through the bottles, real old stuff. [The Min Min pub had burnt down in 1917 or thereabouts.] I remember the flies. Jeeesus Christ! You know the black flies? They ate the corners of your eyes out.'

At night, with Stan and Mary in the caravan, the others lay down on their beds in the truck and listened to the rain hammering on their makeshift tarpaulin roof.

'Rain all bloody night. Just rained and rained and rained,' said Milton.

Finally it eased, and the Joneses were on their way again. They crossed a creek only to be defeated by the 'bloody biggest boghole' on the other side. Just as it seemed another long wait was likely, three graders were seen heading towards them from the west. Apparently word had spread through the area that a bloke by the name of Stan Jones was stuck. That meant something to the man with the graders. Many years before, he'd been helped by Stan, who'd gone out of his way on the long paddock to move some cattle. The result was a repayment of kindness: the bogged vehicles were pulled out, then hooked in a line behind the graders and hauled for kilometres until the going was better. With some handshakes and a belch of diesel the family were on the move again.

Milton wasn't yet ten when he was introduced to Katherine. The region was known by Aborigines as a traditional meeting place for the Jawoyn, Dagoman and Wardaman people, but for Stan and Mary it was the place for pulling apart. Their marriage had become fragile, and while they sought solutions, their youngest children were increasingly left to themselves.

Milton and Terry maintained a close bond. Where one was, the other could generally be found. This, however, didn't mean their relationship was eternally cheerful. On the occasions they went for a drive with Mary, turns were taken to sit in the front of the family's Austin car. Terry's assumption of the prime spot always came at a risk: hair in long plaits was too much to resist for a tormenting brother's hands.

'Mum used to say we fought like Kilkenny cats. We used to fight all the time. That's why Milton is so bald, because I used to lift him up by his hair,' said Terry, laughing.

The pair showed little regard for their education. 'A stash of fags under the railway bridge' was an ample reason to wag on some days. On others, the greatest commitment was shown before arriving at the school gates: Milton and Terry would strip off, put their clothes and books above their heads, and swim across the Katherine River to avoid a longer trip on foot from their leased farm.

The river and its surrounds were their main playgrounds. Thoughts of danger rarely troubled them, and it has only been in adulthood that Milton has reflected, 'When you hear about the crocodiles that have been pulled out of there, I suppose we could have been lucky.'

They were even more fortunate when another incident is reflected upon. The harmless days of an 'itchy bum' waiting to ambush a cowboy with imaginary weapons had been replaced by boys sprinting towards puberty with guns in their hands. In the hierarchy of firepower, the air rifle – some may know it as a pea rifle or slug gun – is a lowly member. Typically it uses compressed air to fire small lead pellets one at a time; some readers who have fired one may be reminded of the tin-duck shooting galleries that were once popular at country shows. However, the desire to win a stuffed toy or a 'World's Greatest Lover' mug wasn't in mind when Milton and a mate, Barry, launched into a river bank war, ducking in and out from behind trees.

'You'll get a flogging. What happens if you turn up with one eye!' warned Terry.

Milton replied with a mix of theatre and aggression. 'You just fish, bitch,' he said, pointing the gun at her.

These days the two make jokes about it, but the seriousness of the incident was emphasised by the heavy hands of both Stan and Barry's father. Terry was right. There were some sore backsides that night.

Cowboys and Indians, swimming, fishing, digging tunnels, riding to the Aboriginal camp and chasing the giggling kids before hauling them up and taking them for a trot . . . the river was a place to escape from an increasingly disturbed home life.

Horses also offered a distraction. Building on the skills they'd been taught by Stan, Terry and Milton commonly rode bareback, sometimes with nothing more than baling twine as a rein and bit. The main exception was when they adhered to the saddle and stirrups convention of the local pony club, where the star was their little blue stallion, Wonga, whose neck was always swathed in ribbons at gymkhanas.

When all four of the younger Joneses in Katherine spent time together, a popular pursuit was pig-catching. Randall and Llawrence were both good riders, and examples for the others to follow as they galloped at breakneck speeds to corner wild squealers.

From afar, it was a free-spirited upbringing, but in reality the cracks were all too wide. Milton was about eleven when Stan and Mary told their two youngest children the marriage was over.

'I can kind of remember that things were going pretty sour,' recalled Terry. 'Mum and Dad sat us down and asked us: "Who do you want to go with?" And Milton said: "I want to go with Terry." And then I said: "I'll go with whoever has the horses." So, that's how we kind of stuck with Dad.'

That afternoon Terry told Milton to pack up some belongings. Then, with Wonga and his stablemate, King Cossack, they left.

'We had a few little goods and chattels in there but we didn't have a lot,' said Terry. 'We were riding, riding, riding. I remember it was wet season because there was plenty of feed and water for the horses. When we pulled up I said to Milton: "Where the hell are we going to?" He said: "I dunno." We didn't know what we were doing; we just wanted to get away from the situation. We went for a few hours, and we rode home again.'

And into a house without a mother.

In piecing together this part of Milton's story, it has been difficult to determine the exact chronology of events. Whether the next part happened within weeks or months of the break-up can't be recalled. At some stage, Jenny's husband, Gavin Dempsey, arrived. He'd given away farming to become a truck driver. After stopping in Katherine, he headed south along the Stuart Highway at night. He pulled up again at Dunmarra, about 300 kilometres away. Within minutes he rang Jenny and told her: 'I've got Milton with me.'

Milton had stowed away, making a nest for himself next to some storage drums. He had no money, nothing else other than the clothes he was wearing. 'I'm comin' with you,' he said to his brother-in-law.

Jenny and Gavin, who were still living in Dalby, again had an instant son, but they only cared for him for a short while before he returned to Stan, who'd taken a job with Randall breaking in horses at Mountain Valley station, about 200 kilometres north-east of Katherine, and bordering on Arnhem Land.

Milton felt he was back where he belonged. Wide open spaces, freedom. Admittedly he and Terry still had to attend school, but it wasn't the sort they were familiar with. This time they were students in a massive classroom that stretched across the backblocks of the Northern Territory. The Katherine School of the Air, the oldest of its type in Australia, broadcast lessons via UHF radio to hundreds of remote children. Teachers gave directions from their central base, while in rooms on cattle stations and in tiny communities, mothers or governesses supervised their students. At Mountain Valley, the mechanic's wife, Mrs McComb, oversaw about a dozen students, including her own son, the manager's son, and a number of Aboriginal children.

'You'd just sit down with your books and go through your day's work. It was correspondence with the occasional questions. If you did it quick you could get out of there. You couldn't go until you'd done it,' said Milton.

The schoolhouse was a Silver Bullet caravan. It was only a few minutes' ride away from where the Joneses were staying in the old Mountain Valley homestead, a donga (makeshift building) made of paperbark with gauze sides, a slate floor and low tin roof. While Milton first preferred to travel to school on a pony's back, he sought modified horsepower after the manager's son, Scott Warren, started zooming around on a small motorbike. Milton wanted one too. Stan obliged, and the trips to the classroom suddenly roared at full throttle. All went well until the day some fencing work was done near the schoolhouse, and Milton, oblivious to the change, came to a skidding halt after he was coat-hangered by a strand of wire that 'pulled me nose and near plucked me eye out.' In scenes befitting an adaptation of Banjo Paterson's poem, 'Mulga Bill's Bicycle', the 'two-wheeled outlaw' was taken away, and the sound of clip-clopping in the dust returned.

Horse or machine? The question had relevance far beyond a boy's wish for thrills. In the previous decade, the haulage of cattle by truck had increased substantially, which in turn had reduced the need for drovers. During the same period, the Commonwealth Conciliation & Arbitration Commission granted Aboriginal pastoral workers the same wages as white workers. Faced with rising costs, the pastoralists had to reassess their business practices. Apart from cutting back on full-time staff in preference for contractors, they considered how they could make mustering, which was expensive in money *and* time, more efficient. This led to the most significant change Stan saw in the bush during his lifetime: the move from horseback to helicopter. However, the skies were still some years away from being crowded, and regardless of what lay ahead, Stan knew there would always be a place for a good horse. So, as he lunged them, 'gentled' them and trained them to carry the weight of a rider, his son hurried from school nearly every afternoon and only then became an eager student who took mental notes while peering through the rails at the round-yard.

The outback education continued during a long holiday break when Stan took Milton and Terry on the road with him. Sitting astride both the present and yesteryear, Stan was part of a back-and-forth movement of road trains that hauled about 7000 cows from Mountain Valley to Mimong station, south-east of Mount Isa, Queensland. After crossing the border, the stock had to be dipped and cleared at Camooweal. (Dips and inspection stations are placed along the 'tick line' in a bid to keep Queensland tick free.) They were then 'tailed' – tailing is the use of horses to control cattle while they graze – on the local common for three days before they were reloaded for the final part of their journey. While Stan came and went with the trucks, Milton and Terry were left to tail about 750 cattle at any one time during a move that lasted several weeks.

There were no home comforts on the trip. The Jones kids camped in a dry creek. It was cold. Every morning and night sixteen-year-old Terry lit a fire and cooked a meal, and they had showers at the local service station: a few twenty-cent pieces placed in a slot would fire up the hot water long enough for the young workers to feel refreshed, although as Terry remembers it, Milton had a habit of keeping most of the coins for himself.

'When we were kids we worked like men. There were no ifs or buts or maybes . . . you just did it. It was a pretty hard sort of life as a kid. Our holidays always revolved around horses. I can never remember going to the beach or anything like that,' said Terry.

The unstable upbringing still had its most unexpected moment to come. After the work dried up at Mountain Valley Stan bought a truck and headed to South Australia to carry pipes that were used in the construction of lines from the Moomba gas field. It was about 1975. Milton, on the cusp of his teenage years, and Terry, more than halfway through them, were sent to Jenny who was only in her early twenties and rearing her first baby, Jody. The new responsibilities that were dumped on her were made even more difficult by the absences of her husband Gavin, whose trucking business demanded he spend considerable time away.

The constant 'shunting around' had begun to unsettle Milton, and Jenny noticed her baby brother became a 'bit withdrawn at school.' He found it difficult to make close friends, and as an outsider there was the problem of being accepted to begin with. When torments and teasing arose, Milton had a standard tactic.

'Kids are cruel and you got to fight your way through everything. Fightin' was my answer. I could handle myself all right.'

He had a nuggety build; not tall, but imposingly broad. In a bid to channel her brother's aggression, Jenny arranged for proper boxing lessons 'every Tuesday and Thursday' with a private trainer.

In between jabbing and ducking, Milton battled through primary and into high school with the growing belief that he would always be 'not much with the pen.' Terry had similar thoughts and left the classroom to begin a hairdressing apprenticeship. She moved out and into a flat, leaving Milton to share painting duties with Jenny as they changed addresses to live in a shearing shed that Gavin had bought and shifted into town as their home.

Gavin continued to have a strong influence on Milton, who was quick to pick up any manual skill: tinkering with machinery; welding; carpentry. He also became adept at driving a full road train, three trailers long. In doing so, he earned an extraordinary level of trust from his brother-in-law, who wasn't against having a sleep while his under-age companion poked along the quiet flat roads.

'I didn't think it was unusual,' said Milton. 'I used to do a lot of drivin'. Gavin used to get fair work out of me, I'll tell you.'

Stan reappeared after about eighteen months. He'd sold his truck, bought two taxis and was setting up business in Kingaroy, an hour's drive north-east of Dalby. He took Milton with him. Jenny and Gavin, and their two children – baby Wade was the latest addition – followed.

They also closed the door on trucking, and added to the newfound family empire by buying two more cabs. They all lived together in a four-bedroom house that Stan bought with cash.

Kingaroy is perhaps most renowned for being the home of controversial former Queensland premier Sir Joh Bjelke-Petersen, who held the reins in his state for nineteen years. One of his favourite responses to the media was: 'Don't you worry about that.' Had that sentiment been applied to Milton, there would have been every reason to doubt its substance. Here was an increasingly restless teenager who'd come from a broken home; been lugged around the countryside without ever staying long enough to spread his roots; worked men's jobs while viewing school as his greatest chore; and 'blued' his way in and out of trouble . . . for all intents and purposes he was a potential adolescent time bomb.

And that potential was fulfilled.

'I was put into school and I wasn't concentrating. I just wanted to be "out there", you know what I mean? I did Grade 8, and I had a blue with the headmaster. I was a cheeky young fella. He caned me and I hooked him back and got expelled, whacked him on the side of the head. He gave me six cuts, he actually broke that finger,' said Milton, pointing at the middle one on his left hand. 'He brought the cane up from underneath and ooh gee, it hurt. So I just drove him, just downed him.'

Milton stormed home and told his father what had happened. Stan confronted the headmaster, but any chance of patching up the relationship wasn't a consideration for Milton. 'I'm not goin' back there,' he said to Stan.

And with those words, he walked away from school forever. He was fourteen.

* * *

While most his age were learning about algebra and the assassination of Archduke Ferdinand, Milton pumped petrol. His first job at a Kingaroy service station enabled him to save up enough cash to buy a second-hand Yamaha 175 motorbike. Never mind that he wasn't old enough to legally ride it; he thought that as long as he kept to the back roads he'd stay out of sight of police. One track led him to Andersson's market garden, where he made some 'good money' picking pumpkins and watermelons. He became mates with the boss's sons, Eric and Dan. Their knockabout pastimes included going to the local rifle range where Milton proved his slug gun antics in Katherine had trained him well. He was a crack shot.

At other times Milton found himself providing precautionary security for Jenny when she was on taxi duty. Although there were the occasional experiences with customers who needed sorting out with a strong word, nothing untoward ever happened. The worst pick-up was a pub regular whose urine-soaked trousers forced Jenny and Milton to drive with their heads out the windows for a twenty-minute ride that shocked the senses for much longer. In winter, the night's bitterness conspired with the stench to make the journey even harder.

Jenny was often the sole driver on duty on Saturdays because Stan and Gavin took off for the local gallops. There are few sports built on as much hope as is horseracing in the bush. Every battling trainer *hopes* the next sprinter or stayer that comes into his stable is *the one* that will string a few wins together before heading to the big smoke and upstaging all the fancy types with a hands and heels victory. Then the hope grows: a horse in the headlines and a trainer suddenly sought after by well-to-do owners. The money flows in, the stable grows, more trophies, a shining reputation, a premiership . . . those days of mucking out the filth with the seat out of your pants are long gone.

Stan never lost hope. But his horses didn't share his sentiments.

'The old fella had some rubbish ones. Jesus Christ, he'd buy anything; he'd have all the worst bastards. Nothin' good. The stables were right beside the school. I used to ride trackwork,' remembered Milton.

Milton was still small enough to be a jockey. He wasn't bothered by what he rode. Not even rogues. Jenny recalls one 'nasty, nasty horse' that was always a risk at the barriers. Gavin put Milton on it.

'I was terrified for him because he had no helmet, no nothing. It wasn't in a yard, this was on the street. A horse with shoes can slip really badly on bitumen. Milton didn't move out of the saddle. His bum didn't move an inch,' said Jenny.

Whether it was always going to happen, or circumstances demanded it, Milton had developed a fearless streak touched with a weighty dose of I-don't-give-a-shit attitude. A larrikin? A confused adolescent finding his way in the world? A cocky upstart? He was all of them.

Terry reckons he was 'good-looking': trim, fit, dark hair, a dominant jaw, wicked grin yet occasionally stormy expressions. On his trips to Dalby he was a regular at the hairdressing salon that Terry was working in; the reason had little to do with brotherly love, but much to do with 'having a perve.'

'We used to go to dances in the area,' recalled Terry. 'I remember one New Year's Milton said to me: "Now Tair, if an ugly chick tries to get me you're my girlfriend, hey." And I said the same: "If an ugly fella tries to get me you're my boyfriend." So we had this little deal. And I remember an ugly fella was trying to get on to me and I thought, Oh, I've got to go and find Milton . . . There he was, doing pull-ups and all these girls were around him. I asked him what he was doing, and he said: "Piss off!" So I had to. Oh, he was a mongrel. I told him: "You're supposed to be my boyfriend, there's a fugly after me." But he said: "You deal with it!"'

Milton was becoming a law unto himself. Although he was still under-age, he would borrow Terry's Datsun Bluebird and turn it from a main-road runabout into a paddock-basher. He'd invariably bring the vehicle back clean, leaving no evidence of the havoc he'd wrought. However, Terry eventually started having engine problems, and inspections revealed a patchwork of dents and scrapes on the car's undercarriage.

As with every other place Milton had lived in, Kingaroy became just another blow-through joint. Next step was Innisfail in north Queensland, where Stan had been lured by the gallops. Again Gavin and Jenny followed with the kids. They set up camp at the racecourse and lived in a caravan which became a popular spot for passers-by to drop in for a cuppa and a yarn. Gavin had become increasingly interested in training, and together with Stan he had a handful of racers, enough to keep Milton busy riding trackwork and doing general stable duties.

They often exercised their hopefuls in the Johnstone River. The sight of a horse with only its head above the water trailing behind a dinghy was common enough, but it never stopped Jenny from worrying about a rib or rump being an open invitation for crocodiles. The only mishap for a Jones horse proved more sinister when a chestnut mare, Goldie, was found in the stables one morning with a wound on a leg. The Joneses believed a rival trainer had taken to it with a rasp, but thankfully had missed cutting the tendon. The culprit was never found, and Goldie recovered to dead-heat for first in her next race.

Milton contemplated becoming a jockey, but steady growth made him too heavy, so he hopped on his Yamaha and found a job sweeping guts at a meatworks. At about the same time, Gavin supplemented his racehorse trainer's hopes with a regular income by labouring for a marine construction company at the nearby Mourilyan Harbour. He soon told Milton: 'There's a start there for you if you want it.'

There was no need to ask the question twice. Milton remembers the incentive was 'good money, it must have been $600 or $700 a week.' Most of the work was in shallow water at low tide under a wharf: jackhammering apart heavy iron casings that protected pylons, then washing them with fresh water, re-bolting them around the pylons, and pumping concrete into them. It was arduous, and by the end of nearly every day, Milton had only enough energy to go home, eat, and fall into bed. He became so run-down that he contracted pneumonia. He struggled through it.

With a steady cash flow coming into his pocket Milton was becoming more independent and confident that he could go his own way when, or if, his situation encouraged it. The defining moment came when Jenny and Gavin decided to go back to Dalby, Stan stayed put, and Milton accepted an offer from the construction company's boss, John Archer, to head south. In his mid-teens, he knew the time was right to stand alone. He was, however, supported by John, who set up his new employee in a flat in Brisbane.

Milton was 'on the grinder' as a trade assistant to a boilermaker in a workshop. His first large project was the building of a slipway on the Brisbane River. It was all underwater work, using chainsaws and pile-drivers.

'I was on a hookah line with air pumpin' down to me through a helmet: you know the ones with rubber across the back and glass on the face? The air just flowed through it, and I had a two-way communication where I could talk to the fella top-side. I couldn't see a thing; it was that dirty, everything was [done by] feel. I had a suit, no flippers, just rubber boots. You didn't have to swim anywhere; just go down with a big heap of lead on you. It was only 4 metres deep or so.'

Milton bent his back. The rewards not only came financially, but in opportunities. He spent about a year working at various tourist spots along the Great Barrier Reef: Townsville; Proserpine; Airlie Beach; Daydream and Hamilton islands. While most of the jobs involved long hours building jetties – some of which required scuba diving – he surely would have been the envy of many a partygoer when he spent a cyclone season on South Molle

Island 'keepin' an eye' on a pile-driving barge to make sure it wasn't washed away.

'That was my job!' Milton said. 'It was a good place to work: full pay, accommodation, big kitchen, plenty of tucker, good nightlife, and plenty of time on my hands . . . I had a few drinks there. It would have been one of the early times I did.'

Despite thriving on the freedom during this period, Milton still had moments when he yearned for family comforts. Having developed a strong respect for money, he was forever the bargain-hunter when it came to eating. After a restaurant at Shute Harbour prevented him from making the most of an all-you-can-eat buffet nearly every day, he rang Terry and asked for some home-cooked meals to be sent to him. Boxes and boxes of quiches, cakes and biscuits soon arrived. Milton promised his sister he would return all her Tupperware. He never did.

In a manner that would have gained his father's approval, Milton had 'saved up a few bob', all in cash. He returned to Brisbane and reunited with an English girl he'd met on one of the islands. The relationship was brief. The effects were long-lasting.

'She ripped me off, the bastard. Stole all my money. She just stung me: six or eight grand, whatever it was. All my savings. Anyway, she worked me out and rolled me. I was flat broke.'

Milton told John Archer what had happened. He returned to manning angle-grinders in the workshop until he again had a heavy wallet. Then, it was time to quit. He packed an army duffle bag full of clothes and headed for the airport with his two most important possessions: a pump-action .22 rifle and a blue heeler dog named Spud. Both went into the plane's cargo hold, while somewhere above them, their owner buckled his seatbelt and looked down at the blur of the runway. Aged about seventeen, Milton was leaving behind a wandering childhood and adolescence. There was only one place he wanted to go.

PART TWO

MAKING SOMETHING

CHAPTER 3

BULLS, BUGGIES AND BLUES

The questions divided the nation: Were they guilty? Or could a dingo really do it? From bars to kitchen tables, offices to grandstands, opinions were voiced on the disappearance of baby Azaria Chamberlain from an Uluru (Ayers Rock) campsite in 1980. History tells us her mother Lindy was convicted of murder and her father Michael of being an accessory. Their convictions were later quashed and in 2012 a fourth coronial inquest ruled that a dingo had indeed killed Azaria. As the case was winding its way through the early stages of the legal process, the sensationalised attention the story received conjured images in the mainstream media of a last frontier, Australia's very own Wild West, where the country was harsh, the wildlife deadly, and the people so tough they could deflect a fired bullet with their glare alone. Such a land appealed to a certain breed of young man who would cross borders, and sometimes oceans, to see if he could make his mark. The Northern Territory was a magnet for masculinity.

Milton flew from Brisbane to Darwin, and was picked up at the airport by his brother Llawrence. They made their way clear of taxis and commuter cars in a vehicle that on first glance was on a one-way journey to the scrapheap. It was a dusty, dented Toyota LandCruiser that looked as though it had run into the back of a road train and come out the other end without doors, a windscreen, a cabin or a roof. However, those in the know treasured such a vehicle. In the 1970s, '80s and beyond, the 'bull buggy' was a moneymaker. (Bull buggies are also commonly referred to as bull-catchers, but to avoid confusion with references to the people who are also 'bull-catchers', we will use only 'bull buggies' or occasionally 'Toyota' to describe the machines.)

Milton had heard from Llawrence and his other brother, Randall, that there were golden dollars to be made from bull-catching. One of the main reasons: the sheer size and nature of the land meant it was impossible to fence all stock, and have 100 per cent success rates during musters. This meant the cattle left behind over many years bred ferals – also known as 'cleanskins' – in large numbers. Numerous problems resulted. They wrecked infrastructure, most often fences; they took valuable feed, particularly during dry spells; and they affected the quality of station herds, often violently. The feral bulls could belt the herd bulls away, and then gang up on cows in season and ride them until they collapsed and died. Heifers could suffer the same fate, and calves were subject to being horned until their blood loss wrote their own death sentences.

Numbers of feral Shorthorn and Brahman cattle (the latter are more prevalent nowadays because of their resilience in the Top End climate) had risen to such an extent that the demand for bull-catchers was high. This was further heightened by the national Brucellosis and Tuberculosis Eradication Campaign (BTEC) which dictated the de-stocking of infected animals, and culling of buffalos in a bid to protect export markets for beef and dairy products. In operation since 1970, it had sparked the initial surge in bull-catchers and contract musterers. All this led to what one bull-catcher, Robert van Kuijck, said was 'every man and his dog in the Territory doing it.'

This upsurge resulted in the establishment of new meatworks across the area to satisfy the demands of the American hamburger trade.

'They were the biggest market,' said Milton. 'US box meat. Buffalo as well. They all went in the same box: red bull and black bull, all the same thing. Grindin' meat, that's what it was. It was about $1.40 per kilo on the hook. You'd get about $300 to $400 a head for a decent bull.'

Milton and Llawrence headed to Katherine and linked up with Randall. Soon enough, the eldest Jones brother took the youngest on his first official bull-run with an experienced hand, Don Pitt. They went south-east, deep into some of the Territory's most remote country near the McArthur River, where they set to work on grass-covered floodplains. Randall's main advice to his novice worker: 'Mate, ya gotta be on your toes working with wild cattle.' The point was thumped into Milton early on when he was charged by a beast in a yard. Milton fell into a dip in the ground, and the bull ran straight over the top of him before crashing into a gate.

A bull-catcher will tell you his job is simple enough: 'Knock 'em arse over head, put a strap on 'em, drag 'em up into a truck and take 'em in.' Although each catcher has his own way of doing things, in fundamental terms the above description means: spot a beast; drive behind it until it is exhausted to the point it can be pushed over by the bull buggy that has tyres attached as bumpers at the front. You don't hit them hard because abattoirs reject damaged animals; bruises and breaks mean no dollars. There is also the matter of animal welfare: those who treat the beasts unfavourably soon earn reputations that will see them out of work. Once a bull is down, you tie its legs, front together and back together, with buckled leather straps similar to belts. Then you cut its horns off with a saw, and 'skid' the animal up by the head or jaw onto the slide of a truck with a pulley block and wire rope; the straps are taken off during this last process. Sometimes if a truck isn't immediately available the bull may only have two legs strapped, and is then tied to a tree and collected at a later time. After that, it is driven with others directly to the meatworks, or is put into a yard to await the same fate when another truck arrives.

This simplistic description does not account for 'squirtin' along at about 30 kay an hour,' in second gear, at full revs, weaving through scrub, spitting sand, trusting wheels on a ridge's edge, while shudders are sent from your toes to your teeth. Of course this all happens before you deal with an unpredictable 500-kilogram animal that has enjoyed a life without rules; any hardened bull-catcher will have his share of yarns about lucky – and not so lucky – escapes, and perhaps some scars and a limp to prove it.

Bull-catching can last for months at a time. 'Your hat is your home,' and at night you might only have your swag, a billycan, a fire, and meat from a killer you've knocked. Milton came to develop a travel pack that included: 'three shirts, three pairs of undies and socks, a pair of boots, a towel, toothpaste, toothbrush and a cake of soap.' The McArthur River adventure introduced him to a way of life that filled him with purpose, and he'd shown enough promise to prompt Don Pitt to tell Randall: 'He's gonna make something of himself.'

After working for a short while at the local meatworks, Milton returned to Katherine with a plan to make enough money to buy his own Toyota and turn it into a buggy.

The first step, though, was more work. Randall helped him secure a job at Katherine meatworks where both older Jones boys were slaughtermen. The industry had recently endured a volatile time with the introduction of contract workers at some other abattoirs. Katherine was a 'union shed', and the threat of outsiders coming in meant blood wasn't only spilled on kill floors, but in pubs as well. Although Milton was to work during a quiet period that was devoid of picket lines and marches, he nevertheless experienced the hardline attitudes of those alongside him.

'To get a start in the Katherine meatworks you had to be a Katherine meatworker. If you went in there and didn't perform they'd get rid of you straight away; the other workers would hunt you because if one fella slowed down, everyone had to slow down.'

The day began at about 5.30 a.m. and finished in the early afternoon. Milton worked on a 'gravity line', a sloping rail with hooked carcasses that hung upside down and moved along through various stages of processing. Using a pneumatic cutter that was suspended from an elastic-type coil to take the weight, he cut off the horns and front hocks, and threw them down a chute. 'Ankle deep in blood all day,' he also tied the weasand (the animal's gullet) to avoid the stomach contents leaking out. It was just one step in a process that eventually led to the carcasses being chilled in freezers overnight before being boned, then packed the next day.

'I remember one day a bull got out and was racin' round the kill floor,' said Milton. 'One old fella there, old Bluey, he got the .22 Magnum and there were no sights on the front of this thing. He's takin' pot shots at it, and there's men on the floor yellin': "Pull up, don't shoot!" He was gettin' a bit excited. This thing did a couple of laps around the floor and down the steps, then gone!'

The work experience, spanning several months, was enough for Milton to vow to Randall: 'I'm gonna own one of these [meatworks] one day.' According to the eldest Jones brother, who would eventually set up a construction business in Port Keats, south of Darwin, Milton was in a hurry to make more money.

In the blue-collar environment Milton had become familiar with, it wasn't surprising that rugby league was the ruling sport. The meatworks participated in a competition that stretched from Darwin to Alice Springs. All three Jones brothers were good players. Milton was a hooker: quick off the mark, except when he needed to stand his ground as fists were flung.

Away from his job, he thrived on good times. A bloke he met during this period remains his closest mate. Kurt Hammer is a year older than Milton. He grew up on his family's station, Bauhinia Downs, near Borroloola in the

Territory's east, and nowadays he runs cattle on 1.2 million acres of land leased from the Aboriginal authorities in Western Australia. He remains a bull-catcher, primarily in Western Australia, and estimates he has caught 81 000 – 37 million dollars' worth – over the last fourteen years. He has a fading tattoo of a riding spur on one arm, and there is cigarette-stained gravel in his voice. When he stands in a doorway there is little room for the air to squeeze past.

Thirty years ago, 'too much beef' was yet to fill his tall frame. He remembers the first time he *saw* Milton. He was driving north along the Stuart Highway when a vehicle passed heading the other way. The sight made Kurt look twice: there dwindling from view in his rear-vision mirror were two young men lying on their stomachs tied down by octopus straps on the roof-rack. Each had a pillow. Kurt found out later who they were. Milton and a mate had become so drunk during a session in Katherine that they merrily accepted the cheap seats for a 250-kilometre lift from a 'good-lookin' girl named Curly' to the Daly Waters rodeo.

Kurt would soon see Milton again, albeit fleetingly. It was at a race meeting on McArthur River station. In one event, some horses were heading for home when Milton, on his way from working with Randall in the area, hurtled across the dirt track in a bull buggy. Although he was a few hundred metres ahead of the field, by the time they reached the finish, the chance of identifying the winner was apparently lost in a cloud of dust.

Finally the two young men met face to face in Katherine.

'I went into a cafe there to buy a drink, and I seen this bloke there with a red cowboy hat on – you just don't wear a red cowboy hat if you're a cowboy – a pair of football shorts, no shirt, bare feet and real well built. I said, "How ya goin'?" I got into a Toyota with him and we've been best mates ever since,' recalled Kurt.

Kurt came to know Milton as 'full of confidence, competitive, and good on the knuckle.' This last attribute still holds weight in the much bigger man's memories: 'I've only had three hidin's in my life and they were all off Milton.'

Embellishment can be an enthusiastic corner man. And perhaps some of the stories involving Milton's pugilism have been boosted by hyperbole. It doesn't matter if they have because there are too many recollections to suggest all are exaggerated. Milton could fight; that's a given. He knew the art, but if he was being outboxed, he wasn't afraid to play dirty. Those who have suffered at his hands include a martial arts exponent who spat out 'Fuck off' in the wrong direction outside a Katherine disco. Spins and kicks may look good, but a driving tackle under the ribs and into a garden bed, followed by a thumb pushed knuckle-deep into the eye can rattle even the surest of scrappers.

Milton did, however, have weaknesses. According to Kurt it was a 'tradition' at the Katherine Show for some groups to gather and drink near the left-hand chutes during the rodeo; unlike in other states, Territory rodeos weren't so much about the competition as about rum, parties and fights. Milton was a reasonable contestant whose strength was in the saddle-bronc and bareback events, in which he won a few dollars over the years. But when his turn was done, the alcohol flowed, and at one particular show he changed from a competitor-cum-spectator into a nuisance *in* the arena. During the saddle-bronc competition he waved a branch at the horses in a bid to make them buck and twist harder. Then, during the bull-ride his sense of mischief crossed the line. The bull-rope is the piece of equipment that wraps around the beast's belly and is gripped firmly one-handed by the competitor. Unbeknownst to one rider who Milton gleefully helped, the rope wasn't only tied around the bull, but to the chute's gate as well. When the gate was pulled open, the bull bucked tight against it, and the rider was going nowhere.

Amidst the laughter, an official rushed over to investigate. Suddenly a 'barney' erupted and the crowd turned its attention from urging cowboys to hold on for eight seconds to watching an older man – Kurt reckons the official was about 50 – show a younger man the meaning of timing. A few good slugs, some blood on the face, and a shaken Milton was taken away by his sister Terry. Hours later, he felt he was sober enough for the second round. He approached the official, but his intentions were swatted away by an experienced man's words: 'We might have a drink instead, Milton.' Handshakes and a beer followed in what was a reflection of Territory culture at the time.

'No one ever really had a blue that kept a grudge, eh. You're a pretty weak bastard if you did,' said Kurt. 'Nearly all the fights were just over piss or somethin' like that. You never see a proper fight anymore, like someone standin' up and havin' a fight over somethin' serious.'

The Katherine Show was one of the main events on the Territory's social calendar, giving people from hundreds of kilometres away the chance to leave any worries at their front gate, come to town and break free of their isolated lifestyles. This focal point was also an invitation for Milton to show he had a knack of escaping trouble, even if he caused it.

'There was a bloke with hair like Don King [the notorious African-American boxing promoter]. A black-fella with a cowboy shirt and jeans on; he had a bit of importance, this fella,' remembered Kurt. 'He hadn't washed his hair for a long time; it would ignite pretty easy with all the oil and grease in it. Milton reckoned it was too good a target, so he lit a match and threw it straight in there while the fella was at the bar. The flame got up off the top of his head but he didn't know he was on fire. So another fella just leant over and took his hat off to beat it out. But the bloke on fire thought he was gettin' bagged down, so he started swingin'. And then she was on. I reckon from everyone havin' a beautiful show mornin' to an all-in brawl took about eight seconds.'

All because of Milton.

Katherine could be a wild town, and whether or not this influenced Milton, there's no doubt he was at times a trouble-maker in an area where Randall Jones acknowledged 'you've got to be a bit of Ned Kelly to be ahead.' In pursuit of owning his own bull buggy Milton scampered onto the wrong side of the law. It may have seemed harmless enough, but it was still telling of his character at the time. He committed his crime after he'd saved enough money to add to his LandCruiser stable; he already had a beaten-up tray-back with no sideboards and two silver exhaust pipes. His second purchase was a wreck. When he showed it to Kurt, the immediate reaction was, 'Jesus, it's got oil all over it.' Milton replied: 'No, that's blood.' It was a 'mangled-up' government vehicle in which someone had been killed in an accident. Though the chassis was bent, the engine was fine.

Milton and Kurt began repairing it at a place close to town that was owned by 'Shorty', an older man who the two youngsters had begun 'kickin' round with.' They didn't get far into their work before they realised they needed more tools. So, they waited until evening then went back into Katherine and climbed the fence of the smash repair business that had sold Milton the vehicle. Minutes later they pushed a wheelbarrow-load of spanners out onto the street, and hurried away.

The next day, Kurt was lying underneath the vehicle with his distinctive feet poking out one end when two unexpected visitors arrived.

'The coppers were straight onto us,' said Milton. 'Kurt has a huge foot on him, and this old policeman, Col, took one look at the track Kurt had left at the smash repairers and said: "I know exactly who this is!" So he went straight out to us. I'm walkin' around the corner and see the coppers right there, and a little lady copper has a photo of a footprint and is holdin' it right up against Kurt's feet. And old Col says to Kurt: "You might want to come out here, young fella, and have a word to me." But Kurt says: "No, I've gotta get this Toyota goin'."

'Anyway, he used to smoke a pipe, old Col. He got the pipe and dumped the hot ash on Kurt's bare feet, and says again: "You might want to come out here, young fella." Kurt shoots straight out and says: "The spanners are over there in the corner, have a look!"

'We got some sort of good behaviour bond. It was very embarrassin'. We had to keep our noses clean, which was a good thing because we were only young fellas, young louts runnin' around – we thought we knew everything.'

At some point, during this age of reckless misadventures, Milton and Kurt went to Darwin on a rugby league trip. They stayed with Kurt's sister, Dominique, who was working as a beauty therapist. She was 21, tall, slender and blonde. Milton was eighteen, and soon to be 'tangled up' in his first serious relationship. Within a few months Dominique moved to Katherine to live with Milton in a 'horrible little caravan in a horrible little caravan park.' They then headed with Kurt to manage Bauhinia Downs after the Hammer family had sold the station, but the new owner wasn't at all against the departing family keeping some connection with it.

Although most of the cattle had been sold off Bauhinia Downs, there were still considerable numbers of ferals that gave Milton the chance to fire up his bull buggy. He had 'knocked the top off it', taken off the doors and blinkers, and replaced the original four-speed gearbox with one of only three gears, believing it was better suited to the high torque 2F motor he had. The results pleased him, and his desire, perhaps his *need* to chase bulls, grew. Like her brother, Dominique recognised Milton's confidence, but she also saw someone who was conscious of his limited reading and writing abilities. Above all, she saw first-hand a devotion to hard work that would only intensify as time went on.

Other jobs on the station weren't as rewarding. For reasons that Milton is still perplexed by – 'the silly, silly things you do' – he and Kurt decided to build a yard to run a few horses into. It was a basic construction: rails shaped with an axe and wire tightened by pliers. No sooner had they finished than rain hammered down, prompting them to push their horses hard for the ride home through some thick tea tree country. They hit some bog and tried ploughing on, only to stick their horses 'up to their guts.' They took off the saddles, hung them in a tree, and then began the hernia-inducing task of pulling their horses out. Several hours later, they arrived home in darkness after walking 15 kilometres with two exhausted animals. A couple of days passed before they drove a tractor out to pick up the saddles. They saw the saddles, but bogged the tractor. So they walked home again. A week passed before they took a Toyota out . . . and . . . 'bogged it to the arse.' It took them a fortnight to retrieve everything.

They worked at Bauhinia Downs for about a year. And all the while, they still found time for mischief. One incident in particular could be said to typify Milton at that point in his life. At the Mataranka show, he came out of a toilet to find two blokes shaping up to each other in a ring of cheering people. Milton sneaked up and pulled one of the fighter's shorts down to his ankles. There were no underpants in sight. Embarrassed or not, the fighter held his stance, 'fists up, balls hangin'.'

Milton knew the feeling. No matter what the situation, he had shown himself to be someone who'd front up and 'have a crack.' That attitude would earn him his next job. It was time to go west.

CHAPTER 4

BLOOD-AND-DUST THEATRE

The way to find work: go into a pub and start asking around. If you're lucky, you'll meet someone who knows someone who knows someone who knows . . . then again, you might meet that someone to start with. Milton can't recall the exact circumstances, but it's reasonable to suggest a chat over a beer led him to working for Kim Walker in the Kimberley region. Today, black-and-white photos of Kim hang on a wall of the Victoria River Roadhouse, less than twenty minutes' drive from Coolibah station. One in particular captures the imagination. It shows Kim wearing only jeans, his wiry torso akin to that of an endurance athlete. He has windswept sandy hair, mutton-chop whiskers, and a moustache. Most telling of all are his eyes. They don't look at the camera. They look through it. Perhaps for years to come anyone who sees the picture may be stirred to think:

Now, that bloke knows his business. Kim Walker did, he was a bull-catcher.

Milton worked with Kim on Cherrabun and Christmas Creek stations, west of Gordon Downs. He now laughs at the memory of catching an average of ten to fifteen bulls a day: 'I was gettin' ten dollars a head *and* supplyin' me own buggy.' Dominique went along as a cook, and when the need arose, she did her share of strapping bulls. This didn't at all concern her boyfriend.

'I credit his growing up with two strong sisters for that,' said Dominique, who now lives in Katherine. 'That was both good and bad because I was expected to do what the blokes did as well. There was never any "You're a girl, you're hopeless." There was never any chauvinism.'

But there was single-mindedness. Milton could be as inflexible as a girder, a bloke who at times didn't think about other people. It was his way or . . .

He 'had a blue with Kim and decided to finish up' after just a couple of months. Milton took a job breaking in horses at Cherrabun, then through someone-who-knew-someone he and Dominique were back on the road to link up with Dick Gill, who was contract mustering at Kimberley Downs, further west towards Derby. Milton and Dominique would be part of bull-catching teams that would come through after the mustering. Dick was one of the early musterers to take to the air in a fixed-wing aircraft. When Milton and Dominique reached his camp near a creek, there was no one there, just a set of portable yards stacked up and about 30 drums of fuel. They waited, with only their deaf bull terrier, Piggy Pig, to keep them company.

'We had no tuckerbox, just some Alfoil and soy sauce,' remembered Dominique. 'Milton made some fish hooks out of a bit of wire, and I think he packed frogs on the end of them and caught these little perch. That's what we lived on for four days: soy sauce and perch cooked on the coals in foil.'

Luckily, one of Dick's workers returned to say everyone had moved to another camp. Milton's buggy was out of fuel, and refilling posed problems because there were no hoses, funnels, or any other suitable equipment. 'So, I ended up usin' my boot. Just rolled a drum over and tipped it in. I don't know how many bootfuls, but I was there for a bloody while,' remembered Milton.

Then he and Dominique drove into a cold night. They reached a homestead in the early hours of the morning; the offer of a coffee from someone there still warms Dominique's memory. They finally reached the new camp, and soon after dawn they launched into a blood-and-dust theatre where those with sensitivities, either physical or mental, would be found wanting. As Milton fell into his second-gear high-rev rhythm, Dominique was still finding her feet, literally, as time and again she leapt from the buggy with bull-straps at the ready.

As formidable as the bull-catching was, Dominique found the camp more intimidating. She was scared of the cook, 'a very rough old girl' who could clog a sentence with expletives. There was little variation to her menu. Steak. Steak. Steak. Steak with a boiled onion or potato. Steak. Steak. Eventually she had to go away for one reason or another, and Dominique took over her job. Suddenly new supplies were discovered, and the camp, comprising about ten men, was treated to tinned fruit and custard. When the regular cook returned and found out, she spat abuse at Dominique for several days before she walked out for good.

While Dominique grew more accustomed to a blunt, sometimes brutal environment, Milton had his own unexpected experiences to contend with.

'I downed this big bull, and I've gone out to whack a strap on him, and this big heavy king brown [a highly venomous snake] is underneath him and he had him on the pizzle, just milkin' the bloody poison into him. Jeeesus! I stepped back and jumped back in the buggy and let this old bull up. He stood up and the snake fell off. It went on its way and we went on ours. I took the bull out a bit further and downed him. I watched that bastard; I wondered if he'd be dead when I came back. It didn't affect him at all. He went on the truck to the meatworks that fella, away he went.'

The incident may have initially surprised Milton, but in the harsh environment of outback Australia it wasn't to be completely unexpected. Regardless, it did nothing to shake the student bull-catcher and his belief that he had chosen the right professional path. He was inspired by some of the men he met, none more so than Billy Fulton, a well-known stockman of mixed Aboriginal and white heritage whose most famous deeds were away from bull-catching: in 1968, Billy played a prominent role in tracking down Aboriginal fugitive Larry Boy Janba, who evaded Northern Territory police in swampland for 40 days after murdering his tribal wife on Elsey station, south of Arnhem Land. At the time, it was one of the most famous man-hunts in Australian history.

'He was a bloody brilliant old man, old Billy,' said Milton. 'He actually was one of the first fellas to ever start catchin' bulls with a Toyota. He used to throw bulls off horseback, and then modified Toyotas and started doin' it. He was good. He was a steady old driver; he'd never go fast unless he had to. He taught me what to do: "Do it this way and go that way, look at this country here and that kind of tree there." Teachin' me how to tie a knot properly; I knew how to tie knots, but [he taught] short cuts, you know. He knew the bush properly. Tucker: taught me how to find sugarbag [native honey], yams and witchetty grubs. Old Billy was a good bushman, one of the best. He was 50-odd years of age then. He's dead now. Bloody laugh, God he used to laugh. He used to frighten the shit out of me all the time. "Look out!" he'd sing out. Always givin' me a start.'

For the rest of the 1980s, bull-catching would be Milton's main earner. Looking back, he says so many of his experiences have merged into each other it's often difficult to pin them to a particular time or place. Perhaps the following incident happened during his stint with Dick Gill. Even if it didn't, it still signifies what Milton needed to accept, even embrace, if he was to profit from such a dangerous lifestyle.

'When I was young, real young, I downed this bull once, a big Brahman bull he was, a sharp-horned bastard. I jumped out of this Toyota and it was on a bit of a ridge and I grabbed this big bull by the tail and he just had his second wind, the bastard; he was as fresh as he was when I started with him. Anyway, he just flipped me straight off and tore my shirt near me hip. And I had a pair of shorts on, and he tore them and near opened me up. So, I was gone, flat [sprinting]! I jumped straight under the Toyota and this bull has hit the Toyota a couple of times and the bastard motor car took off with me down this ridge. Here I am draggin' underneath with this Toyota on top of me and I'm hangin' onto the bullbar. Lucky it wasn't far; if it was a big ridge it would have killed me, you know. But I would have gone about 10 metres. Tore all this skin off my back but I ended up catchin' that bull, don't worry. I think I've still got his horn tips today. A big fresh Brahman bull he was.'

One of the worst troubles Milton encountered during his first full bull-catching season was one that wouldn't be imagined by the uninitiated: 'Barcoo rot', a bacterial infection of the skin. Milton's hands were the worst affected. They were constantly being squeezed, rammed, trodden on, sliced, pierced and knocked. Then add hair, dust, blood, animal urine and faeces to the wounds, and with a diet deficient in fruit and vegetables it is not surprising he had infected cuts and scrapes that would take forever to heal.

Dominique recalled that they lived for months on little more than corned beef and onions when the camps were split and she and Milton were part of a group that worked at Millijidee station. A pure luxury was when someone returned from a rare trip into Derby with a block of butter to spread on the dampers Dominique made.

The season began in about March and finished in November. Nine months of a very basic existence; not one town was visited by the couple. On their way back to Katherine, Milton and Dominique stopped at Fitzroy Crossing, a small, predominantly Aboriginal settlement. They bought some Coke and a chocolate bar, but after so long without sugar their bodies couldn't handle the sudden hit, and they both vomited.

They had 1100 kilometres yet to travel along mostly bitumen, and there was a problem: the bull buggy couldn't be registered. Hoping to avoid the police, Milton decided he would only drive at night, and in the irresponsible way a young male's mind sometimes works, he also had a strategy should the law enforcers notice him.

'Milton was going to throw me out somewhere, and then cut bush and come back and get me later. He was determined he wasn't going to get caught,' said Dominique.

They finally arrived in Katherine. It had been a profitable time away, and Milton and Dominique felt 'rich' with the money they'd earned. They bought a second-hand caravan which they lived in at Shorty's place where Milton had made his bull buggy. In its contradictory manner the wet season brought rain, but the work dried up. Milton began planning for the next bull-catching year. He rang around offering his services, and with Dominique providing the legible handwriting and business etiquette, letters were also sent. They received some interest from the Tennant Creek area to the south. Milton went to inspect, and returned with the assessment: 'A lot of rubbish country, wattle and sand, but full of bulls, just full, thousands of the bastards.'

The year in the west had already taught Milton that if he wanted to line his pockets heavily, he needed to work for himself and deal directly with station owners or managers. This meant he had to expand his operations.

Stan, who was still living in Queensland, lent Milton several thousand dollars at interest to buy a second-hand truck with a crate to carry cattle in. The act was a revelation of traits: 'Milton told Dad: "I'll pay you back in six months," and he did,' remembered Jenny Jones. 'Dad always spoke about that. He was a bloke who believed that if you borrow a cent, you pay it back.'

Stan joined his youngest son and Dominique for the first part of the season on Kurundi station. Billy Fulton's son, Harold, and his girlfriend made up the rest of a small operation that would grow from time to time with other contractors when necessary. In a tragic reflection of the dangers of bull-catching, Harold would later be killed while working for someone else when his buggy's bonnet flew up and hit him.

The trip to Kurundi was a misadventure after Milton accidentally cut his leg with an axe and in the absence of proper first aid Dominique gave him antibiotics used for dogs. They then encountered heavy rain, and were forced to set up camp for about ten days underneath a tarpaulin stretched out from the truck. Five people in a small space was crowded enough, but with Milton unable to bend his leg it was even more cramped. They cooked their food on a fire they made in a 44-gallon drum that was cut in half. The curling, lingering smoke added to the discomfort.

But those dramas soon passed, replaced by landscapes that harboured the untamed dollars. The area was to be

Milton's main office for two or so years. He negotiated with several stations: Milton would catch the bulls, then pay 50/50 with the stations for freight costs, and split the cheques that the abattoirs paid. The average price per beast was about $380.

Each operation was different, but typically the process involved three to four days of 'goin' hard' catching and yarding, then a day of trucking about 'three decks' (60 beasts) to the meatworks at Tennant Creek. One of the main variables was the availability of yards. It was imperative to keep the animals near water, usually a billabong or creek, from which pipes could be run to troughs. If there were no yards in suitable locations, temporary ones needed to be made. These could be as simple as hessian wired around a grid of trees, or the more sturdy construction of portable 8-foot-long steel panels (the cause of too many blisters for all who've lugged them across northern Australia's cattle country).

While he grew more accustomed to 'the art of bull-catchin'', Milton was keen to explore new ways of making his operation more efficient. At Willowra station on the eastern edge of the Tanami Desert, he worked in with helicopter muster pilots. At this stage, he had no immediate wish to fly choppers, but he saw the chance to use them as a different style of buggy. With a Bell 47 moving in low over the ground, Milton would stand on a skid, reach down and grab a tiring beast by the tail, then jump off and pull it down, often by throwing his legs between the bull's hind legs.

'He was an amazing man on the tail. A tough nut, a ton of guts,' said Robert Parkinson, a catcher who worked with Milton at that time.

Milton accepted the risks of falling badly or being trampled as all part of the job, but he didn't factor in the surprise he received on one chase.

'Dave Norris was my pilot. Old Dave, he was a good man. He dropped me in low over this bull, but when I touched its tail, there was some static electricity in the Bell 47. I got shocked and the bull got shocked, and I let go of its tail in a hurry. But Dave thought I was on the bull so Dave was pullin' away, but I still had an arm hooked around the skid, and I was hangin' about thirty foot up in the air before old Dave noticed.'

Such an incident only enhanced the image of bull-catchers as being a breed apart. Living conditions at their camps were elementary at best. Everyone slept in swags – tarpaulins were used as cover when it rained – and a flour drum with water heated up on a campfire became both the shower and washing machine; the nature of the work assaulted the clothes that Dominique had mostly bought at St Vincent de Paul's.

'All men's shirts. We'd just swap between us. Jackets, jumpers, whatever. Everything we owned was basically in the back of the buggy. We were living like dogs really. It was long, hard times,' said Dominique. 'And cold, so cold! The water would freeze in the poly pipes running up to the yards.'

Apart from the regular meat provided by a 'killer', food supplies consisted of little more than potatoes, onions and flour carried in a cardboard fruit box. The flavour of the meat wasn't always as expected. One night, Milton surprised Dominique by offering to cook, something he rarely did, after arriving late at a new camp at Epenarra station. The one-off stew was eaten. The next morning, when Dominique went to clean the cooking pot she discovered it was full of maggots. She confronted Milton, who replied: 'I knew the beef was full of 'em, but if you'd cooked it you wouldn't have eaten it, and then you would've been hungry.'

'I suppose that was actually him doing a nice thing for me,' recalled Dominique, smiling.

There were, however, some moments of relative luxury: occasional stays at the Goldfields Motel at Tennant Creek, and for a while at Epenarra they lived in their caravan.

On another occasion at Epenarra, when they were back to basics, they set up camp near the schoolhouse, where they became favourites of the children. 'It was all black kids at the school, and we took 'em out for a day when we were bull-catchin',' said Milton. 'They all sat up a tree and we tied these bulls around the tree. It was a real big excursion day. I don't reckon many kids get an excursion like that.'

Milton and Dominique established friendships with the school's husband and wife teachers, Gerry and Dawn McCarthy. Gerry is now the Northern Territory's parliamentary member for Barkly, and a government minister. Initially, he'd been just another young man lured from down south, but his reasons for crossing borders and cultures were vastly different from many his age. He grew up in Sydney, and hadn't experienced any degree of rural life until he underwent his teacher training at the Teachers College at Armidale in the northern tablelands of New South Wales. He then went further west when he accepted his first posting at Walgett, a wool and wheat town with a large Aboriginal community. By the end of a two-year stint he had 'started to get a taste for the bush and wanted to see some country that had no fences.' And that took him into the Territory where he was involved with a federal program to establish remote-area Indigenous schools.

The memories of Gerry's experiences at Epenarra are coloured with stories about Milton and Dominique. One of the highlights of every remote-area school's year was a sports carnival that was hosted on a different station each time. In preparation for staging the event at Epenarra, Gerry invited some members of his family to visit. Among them was his elderly aunt, Aileen, who was busy making sandwiches when Milton's crew came back from a day's work. She saw Dominique covered in grime and dressed in a shirt, trousers, boots and a hat pulled down over her face 'like a Territory stockman.' They chatted to each other for a while. Then that night, when the students performed a concert, Dominique attended looking 'like a stunner in a leopard-print dress.' Her entry turned heads and prompted whispers: 'Who is that?' Aileen's immediate reaction was to ask: 'Where's the bloke?' All along she had thought Dominique was a man. It was a mistake that Aileen re-lived, at her own expense, in the stories she told for years afterwards.

Gerry remembered Milton was 'such a character, the kids loved him.' His presence also left its mark on the adults, particularly the former Sydneysider who was still learning about authentic bush life.

'At the same sports gathering, we had a barbecue and were all sitting around late,' said Gerry. 'The kids had been put to bed and everybody was relaxing. Then in through the stock fence and into the school compound came the biggest mob of camp dogs and they started having a blue. Everybody was a bit timid about this; these dogs were pretty savage and they were all having a go at each other. Milton, from a sitting position, just leaned over, grabbed this big camp dog by the tail, and without losing his balance – and it shows you the strength of the guy – he was just able to flip this animal into the air back up over the stock fence. It hit the dust yelping and screaming, took off like a shot out of a gun into the scrub, and that commotion completely dazzled all the camp dogs. They all got the idea that they'd be next, so they all took off through the fence. As all that happened Milton did not miss a beat in the conversation that was going on.'

Later, Gerry witnessed another example of bush pragmatics after Milton, Dominique and their crew had moved on to Elkedra station. The McCarthys received a call over the radio that a party was being organised to celebrate Milton's twenty-first. After arriving on the banks of the Elkedra Creek, Gerry was soon taken away by Milton for a fundamental job.

'They used to call me "schoolie",' recalled Gerry. 'And Milton said: "Come on, schoolie, we'll go and get the firewood." So, here am I thinking in the mainstream that we'll grab an axe. We headed out into some mulga country and found a couple of really good, big old dead trees. Milton stopped and said: "What d'ya reckon, mate, are you gonna get the wood?" And I said: "Yeah, let me out here." I was trying to impress the boss. Well, he just laughed. I jumped out and he took off in the Toyota and belted those trees, knocked them over flat, split them, and broke them up all with a couple of quick manoeuvres with the bull-catcher and we had a load of firewood we couldn't jump over. And here's the schoolie standing there with a bloody axe! I was learning every step of the way.'

The McCarthys helped to swell party numbers that also included Milton's crew, and some Elkedra workers. Celebrations lasted a night; the hangovers perhaps longer. Dominique recalled one particular delight of the occasion: instead of slabs of steak or chunks for stew, they enjoyed mince that was chopped up finely with a butcher's knife by one of the youngest, and no doubt later sore-wristed, men in the camp.

Milton may have formally come of age, but the moment was nothing more than an excuse for a get-together in a place where manhood wasn't determined by years but the ability to take a knock, dust yourself off, and stand squarely on your feet again. Every single day of bull-catching threatened to break even the strongest of characters. Most troublesome incidents happened in seconds, such as when Milton tied a Shorthorn to the front of his buggy while trying to pull the brute over; the bull took off, and when it came to the end of the rope it snapped around, drove its horns into the front seat and tore it straight out. One frigid morning Milton tried running some Herefords with pink-eye (inflammation of the eyes) into a truck. After 'jobbing this old bull on the arse with a stick' he was suddenly hurled to the ground. The bull ripped some flesh off his left hand with a hoof, and then tried to kneel on him. The end result: a couple of broken toes and 'a fair sort of livenin' up right on dawn.'

All in a day's work.

And it could happen to anyone, even the ever-reliable Billy Fulton, who'd taught Milton the basics in the west and joined him for part of the time around Tennant Creek. Billy epitomised the manner of many an old-fashioned bush character: don't bother complaining, just get the job done. As Milton discovered when dealing with the bulls with pink-eye, one of the risks of bull-catching is the loading of the animals onto a truck. In makeshift yards without crushes, a common technique is to push three or four bulls forward at a time with a buggy while someone stands in a safe position with a stick to steer the heads in the right direction. When it works, it's just a matter of bolting up the back of the truck and driving away. When it doesn't . . .

'Old Billy was there in the buggy and pushed one bull up and another come up and over the bonnet, put its legs through the steerin' wheel and jams the old fella in the front seat. It messed him up a bit, but he was right,' said Milton. 'Billy was as tough as there was. I remember once, he had an eye all bunged up. I had to take him into Tennant Creek. I left him at the hospital and he's gone straight in there, and I went off to buy a part or something and told Billy I'd meet him at the pub about two blocks from the hospital, not far anyway. I get to the pub and there he is with a wattle seed in a jar, and it had a little green shoot comin' out the tail of it where it had been sittin' in his eye. Billy's there with a rum, and his eyes wide open. I said: "Are you right now?" And he said: "Yeah, I'm right now, that rum was the eye-opener." I think that one drink led into about three days of it. That's all we needed, then back out again.'

In this precarious yet fruitful land, one danger could haunt the mind long after machines had been repaired and broken bones healed. When Kurt Hammer began working for Milton at a separate camp at Kurundi his only motivation was converting bulls into bucks. Was he single-minded or selfish? A visiting policeman had reason to think the latter after he asked Kurt to join a search for a man who'd been working with Kurt, but who had decided to leave and had gone missing. Kurt refused.

'One day you might be stranded or lost,' said the officer.

'Yeah, well, I'll get meself out of it,' answered Kurt.

A week later, Kurt drove to neighbouring Elkedra to visit Milton. He stopped first at the homestead where the owner, Roy Driver, gave him directions. It was a matter of following tyre tracks. But desert sands and winds can be wicked conspirators, and in the confusion of altered routes Kurt ended up missing the turn-off to where Milton was working. None the wiser he drove on, looking but not finding until he was stopped by the unexpected.

'A front shaft come off the buggy and put a hole in the sump,' recalled Kurt. 'So I started walkin'. I was pretty fit back then.'

Without a radio Kurt had no way of contacting anyone. It was only when Milton drove to the Elkedra homestead to truck away some bulls that he was asked by Roy Driver: 'Did Kurt catch up with you?' By that stage Kurt, wearing jeans, a shirt and no boots – 'never wore boots back then' – had been out on his own for two nights in the sparse sand and mulga country where temperatures dropped quickly from the high twenties (Celsius) to low single figures at night. He had no food and 'only a bit of water.'

Milton immediately began to search. In trying to follow Kurt's tyre tracks, he came across a group of Aborigines; initially he was tormented by the thought that one of them may have mistakenly shot Kurt, believing he was a kangaroo. Tempers flared but subsided, and it was soon agreed the Aborigines would join the search. One of them sat on the bullbar of Milton's buggy and read the patterns in the sand. They found Kurt's footprints and then discovered a camp where the missing man had lain in the middle of a ring of wood that he'd stacked up and lit to keep him warm at night. Milton and his helper eventually found the abandoned buggy several kilometres away from one of three bores that Kurt had been walking between, but the footprints were inconsistent, at one point disappearing off the road and into the bush. Milton towed Kurt's vehicle back to the closest bore, and then returned to set up camp where the footprints had vanished.

'I was gettin' real worried by then,' recalled Milton. 'I thought he'd be gettin' buggered. Freezin' cold, and stinkin' dirty water, all arsenic water out there. Ooh, it scours you when you drink it, and Kurt would have been drinkin' it.'

Kurt *was* deteriorating. His tongue had swollen up, making it impossible for him to close his mouth. Until the point he'd turned off into the bush, he'd stuck to his plan of continually walking between the bores in the hope he'd be found by a station hand or mechanic on a regular round of inspecting the stock watering sites. However, his decision to go bush signalled his growing desperation, albeit with acceptable logic: he wanted to climb a hill a couple of kilometres away to see if he could see a homestead or a main road.

'I reckon I would have walked about 60 miles by then,' said Kurt. 'Oh mate, I'd gone all that distance and I was a good way from water. I was nearly perishin'. So I got off that hill and it was about eight mile back to the nearest bore. I thought I was gonna die. So I decided I was gonna jog the whole way back to the bore.'

The next morning Milton decided it was time to call the police. He rolled up his swag and went to the bore for a final look.

'And there in the front seat of the Toyota was Kurt, asleep. I was glad it was over. That was a bit frightenin'.'

The other lost man had also been found. According to Kurt this other bloke was 'half dead' after he resorted to drinking radiator fluid.

Normality resumed, and both bulls and bucks did indeed mount up. At this stage of his life Milton was mostly a 'handshake man' when it came to business deals, but there were moments when an extended hand needed to be changed to a cocked fist. One person who tried to 'hoodwink' Milton came in for special attention. A disagreement led to some purposeful steps behind a building, and by the time the accused came out the other side all that remained of his sloppy-joe jumper was a collar and sleeve.

Soon afterwards, a briefcase with the money owing was delivered to Milton by a third party. At the time he was staying at a motel in Tennant Creek, lodgings he regarded as being 'pretty modern then' because he needed only to press zero on his telephone to get an outside line, as opposed to going through an exchange operator.

Money to save. Money to blow. Milton had both. During wet seasons he returned with Dominique to Katherine, but the town became nothing more than a revolving door for a young man who was conditioned to life on the move, and the opportunities *and* trouble that came with it. Longreach, where some of his cousins lived, was among his favourite places. Returning from Brisbane where he'd bought a truck and trailer, Milton stopped at the central

Queensland town with Kurt. While there, they were fascinated by the kangaroo-shooters who drove by with the results of their work hanging off hooks on the backs of their four-wheel drives. It made Milton think.

'You see, Milton's always gotta do somethin' bigger than someone else,' recalled Kurt. 'He thought, These blokes are only goin' and makin' 100 bucks a night. We'll do better than that. We'll do this properly. So he built this huge frame with hooks on his truck, so he could put 200 kangaroos on the back, not ten. And away we go out on the plains. And everyone else is shootin' roos with .222s, but Milton's got a .270, a big gun, so you only gotta shoot 'em once; you see, he's gonna kill his kangaroos better than anyone else too. Usually you shoot a roo, gut it and hang it up, but Milton thought, We'll just shoot the biggest mob of 'em, throw 'em on the trailer, and we'll gut 'em all after.

'Anyway, we done 'em all and we got about 50 kangaroos, all hung up. Proud as punch we are. Now he's gotta drive up the street so everyone can *see* he's done it better than anyone else. And when he went around the corner the whole rack wasn't tied to the truck, so it fell off and scattered kangaroos all over the main street of Longreach. That doesn't worry Milton. He pushes the rack into the car park, throws all the roos onto the truck and away we go to the freezer box where they hang 'em up. This old bloke comes out and he reckons: "What the hell is goin' on here?" We thought we were gonna get this cheque for a couple of thousand . . . Eighteen dollars I think we got.'

Longreach became well used to Milton's antics. Inevitably, his self-assurance – some might say ego – collided with too much alcohol, testosterone, and some police officers trying to cool a heated confrontation outside a pub. Milton ended up in the back of a police car – he refused to get into the paddy wagon – and on his way to a cell. Of all the yarns Kurt tells about his mate, none tugs at the corners of a deadpan expression more than this:

'This other big mate of mine, Bill, and me, we're gonna get Milton out of jail. He's just had a blue with someone, that's all. So we go down to the station and we're lookin' through the window and they got Milton and they're gonna charge him, and he's sittin' there and one of these junior cadet fellows is doin' the writin'. And the sergeant's there and Milton's just walkin' round while they're askin' him questions. There's a drawin' board there with all pins on it. And Milton pulls one of them pins out and he's got that pin and this little police cadet he's as nervous as hell. Anyhow, Milton just goes past and jabs him with that pin. And he lets out a scream and the sergeant says, "What the hell is wrong with you? Just do your thing." So he'd be writin' again and next thing you know Milton would lean over and stick that pin into that little cadet fella.

'Anyhow, they reckoned he was a danger so they locked him in the padded cell. Me and Bill were outside and we knocked on the door and the sergeant says: "What do you want?"

'"Oh, we've come to get that Milton Jones."

'"Well, you can come back in the mornin' and get him."

'"Oh mate, he's our boss. We've got 1000 head of cattle out here on the common, we're drovers and we really need him to run the show."

'"If you need an idiot like that to run the show you're all in a bit of trouble aren't yers?" . . . He ended up handing him over.'

It wouldn't be Milton's last brush with the law. His next wasn't only over a border, but an ocean.

CHAPTER 5

TEXAN HOSPITALITY

Kip Glasscock lived at the end of a road near swampland on the Texas side of the border with Louisiana. It was a 'dark and lonely' place, perhaps fitting for the mood of a recently divorced middle-aged man. But Kip was upbeat. He'd just received a surprising phone call from someone by the name of Milton Jones. Until then, he had never heard of him. But there was a connection: a couple of years earlier Kip had visited Australia on a motivational speaking tour, and one of the friends he'd made was linked to Milton in the someone-who-knows-someone way. That, in combination with a heartfelt sense of Texan hospitality, was more than enough for Kip to feel excited after Milton asked if he could come and visit.

'Well, that just sounds great,' said Kip.

It was December 1985. Milton and Dominique had broken up, and with the wet season ending another lucrative year of bull-catching Milton felt the time was right to see what life was like looking over a car bonnet on the other side of the world. So he flew to Los Angeles, freshened up in a hotel, then 'whistled into a car yard and bought an old Dodge Aspen with a 318 V8 in her, two-door.'

'Nineteen hundred she cost me. I paid cash,' remembered Milton. 'Then I was straight out there and gone. It took me three days to get out of LA. You can imagine straight out of the bush and into the big city, Christ Almighty! I didn't know where I was goin'. I didn't even have a road map. I just went. I must have done a few circles at one part there, I'll tell you.'

The early stages of the holiday challenged Milton to the point where he asked himself, Why the hell am I here? Homesick, he rang his sister Jenny to hear a familiar voice. America was just so . . . cars, cars, cars, horns, blinkers, stopping, starting, move-over-get-out-of-my-way; smog, graffiti, grime; fast-food joints, dodgy tacos; TVs with a lottery load of channels; boom boxes; basketballers with swaggers; swaggerers with basketballs; neon turning night into day . . . whooh, take a breath . . . America was, well it was just so different, not least Las Vegas where one high roller boasted to Milton that the key to success was a 'pocketful of money and a hard dick.'

Milton headed back to Los Angeles, where he picked up a tonic for his homesickness: his bull-catching mate, Robert Parkinson, who had worked with him at Willowra. It had been a joint decision by them to come to the USA, but passport paperwork had prevented Robert from flying out at the same time as Milton. Now that they were together, any thoughts about what they'd left behind were shoved aside by the two young men chasing good times. Eventually, the road led them to that dark, lonely place near swampland on the Texas side of the border with Louisiana. At last a spot Milton could relate to.

'I can remember the first time Milton's looking at a squirrel, just a squirrel, and he's giggling,' said Kip Glasscock. 'Here he is with these massive shoulders, these kinda sleepy eyes, and a big cowboy hat that looks like nothing anybody has seen around here. I have a 2500-pound bull, the biggest damn thing you ever saw. Some kind of Simmental-something that was shipped in, and I'm so proud of him. Milton jumps over the fence, runs after this bull, grabs that poor sucker by the tail, runs up beside him and pulls him down just for the fun of it.'

When told of Kip's recollection, Milton smiled before adding: 'We knocked him up first. We couldn't get him in a yard. Kip had about 30 head of cows and this old bull, and we upped him with a Kubota tractor. We chased the bastard round, Robbie and I, then we jumped off and threw him, put him in the bucket of the tractor and then put him in the yard.'

To Kip, the bull-throwing underlined Milton's 'wild, frisky, mischievous spirit that was all of a sudden let loose in Texas.' Perhaps in some strange twist of fate

Milton was always destined to have a relationship with America's biggest livestock state. Wind the clock back to his childhood, and somewhere along his trails he would have heard his father crackle out a line or two of his favourite song, 'The Yellow Rose of Texas'. Now, in a small way, he had another father. Certainly Kip felt as though he was 'Daddy', explaining an 'alien world' to two young men.

Kip was a lawyer with a practice in nearby Beaumont, a small city 120 kilometres to the east of Houston. He had bought a piece of land because 'in Texas, it's the sort of way one validates being a Texan. As soon as you get an extra nickel you have to go and buy a few acres so you can sit with everyone else and talk about cattle.'

Whether in Texas, the Northern Territory, Los Llanos in Venezuela, the thorny stretches of Paraguay's El Chaco, or anywhere else dictated by the paddock-to-plate cycle, there is a common link: cattle people like talking about cattle. Weights, ages, diseases – 'bloody ticks' – markets, ear tags, seasons, what to do with old cows, how many to run in a herd . . . It's not a job, it's a lifestyle. Milton and Robert were in their element. They helped improve Kip's yards, and became familiar with some local bars where a popular method of introduction was to talk an honest load of bull. They visited numerous ranches, including the renowned 'Doc McKellar's', where they learnt about artificial insemination (AI), which was becoming an increasingly important process in the breeding of Brahman cattle in Australia.

Kip was 'tickled to bits' with his guests and showered them with hospitality to the extent that Milton thought 'it was just like being in a new paddock: you didn't know which way to turn.' There was a trip to Florida; duck-shooting with Kip's teenage son, Rian; Christmas dinners; an introduction to eating the not-so-delicate catfish; there were meets-and-greets with seemingly anyone and everyone in Beaumont. Kip even took Milton on a private tour of the Jefferson County Courthouse, where he met a number of police officers. And all the while word spread about Milton to the point that a local newspaper, the *Port Arthur News*, wrote a feature piece about him:

> *He's young, muscled, strong and yes, brave. He's a 'real' man in a rugged man's world. He's one of a breed that may be extinct in coming years. He's a cowboy – in Australia.*
>
> *He makes his living – and a very good one at that – by catching wild bulls and shipping them off to America where they end up as that staple of American diets – the hamburger. Yesireebob, he does . . .*

Several months later, Beaumont's curious fascination with the 'Ossie' outback character was magnified across the United States, and indeed other parts of the world, when the movie *Crocodile Dundee*, starring Paul Hogan, was released. The American and international version was different from the Australian one: much of the outback slang had to be replaced with more widely understood references. The same couldn't be said for Milton. He remained authentic in every way – which literally wasn't the right way the night he swung his Dodge out of a car park after he'd been drinking at a local bar. Robert Parkinson was in the passenger seat. Next, the flash of blue lights and a shrill sound couldn't be lost in any translation.

'I went out on the wrong side of the road, you know Americans drive on the right and we drive on the left,' remembered Milton. 'When the coppers pulled us up, one of 'em said to me straight away: "Mister Jones." We never had that in the Territory because in the Territory they'd have to get on the radio to find out names, but in the US they just had to press a button and it brings up your rego and who owns the motor car. So, he says: "Mister Jones" and I said: "How ya goin', mate, I must have met you in the courthouse, did I?" Because Kip had taken me on that tour, see. Anyway, they put us in the car and drove us around – they couldn't stop laughin' to have these two Aussies there – and that was pretty good because we sobered up a bit. We wanted a coffee and a hamburger and they got us all that. They were in the shop, and we were left in the car, not cuffed or anything. And Robbie's got on their radio and started talkin'. Anyway, they put us in prison in there in Jefferson County Jail.'

The cell was small, and already had one inmate, a sleeping African American whom Robert had no intention of disturbing.

'His feet were hangin' off the end of the mattress about a foot and a half. He was snorin' away and Milton kept slappin' him on the belly and tellin' him to quieten down. And I'm tryin' to keep Milton from doin' that because I didn't want this fella to wake up. There wasn't enough room in the cell to get away from him. I think we were put in there for a reason. He was a big boy, and I was quite happy just to let him snore.'

Within hours Milton was reacquainted with the courthouse, and Kip was there again to guide him through an altogether different inspection of the American justice system. He received a fine for reckless driving and had to dig deeper into his pockets to get the Dodge out of a compound. He knew being a foreigner who adhered to different road rules helped his cause. Nevertheless, he received a strong warning from the judge who 'put it through the motions, slammed his hammer, and punted us.'

The rest of the stay in Beaumont passed without too many other 'incidents', other than the night in a bar that led to a disagreement, a wrestle on a pool table, an all-in, and then an all kicked out.

Despite his wildness – or perhaps partly because of it – Milton endeared himself to Kip in a manner that would have extraordinary repercussions in the future. But that wasn't in either man's thoughts as Milton and Robert farewelled Beaumont and pointed the Dodge towards adventure. In Austin, Texas, they played Paintball, where Milton 'must have done a good job because they wanted to sign me up for a team. I shot the lot of the bastards.' And in Taos, New Mexico, they saw snow for the first time, and then disregarded the advice of ski resort staff by choosing a chairlift over lessons. The sight of two men in jeans, jackets and cowboy hats was surely a warning for others on the slopes to be wary. If not, then the sight of two men in jeans, jackets and cowboy hats edging their way down a hard, icy mountain on their backsides most surely was. Faced with the choice of trying to work out what the different colours at the top of each run meant, they'd decided on a simple approach: pick the run closest to them. It was colour-coded black; the domain of only the best skiers.

'Yeah, it was an awful deal,' remembered Robert. 'I ran into some fella. He must have thought I could ski a bit. He was cuttin' across in front of me and I was totally out of control, and I whacked into him. He ended up pretty crook, that fella, I think.'

Milton wasn't as daring and 'skidded down all the way on my arse.' His assessment of his experience took a mere frosted breath: 'Bugger that!'

They aimed to leave early the next morning, only to wake up and discover the Dodge's windscreen was covered in ice. Hot water hurled from a bucket added to the problem: the glass shattered. The pair kicked out the windscreen and drove to Albuquerque with the winter air blasting their faces for two hours. The only car-wrecking business they could find didn't have the right sized replacement, so they compromised by fitting a smaller windscreen and filling the two-inch gaps on either side with plastic bags and duct tape. On they went towards Mexico, stopping at a roadhouse for a meal of fried chicken. Or so they thought.

Milton recalled, 'I've eaten it, and I've pulled out a shoulder blade, and said to Parky: "I've never seen a chicken with a shoulder blade in it before." Next minute there's a road block, and these coppers pull us over. They were laughin' at our windscreen. No worries, we actually had a cup of coffee with these fellas. They had a demountable in the middle of the road. Told us we were goin' the wrong way. I said to 'em: "Tell me somethin'. I bought this chicken back there, and here it is – what am I eatin'?" One of 'em said: "You eatin' armadillo, boy!" It didn't go down too well, you know.'

Milton and Robert hired a guide in a 'big old Yank Tank' to take them across the Rio Grande and into Ciudad Juárez, Mexico. Ample samplings of cervezas (beer) followed, and they each bought a saddle. On the way back to their guide's car, they were hounded by a boy who was probably well versed in playing the role of the wretched soul seeking sympathy from gringos. Milton followed the script and allowed his new friend to lug his purchase that looked so mountainous in little hands. Once the job was finished, Milton handed the boy his payment. The boy's eyes widened, and then they narrowed as he clutched the cash to his chest. In the green confusion that a wad of American dollars can bring, Milton had accidentally handed over a 100-dollar bill. As the boy dashed away, Milton watched others 'peel out of the woodwork' and give chase. The pack disappeared into a throng of people, leaving Milton to feel he had done the wrong thing; in the travel lessons taught by comparing one way of life with another, chasing bulls for a living had never seemed more appealing.

In all, Milton was away for three months at the end of which there was only one answer for a second bout of homesickness. He and Robert drove back to Los Angeles, the Dodge was sold, bags packed, passports stamped. America had opened Milton's eyes. He liked it, but 'There were too many bloody people.' The same couldn't be said for what awaited him.

CHAPTER 6

HELICOPTER OVER HORSEBACK

The scene is as if from a movie: in a remote landscape a husband and wife are prospecting in a river for gold. They work silently, picking through their sieves with such focus that nothing else in that moment exists. They are a long way from civilisation; the middle of nowhere springs to mind. Suddenly the silence is broken by the thunder of machines and they look up to see several vehicles and their occupants – men who are dirty, unshaven, and look as rough as a prison stretch.

'What time is it, mate?' asks one of the men.

The answer comes from the husband.

'What day is it?'

The answer comes only after a raised eyebrow.

'What month is it?'

It is too much for the prospector and his wife to believe. But it is true. The men have lost track of time.

'I reckon we'd been bush for about three or four months,' recalled Milton. 'I was tryin' to line up the Katherine Show; I had no idea if I'd missed it.'

Milton and his workmates had been catching bulls in the Kimberley region near the Bungle Bungles, the sandstone ranges that rise like gigantic termite mounds on grass-swept plains north of the Ord River. By the following year, 1987, the area would become part of the Purnululu National Park. Milton and his crew had put a road through from the Ord, bashing up next to the Osmond River. The result was a bits-and-pieces track that enabled them to get about 900 bulls off to the meatworks. In the same vicinity, the Argyle diamond mine may have been a lure for other young men trying to make a 'good earn', but for Milton, the money was all to be found above ground.

'Where I made a great quid was Ord River. That's where I did real well. It was all just dead flat, beautiful goin' and plenty of cattle. I think we averaged about 32 bulls a day there for five years.'

At the heart of the area was the Ord River station which was operated by the Western Australian government, whose agriculture department had been significantly regenerating the land since the 1960s by planting grasses. Milton was granted a three-year contract to 'clean it up.' He also worked on surrounding stations in what was a 'picture of a place. Mitchell, Flinders and buffel grass as far as you can see, and beautiful big rivers runnin' through it. The Osmond, Ord, Linacre, the Turner, Panton . . .' To this day Milton considers this his favourite country.

The scenery provided some relief from what remained a raw way of life for bull-catchers. For those who weathered it, years of reflection have given them an appreciation of experiences that helped build their characters.

'Being a young fella it just makes a man out of you real quick, you harden up quick, you know,' said Robert van Kuijck, who spent three years working with Milton. 'You might have five or six or ten in a camp with you. You've just gotta all work together. If you have a fall-out you'd have to sort it out there and then around the campfire. You'd have a big knuckle-up, then you'd sort it out, shake hands and get back into it [work] again. That's part of living in the bush.'

Robert, or 'Camel' as he was known in the camp, now runs a roadhouse in Condamine, a Queensland town of just a few hundred people. Born in Longreach, he received a typical education on the land: cattle and sheep mustering on horseback. Partly inspired by the *World Safari* movies that at the time made adventurer Alby Mangels a household name, he sought his own 'living on the edge' by moving across the border as a young man to catch buffalo in Arnhem Land. During the wet seasons he worked as a bull-fighter at rodeos in South Australia and Victoria. He met Milton in a pub, and once they got talking, the offer came up to go bull-catching at Ord River, and Robert thought it was time to try something new. Others who worked for Milton during this time included 'Pat', 'Old Man', and 'Pinky', all with the same approach as Camel: 'having a crack at making money with wild cattle.' And these were, to a considerable degree, wild men. Camel acknowledged that when given the chance they 'would come to town, have a big blow-out, have a gutful of grog and go back out again. It was all part of the adventure.'

Work hard, play hard. Milton remembered the plans he and others had of making it to the Katherine Show, about 750 kilometres' drive from Ord River. They travelled the first 500 to Timber Creek without problem, but . . .

'We got to Timber Creek and that was it. Got drunk there for about four days, then turned around and went back again. A bloke by the name of Maxey Duncan – he's dead now, he's gone; geez, a lot of people are dead and gone when you start talkin' about it. He had the Timber Creek pub. We were parked up there for, oh geez I must have spent ten grand there I reckon . . . Just grog for the blokes. It was cheaper to pull up there and get drunk than go to Katherine. And we were catchin' a lot of cattle and makin' a lot of money, so I shouted everyone. Anyway we were there and Old Maxey said: "You know, I've been thinkin' about makin' this pub 24 hours." I said: "Why don't you?" "Oh well, I bloody should," he said.

'Well, with that, I had a couple of mates and we looked at the doors, grabbed the top hinge and jerked 'em clean off, pulled the two doors off, threw 'em straight out the pub and into the back of the Toyota and said: "Now she's open 24 hours!" It had no doors on her, so he couldn't shut her.

'Anyway, when we did go they put me in the back of a truck, the buggers. Camel, Pinky and that. I'd been drunk for about three or four days. I had an old Mack with three trailers on her, and it was headed back west, and I was in the back trailer in my swag goin' back to Ord River. Oh it near killed me. I had to climb from trailer to trailer and I reached over the old window and grabbed the truck driver by the throat and threatened to kill him for puttin' me in there while it was drivin' goin' down the Duncan Highway. I was havin' a camp on the bitumen but as soon as I hit the dusty road it wasn't real good. Yeah, old Pink and them, the rotten bastards!'

When bull-catching, everyone's need to 'stand on their own two feet' was underlined by the realities of machine maintenance in the outback. As Camel suggested matter-of-factly, yet with tones of deeper meaning: 'You couldn't just go round to the corner store and say you wanted a spare spring for the motor car, or send it out on the bus.'

A broken-down or inefficient vehicle wasn't just lost time and money, but a dangerous liability should a medical emergency arise. The only form of communication was by VJY or UHF radio to surrounding stations.

By this stage, Milton's inventory included three buggies and two blitz army trucks that were used for picking up the bulls and storing supplies, such as drums of fuel and spare parts. Because of the daily bolt-jolting strain on them, the buggies needed most attention. In camp, there was a welder and an air compressor. 'We did plenty of tyres. Jesus Christ, we were always changin' tyres.' When a buggy needed servicing, Milton had a set routine: run the vehicle until it was nearly out of fuel; knock the plug out of the tank; drop the oil out of the engine; hook a rope to it and use a truck to pull it on to its side; then it was ready to work on. New U-bolts, change a spring, a tail-shaft, do some welding . . . all done just by 'jerkin' 'em' to begin with.

'I could just about tell you every nut and bolt on an '83 model Toyota,' recalled Milton. 'That's all I used to try and buy was '83; they had the disc brakes and power steerin'. They were a good thing. When you had the old drum brakes and you were there pump, pump, pumpin' with no brakes, she wasn't much fun. You gotta have good brakes when you're bull-catchin'. Good brakes and power steerin' was like gettin' on a good camp-horse. Them old hard-mouthed bastards with no power steerin', I've got chips off both elbows from the steerin' wheel beltin' me. When you were drivin' them old ones you'd hit an ant bed and *bang*, it would take the end off your elbows. I found a receipt the other day for a new Toyota. Fourteen thousand five hundred dollars for a brand new one. That must have been goin' back to the '80s. I used to buy a couple of new ones each year. Brand, spankin' new ones. Rip the gear off 'em, sell the cabins to a wrecker, and go!'

It's hard to determine who was more resilient: man or machine. One possible answer came the night Milton and his crew – he can't recall who, but maybe 'Wayne Long and a couple of blackfellas' – camped on the higher of two tiered banks on the Ord. It was a tranquil setting: a carpet of couch grass, lazy paperbarks spreading shade, and blue skies caught in the reflections of waterholes. Perfect, thought Milton. They stretched a tarpaulin above the camp that included a brand new '83 model bull buggy, a 'couple of old girls' (other buggies), a blitz, spare parts and about 30 drums of fuel.

In the late afternoon it started to rain . . . and rain . . . We'll be right, thought Milton.

They built a campfire, started a generator to shed some light, and settled down for the evening. By the time they rolled out their swags, the rain had eased to a drizzle, a bush lullaby on the tarpaulin that belied what followed.

'About one o'clock in the mornin' I heard the bloody roar,' said Milton. 'I didn't know what it was. I raced around and got a torch, you know, pitch black, and there was a wall of water comin' down the river. All I've got is me swag. The bank was real slippery, a red bank. We scrambled up, got out of there with our swags and the bare minimum. We couldn't get any vehicles up there, we were slippin'. Anyway, the water took the new bull buggy, just rolled it, wrecked it, and all our fuel and all our tucker – the whole lot. In broad daylight in the mornin', Jeeesus there was some water there all right! We went and got some of our gear and tucker back. We were lucky to get away with that one.'

Although the water subsided quickly, Milton and his crew were forced to stay there for a week or more. They were still able to go and catch bulls, but they couldn't get their vehicles across a large sandy stretch reaching to the other side of the river. This led to Milton adding Marsden matting to his essential equipment for his next trip to the area. The perforated steel strips, commonly used on old air force runways, provided enough support and traction for the blitzes to idle across without getting bogged.

Whether it was making temporary roads, servicing vehicles, or finding answers for any unexpected situation, Milton and his workmates proved adaptable. Bull-catchers had to be. This trait impressed one man in particular. Texan lawyer Kip Glasscock was there when Milton laid the Marsden matting for the first time.

'Here was a relatively uneducated yet very bright man. He was shrewd,' recalled Kip. 'And Good Lord, I'd never seen such absolute focus. Make it happen, no matter what. The damn axle breaks in the middle of the river, fine, make things happen because there's nobody to make an excuse to. Of course I'm just doing it for fun, to learn something. It was his turn to be the tutor and for me to listen. He'd explain everything, even the very basics like: "When you see this kind of tree it's sweet. That means it will support a lot of cattle." He explained things that my forefathers probably knew, but I didn't.'

Kip went to Australia with his teenage son, Rian, primarily to experience bull-catching. He'd been so intrigued by the seemingly indestructible natures of Milton and Robert Parkinson and the stories they told on their trip to Beaumont that his curiosity had become an itch that couldn't be resisted. From the moment Milton picked them up at Darwin airport in a LandCruiser they were launched into a so-called vacation that both enraptured and shook them. One of Kip's clearest memories remains the trip into the Ord area. He and Rian, and an 'Aboriginal fellow' sat on top of a generator, boxes of spare parts, swags and other bits and pieces in the rear of a Toyota tray-back.

'We're hanging on for dear life as we're screaming down these gravel roads, and I'm thinking, What the hell is a man my age doing here with his precious kid?' recalled Kip.

He had reason to again question his decision to experience outback life after he'd been part of a catch for the first time. It had begun well. The bull had been spotted, the revs were lifted, and the chase was on. It ended tragically. The tired beast found a second wind, charged the buggy, and broke its neck.

This was a powerful moment, a brutal fragment of a way of life that few people, beyond the bull-catchers themselves, had ever experienced. Kip knew he and Rian were privileged to be there. Some people went on cruises to Alaska, others saw Big Ben, the Eiffel Tower and the Colosseum on holiday-of-a-lifetime package deals, but bull-catching in the Ord . . . well, that was something that couldn't be summed up in a scrapbook or on a coffee table of knick-knacks. There were of course the gentler times, none greater than sleeping under the stars in a swag. Then there were the experiences destined to be told and re-told back in Beaumont.

'I remember Milton thinking we'd all smell bad after a couple of days, and he said: "You gotta dip your pills, you gotta dip your plums," said Kip, laughing from the end of a crackling phone line in Beaumont, where he still practises law. 'He made us do it, but I didn't take a bath, a full bath because the waterholes had little freshie crockies [freshwater crocodiles] wherever we camped. So, you'd only splash up on yourself.'

After about four weeks Kip and Rian headed back to Darwin. Milton arranged a lift for them on a meat truck. They barely made their flight to Sydney. Pre-cooked packaged meals and seats with little leg room were a blissful step back towards a comfortable life, although Kip remembered that at least one other passenger wouldn't have been relishing the trip.

'She leaned over me to put her fancy hat down, and I saw her reflected in the window glass. She had a look that said, "Did you get a whiff of these two!"'

As the Texan lawyer returned to his sedentary job in which bills could be charged in increments of minutes his bull-catching friend remained in a workplace where the dollars were determined by endless hours of personal risks. But it was worth it. Milton was making money. Lots of it. On a trip to Mataranka, he spontaneously bought two blocks of land, one with a house already built on it. These were the first pieces of dirt he owned. He also wanted a piece of the sky.

'The first chopper I bought was a little Robinson 22 from Slingair at Kununurra. It was a brand-new rebuild out of the States,' said Milton.

The R-22 is a lightweight single-engine, two-bladed helicopter that seats two people. To this day, more than half those registered in Australia are used for mustering.

The rounding up of cattle by helicopter was first trialled in northern Australia in the late 1960s by ex US Navy pilot Stuart Skoglund. It proved successful, and from that moment on an increasing number of pastoralists turned to the air to sort out matters on the ground. By the 1980s heli-mustering was common, in no small part due to BTEC, the ongoing national campaign to eradicate brucellosis and tuberculosis from herds.

BTEC was an ambitious program that created a logistical – and often economic – nightmare for the owners of large stations where even a block of a million acres was considered 'small'. The process required the mustering of paddocks of cattle into yards where veterinarians, under the supervision of government-employed inspectors, tested the stock for TB by injecting a purified protein derivative into the skin under each animal's tail. Three days later, the vets would search every injection site for adverse reactions, primarily extensive swelling. Any affected beast would be shot and examined post-mortem. If it was found to be a disease carrier, the entire paddock from which it came had to be de-stocked.

'All sold to the abattoirs. Cut their heads off, calves, cows, the lot,' remembered Milton. 'On top of that, any stock left behind after a muster in a paddock had to be shot. That used to play a lot on the musterers. You had to have your wits about you. You could look like a complete bloody idiot if you left a lot in a paddock, and you had the stockies [stock inspectors] comin' back the next day in a chopper and shootin' behind you. They'd run through and shoot everything that moved in it.'

Owners were compensated for the losses, provided they were part of approved programs between themselves and the Northern Territory government. If they weren't, they received nothing.

More and more stations turned to contract musterers to do the work. These were enormous operations. Even after the yarding of the cattle was completed – and there were a number of places where portable yards had to be dropped in as well – there was the responsibility of looking after the stock for the period between the testing and analysis of results. The cattle needed to be let out to feed, so this required further control.

Hundreds of millions of dollars were poured into BTEC; it was 'bloody huge money' that Milton wanted to have a part of. The purchase of a helicopter and acquisition of an Air Operator's Certificate allowed him to do this, albeit as a fledgling member of the heli-mustering community. Milton wasn't yet licensed to fly, so he contracted pilots. His very first was Tim Anderson from Victoria's Murray River town of Swan Hill. After doing his training at Maroochydore on Queensland's Sunshine Coast, Tim, in his early twenties, gained work with Kerry Slingsby who ran a helicopter business, Heliworks, in Kununurra. While there, he was leased out to Milton, and it didn't take him long to ask, 'What the hell have I got myself into?'

The flying was different from anything he'd ever done. It was 'intense', mustering from dawn to dark and eating 'pretty much just a bag of onions and whatever we could pick up.' Tim, who now owns an aerial agricultural services company in South Australia, acknowledges the three or so years he worked with Milton were integral to his development as a pilot.

Aside from mustering, the chopper gave Milton greater scope as a bull-catcher: finding cattle in scrub at ground level could be difficult, so having a set of eyes in the sky, and another means to steer the bulls in particular directions or run them into yards was advantageous. Despite the BTEC culls, stock still got left behind, and Milton capitalised on this. He split his time between the Ord and other stations across the Kimberley and the Territory's Victoria River region.

'Through BTEC, I worked on a lot of stations,' remembered Milton. 'You'd go there after the stations had had a run at 'em [bulls], but couldn't get 'em, so we'd go and catch 'em. Get the money out of 'em before they got shot. There were lots of helicopter hours and lots of feral cattle, lots of cattle left behind. So we'd go and do deals. Like at Ord River I was goin' and buyin' them for 30 or 40 bucks a head, or somethin' round there.'

The late 1980s was a boom time for Milton. Yet some tallies belied his growing wealth; for a man who spent months on end working away from any type of home, it would be expected his food expenses alone would be sizeable. After either his first or second season in the Ord, he claimed just $83 on his tax return. There'd been few shopping runs, but many 'killers'.

The money gave Milton choices. More choppers? More buggies? Trucks? The answer came at 1000 feet above the ground.

CHAPTER 7

A ROUGH LITTLE BLOCK

Milton had become a competent reader, but there was never a need for him to follow lines and pages. Paperbarks, hardwoods, and the landscape around them were more his choosing *and* his educators.

'You're screamin' through the scrub at 30 or 40 kay an hour after a bull and you see a different shade of grass, you know your wash-outs [holes or breaks produced by washing out of earth by rain] and stumps, you can see things before you actually see 'em. Knowin' what sort of timber grows there and what sort of grass is that, whether it's rough or smooth. You know to stick to the red country, that's the better goin' so you look for your red country grasses when you run the bull, or you run him back to the road. Just the things you learn. I don't read a book real good but I read the country well.'

In his R-22, where those unfamiliar with the country would see little more than colours determined by land, vegetation and water, Milton interpreted deeper meanings. An area that had a mix of both red and black soils was 'strong': after rain the red country would 'come away green', and the grasses on the black would take longer to respond, meaning continual feed. But beware the straight black soil with few stones. It could be deficient in phosphorus. In the worst cases, cattle without the adequate amount would die: it was so horrible to see a cow with 'peg leg', having drawn every last nutrient it could out of its bones, barely able to stand while a weaner suckled it for milk. Elsewhere, dense thickets of shrubs with broad purple and green leaves and red flowers lived up to their name, Bellyache Bush, another killer. Nutwood, bloodwood, silver box, snappy gums on red ridges; 'good mimosa' in the Ord, 'proper bad mimosa' in the Top End; plains, ridges, swamps . . . Milton had learnt to read them all.

On a trip back from the Ord to Mataranka in 1988, he surveyed a particular piece of land below him in the Victoria River region: spectacular escarpments with some 'rubbish country'; a lot of bloodwoods and coolibah trees; bauhinia and some rosewood on the black soil . . . 'very sweet.' But most of all, he looked at the river that split the land: 'good water.' And the banks were sandy and shingly: 'not steep.' That was a bonus, especially at the end of a dry season when poor cattle would still be able to have a drink and get out again, unlike other parts of the river, or on different waterways where precipitous muddy banks trapped many a weary animal – 'and that's where the poor buggers would stay.' Milton noticed several crossing areas where cattle could walk from one side of the river to the other, and there were lots of couch, buffel and urochloa grasses – 'good herbage.' As was his professional and personal habit, he also surveyed the landscape for cattle. There were no branded ones, just 600 or so ferals.

Soon after arriving in Mataranka, Milton heard on the grapevine that the 'rough little block' he'd seen was for sale. With his finances soaring, he'd been advised by his accountant that he should consider buying some land. So, he contacted the selling agent, Elders, and was taken on an aerial and ground inspection of the 700 square kilometre station. He knew next to nothing about the operations of the place; nevertheless his mind was made up in a matter of hours: 'Stuff it, I'll buy it!'

Elders flew Milton to Darwin where the auction was held at the Crowne Plaza Hotel. He was one of a few interested buyers.

'I was pretty myall. I'd never been to an auction. I had about 380 grand in the bank, all from bull-catchin'. Anyway, the auction slowed right down, and I ended up gettin' it for 450 grand. I borrowed a bit off Elders, and there you go. It was a good spot because it was right in the middle of everything. It was a Small Purpose Perpetual Lease, close enough to freehold, unlike most blocks that have a 99-year lease on 'em. It was mine, and that was it.'

The station was Coolibah. Like so many pastoral blocks, it came with its own rich history. Originally, it was part of Bradshaw's Run, an enormous pocket that stretched all the way to the Victoria River's mouth on a remote and inhospitable stretch of coast that looked out over Joseph Bonaparte Gulf. It earned its name from Joseph Bradshaw, who acquired a lease for the land in 1894 just a decade after the area had first opened up to pastoralists with the establishment of a handful of stations, including the mighty Victoria River Downs and Wave Hill. The belief that the land held promise for the pioneers was partly due to the assessment of explorer and surveyor Augustus Gregory who, with a highly qualified team, travelled through northern Australia from west to east in 1855–56. It took them fifteen months, during which time Gregory identified the good grazing land he saw. Both the upper and lower reaches of the Victoria River were included. And so both the cattle and sheep industries were launched in the area, thanks in no small way to the epic feats of the hardened people who 'overlanded' stock from South Australia and Queensland.

Since those earliest times, Coolibah underwent various boundary shifts, changed ownership several times, and played host to some incidents that ensured its character wasn't solely moulded by its cattle and country. Of all its incarnations, none was more notorious than during the mid-twentieth century. In 1949, a commercial pilot was killed when his plane crashed at Coolibah while on a mail run. A few years later the station was used extensively in the filming of *Jedda*, the first feature film to cast Aboriginal actors in the lead roles.

One of the whites who appeared in the movie was Wason Byers, manager of Coolibah at the time. He was a strongly built man with a reputation for being horrendously cruel to Aborigines. With the passing of years the reliability of some accounts can be questioned, but there seems little doubt he was responsible for some appalling acts, including ordering two Aboriginal women to sit naked on a galvanised tin roof in the middle of the day, and firing gunshots near the feet of Aborigines. Later, Byers was arrested for stealing cattle from Victoria River Downs station. At his trial he blamed his Aboriginal stockmen for 'cross-branding', the process by which one brand was burnt on top of the original one in a bid to hide ownership. He was acquitted.

Milton knew next to nothing of Coolibah's history when he bought the station. His knowledge of the block's past stemmed no further than the previous owner, Ian MacBean, a former New South Welshman who worked up from being a ringer in the Territory in the 1950s to become a highly successful cattleman. And that's all the

ABOVE: A man, his mates and his machine. Milton was always destined for a life in the bush. (JENNY JONES COLLECTION)

BELOW LEFT: A multi-ribbon winning combination. Milton and Wonga at Katherine. (JENNY JONES COLLECTION)

BELOW RIGHT: Stan Jones had a way with camels. The sounds of '*Whoosh*' (get up) and '*Gyeeee*' (get down) are still vivid in Milton's memory. (JENNY JONES COLLECTION)

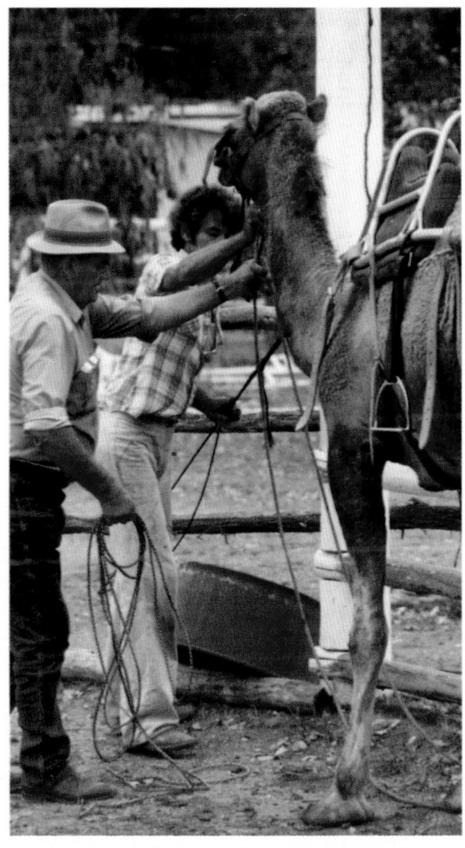

ABOVE: On the road with a bull-catching crew in Western Australia. *From left to right*: Camel, Milton, Craig (on bonnet), Pinky and Abo. (JENNY JONES COLLECTION)

BELOW: Sliding a red bull up onto a blitz. (JENNY JONES COLLECTION)

ABOVE: First trip to the USA. Milton and Robert Parkinson. (JENNY JONES COLLECTION)

RIGHT: Stan and Llawrence. (JENNY JONES COLLECTION)

BELOW: The Jones family. *From left to right*: Mary, Terry, Randall, Jenny, Stan and Milton. (Missing from the picture is Llawrence.) (JENNY JONES COLLECTION)

ABOVE: Milton at Coolibah soon after he'd bought the 'rough little block.'

(JENNY JONES COLLECTION)

RIGHT: The remains of a helicopter crash Milton was a passenger for. This was the start of a series of unexpected events.

(JENNY JONES COLLECTION)

ABOVE: The perils of crocodile egg-collecting mean you sometimes have to move fast.

BELOW: Helicopters make accessing crocodile nests a little easier, but it definitely isn't a simple day at the office.

ABOVE: One of the few times Milton has dressed in formal attire was for his wedding to Cristina.

INSET: The results of the 'cock-eyed bob'. Milton thought Cristina was joking when she called and told him the roof of the house had blown off. It wasn't a joke.

ABOVE: Farming life starts early! Milton and Little Milton.

INSET: Father and son inspecting a catch of water buffalos.

ABOVE: Jim Dooley has lived on Coolibah for over twenty years. Here he is with little Milton.

BELOW: During muster, Milton and Cristina's brother Hamish worked up a thirst.

confirmation Milton needed. He too was now a cattleman. At the time, Coolibah had little more than an abandoned homestead, a red tin shed, a yard, and scrapheaps that were seemingly as full of snakes as they were of rusting steel, pipes and wire.

'Coolibah was pretty run-down. Cattle were livin' in the house when I come here. The gauze was all kicked in. Had horses livin in it too,' recalled Milton. 'We had no phone or nothin'. You'd just have a two-way radio: Flyin' Doctor 5365 was the frequency. And you'd get on that and go to the Flyin' Doctor base and tell 'em what phone number you wanted to ring – that was always the difficulty because you had to have the numbers, you couldn't just ask for 'em – then they'd put you through and you could talk, but everyone could hear you. Everyone in the area was on that frequency so you couldn't say much. I was with a Kiwi girl then, Phillipa. She was in Mataranka, so we used to talk in puzzles there sometimes. You know, "There's a big storm comin'," or "There's a bit of trouble in the wind."'

Milton didn't have any immediate aim or a business plan for Coolibah. First and foremost his new purchase was a central base for his bull-catching and contract mustering. It just so happened it was a bonus that police stations were few and far between in the area, meaning he could 'bounce through' towns in his buggy with little worry of being caught. However, he still laid tracks, most conspicuously in his army blitzes, which became a source of curiosity and perhaps confusion for some other people in uniform. The tail end of the 1989 bull-catching season in the Ord region coincided with 'Kangaroo '89', an extensive Australian Army military exercise involving an 'invasion' of northern Australia by an 'enemy' from the mythical country of Kamaria.

'These bastards would see our tracks and they must have thought we were the Kamarians,' recalled Milton, slapping his left thigh. 'We used to get a few visits from the army. Anyway, one time they dumped a heap of tucker . . . we found it and picked it up. It was all unmarked. Bloody hell, a lot of carrots! We must have lived for two months on them tinned carrots and beef. And peas. It was a bit of a lucky dip what you had out of the tin. I suppose it was all out of date but we were into it.'

Peas and carrots, carrots and peas, the monotonous clickety-clack of existence on the bull-catching line. Although it caused moments of concern – Jenny Jones thought Milton often looked 'malnourished' when he visited her in Dalby at the end of a season – the rewards outweighed the disadvantages. Terry Jones, who by this stage was living in Katherine and raising two daughters from a broken marriage, helped Milton do his paperwork, together with their mother. Terry wasn't surprised that her brother, who was 'hard-working adrenalin on legs' had become so successful. She was, however, stunned when he suggested that he buy half her hairdressing salon to save her making bank repayments. It proved to be only a short-term deal, but long enough to help Terry.

'Milton turned everything into fruition,' said Terry. 'He made everything happen. I mean, *he* made it happen. He was always uncanny with incredible foresight.'

Milton's rising fortunes were a talking point in the Jones family. Yidumduma Bill Harney recalled when, he thinks in the late 1980s, Milton's father Stan returned to Katherine to live and caught up with his former head stockman.

'Old Stan and his boy Lawrie (Llawrence) come up and Stan said: "Can you take us down the river to look at your country." And I said: "Yeah, all right." So the three of us jumped in the car and away we went and camped down the Flora River. And old Stan said: "Good to be like this, watchin' the stars like back in the early days." And I said: "Yeah, it is great." Anyway I went away and I come across him again and we sat down and talked, and this is what Old Stan said: "Milton, he's a rich bastard." I said: "What do you mean, rich?" Old Stan told me: "He's got his brain real switched on. He knows how to make money. That boy will be bigger than Kerry Packer," he said.'

Stan had seen Milton at work in the Ord when he went with Terry and her youngest daughter, Brooke, on a bull-catching trip. He'd expected nothing less than the tough, long hours he saw his son put in. It was, after all, the Jones way.

As the dollars continued to mount, Milton was also able to build up his own stock in a manner that would be illegal today. Currently in the Northern Territory any transportation of stock beyond a property's boundary requires a waybill, the documentation that shows the station of origin, and which can be used to trace stock movements. All cattle must also wear an NLIS (National Livestock Identification Scheme) ear tag that carries a code which identifies the station of ownership. However, no such legislation was in place when Milton, with the permission of the stations he was working on, occasionally brought ferals back to Coolibah.

'I started a little herd of cattle. I got 100 head here, 100 head there, and put them together. It was good because I had my own brand by then: TSK, Territory Stanley Knight. We had an abattoir right here at Victoria River, so we basically brought a lot of cattle from where we were catchin' back to here, and sold 'em to the meatworks from here. It was a licence to print money.'

Milton expanded his business further when he bought his second R-22 helicopter. Time for the pilots was spent between mustering, running bulls for catching, and 'lining up' the overlooked stock in paddocks for shooting during the BTEC period.

It was inevitable that Milton would eventually gain his helicopter pilot licence. He began his classes by sitting in the passenger seat and operating the dual controls under Tim Anderson's supervision. The lessons provided a new sense of freedom. Milton was no longer restricted to life in a stock camp; now he had options for escapes: a trip to Mataranka or Katherine, even Darwin. Throw in a 'bit of work this way and a bit of work that way,' and Milton 'did quite a bit of bloody time on the duals.'

He did his formal training with Howard James, the chief instructor at Heliworks at Kununurra. It took about three months, 'doin' engines and systems and learnin' everything inside out.'

Milton's ability to read the country enabled him to take some short cuts during his lessons. On one flight he was asked to fly to a set of yards that were marked on a map as being on a stony ridge on one side of a river. Milton deduced the area was too hard for the building of yards, so he flew to softer country on the other side of the river where he discovered where the yards in fact were.

Throughout his working life Milton has adhered to the six P's: 'Prior preparation prevents piss-poor performance.' Never is this more essential than when undertaking heli-mustering in its various forms. Whether running in bulls or doing a full seasonal muster the operation begins before any stock is stirred. It was the same when Milton was clocking up his early air miles.

The first steps involve inspection of the area to determine what, if any, infrastructure is needed. This may be a yard with a crush, a draft and a loading ramp. At times a road may also need to be graded or at least improved enough to allow truck access. The placement of the yard can be determined by where the cattle are and where there's access to water. Unless there is prior knowledge, this is best done by an aerial inspection, which also allows the pilots to 'know the paddock.' In the largest cases these may be 700 square kilometres, as big as the whole of Coolibah station. Considering the vastness, maps may be used to explain each pilot's role: 'You go this side of the creek, and I'll go the other.' At times as many as four machines may work a paddock.

Once the muster is underway, the pilots begin working their dedicated areas 'high and wide' at as much as 1000 feet. But as the day moves on, the flying becomes lower and harder, backwards and forwards, moving tiring cattle towards the yard or another destination. Noise is the key. The pilots must put themselves in positions where the cattle will run away from them. The images can be captivating and often so richly Australian: curling fingers of red dust slapping rumps; silhouettes of gum trees and broad hats; and above all, machines that change direction in less than a blink, giving the impression they could be toys suspended from a piece of string that are being blown on by a powerful breath. Concentration is intense.

Weaving among trees while watching and reading the cattle: a cow that has lost its calf, a rogue that lies down under bushes. It is a draining job, aerobatics without the gaping crowds.

'If you want to find your cattle you get up a bit higher and have a look where your lead is,' said Milton. 'In scrubby country you won't see it. You gotta work yourself a lot more, read your cattle. If you think your cattle are gonna pull up or turn around, you gotta be watchin' that . . . that's what you gotta be lookin' for to be a good musterin' pilot. In scrubby country you gotta think, Righto, there's three here, and there are four there on the tail. When you get to the end of the day you say: "There's my three bullocks I started with way back there, and there's that bastard I thought was gonna lay down." When you're threadin' 'em through into the yard and you start seein' the cattle that you thought you might lose, that's when you've done a good job.

'There's lots of rules with choppers and cattle. The biggest thing is you don't want 'em to move too far too quick, which is hard because you're movin' so quick. Same as on a motorbike; I hate motorbikes because they end up in the lead all the time, they go past the cattle. And it can be the same with a helicopter because you can fly over a lot of cattle. You've gotta take your time and slow right down, steady, steady. You get right on 'em if you have to, touch 'em with the skids sometimes to get em goin'.

In the earlier days there was a lot more Shorthorn cattle while they were still introducin' the Brahman. So you'd get a big lead when you were chasin' with a helicopter because the Brahmans would cover twice as much territory as the Shorthorns. Shorthorn cattle would pull up but the Brahman cattle would just go. You'd really have these two different classes of cattle to muster which made it bloody difficult. Now, you've just got all Brahman cattle or all Shorthorn cattle and away you go at the one pace. Whatever you're doin', all you really have is a noise and a position.

'There's a lot of skill in it. You know most of these paddocks you'll finish by two o'clock, somethin' like that. You start at daylight. At Ord River, where I did most of my early flyin' every yard you'd run a thousand up the river, then you'd go back and run a thousand down. You might be a week handlin' one, then a week handlin' the other. Then move your yard.'

Relentless, rewarding – and dangerous. The first helicopter Milton owned was the first one he crashed in. The reason was: 'too much fuel, too heavy, too hot, two of us in it, and inexperience.' Milton was in the passenger seat spotting bulls near Bullita outstation, which is now part of the Gregory National Park in the Victoria River district. As it turned out, the accident was only the start of a comedy of errors.

'The helicopter just stalled. We were hoverin' actually and it rolled over, that's what wrecked it. The machine hit the ground and dropped over. I buggered my knuckles up tryin' to punch the bubble out, they're tough bastards. I was on the bottom side, and I could hear all the fuel runnin' out. I undid the buckle and the old mate [pilot] he was hangin' sideways with the seatbelt on top of me. He was right. I kicked me way out of the bubble and got out and told the pilot I would go and get help. Then I had to run out to the road about 4 or 5 kay.

'There was two truckloads of bulls comin' and I blocked the first truck, and Kurt [Hammer] was drivin' it. I caught him, otherwise I would have spent the night there. It was late afternoon. Anyway I started vomitin'. I must have run too far, I was just havin' a big drink of water when we crashed, actually. I had the water bottle up to my mouth, a big gutful of water. Kurt sat me down and said: "Don't panic, don't panic," and I told him what happened. He'd pulled up on a dirt main road goin' into Bullita, and I knew the pick-up truck comin' in behind had no brakes, very limited brakes. It was one of those ex-army trucks and it had a full load of heavy bulls on it.

'Kurt had me sittin' down right beside the muffler of the truck. He kept sayin': "Don't panic, don't panic." And I looked up and I see the second truck comin' down the road flat and it was like you see in the movies. I sang out: "He's got no brakes, he's got no brakes!" Kurt ran over the top of me to get away, and I just made this dive. This truck went *wssssh*, and all I could see was the rocks flyin' up; he had to straddle the windrow [a ridge of pushed-up dirt or debris found in the middle of outback roads], you know. There was a tree, a good big bloodwood tree and she [the truck] just cut her clean off.

'This fella, the driver, has hopped out and he puts his hands on his hips, all bailed up and says: "What the fuckin' hell's goin' on here?" When he'd found out we'd crashed the helicopter, that was all good. I think we've had to walk back in there and get this other fella [the pilot]. It was nearly dark. And we walked out again and they made me drive this truck back to Coolibah because the other driver had got too big a fright. I had to steer this old six-be-six that didn't have brakes on it all the way home. It was a pretty common thing in them days, no brakes. There wasn't much maintenance . . .

'Anyway, those bulls went back to the Vic River abattoirs. And there was twelve bulls and I think eight of 'em had TB. Just one particular load, that's how thick it was in different areas. So, no money for 'em, no pay, just down the chute. We crashed a helicopter, near got run over by a truck, and no money.'

Thankfully for Milton – and no doubt any future unsuspecting truck drivers – such incidents were rare. With each flight he took in his early years as a pilot, Milton gained a greater understanding of, and respect for, the ways of the air. By the end of the 1980s, helicopters would become integral to his business. At that stage he still had no concrete plans. It was a 'see what happens' approach. But this belied his shrewdness. Milton knew how to grab *and* make opportunities.

CHAPTER 8

ROOM FOR IMPROVEMENT

In general, bush dogs don't whinge. On as little as a hatful of water and a handful of love they'll be at your side all day, just letting you know with an occasional nudge of their nose against your skin or a gentle lean against your legs that they're there, ready to do whatever you, the boss, tell them to, or at the very least they'll support you with a panting smile – or smiling pant – while you are working. That is, unless it's a hot day and the shade under the Toyota makes an all-too-inviting spot to curl up and sleep until a whistle or the calling of a name prompts an ear to be pricked, an eye to be opened, and a body to bow under the bullbar before shaking out the dust and come trotting towards you with here-I-am purpose.

Milton has had many canine mates throughout his life: Spud; Lucky; Boofit; Tige; Piggy Pig (deaf); Squirty (three legs); Lolly; Dozer; Gypsy; Eighty (found 80 kilometres out of Katherine); and there was also the long-serving Smiler, a white-speckled blue heeler–bull terrier cross.

'Smiler was a beautiful dog,' recalled Terry Jones. 'When Milton came to the hairdressing salon he'd leave Smiler out the back, but after he bought half the salon, he said Smiler was allowed inside. I sometimes think that's why he bought the place.'

Smiler was alongside his boss at Ord River when Milton caught a pig and hogtied it in the back of his buggy. What should have been a cheerful drive back to camp with different meat for the menu turned abruptly into a dangerous situation.

'I looked around to make sure the pig was right, and I hit a gully, went straight down a hole and it swallowed the whole Toyota, that's how deep it was,' said Milton. 'It knocked me out. I can remember goin' over the front of the Toyota; lucky it didn't keep goin' like that or it would have squashed me. The motor car basically ended up at 90 degrees, and I ended up under the bullbar that had stopped on top of a vee in the gully. It was just on dark when I come to; two hours I reckon I would have been out for. The radiator scalded my arm, and I hurt me knee and bent the steerin' wheel. The accident sheared all the mounts off the engine and the engine went straight through the radiator. The fan was sittin' on the bullbar. That's how hard it hit. I wasn't goin' that fast, probably first or second gear, but *boof* straight down! My old dog was layin' there with me when I come to. I had him for a long time, Smiler. A bloody good dog.'

The relationship between humans and animals is at the core of bush life. As he continued working in the Ord and beyond, Milton had so many experiences with nature in all its guises that an outsider could be excused for thinking his stories could only be conjured by a vivid imagination. But to Milton, nothing was to be unexpected, although this didn't prevent him from being surprised when the unexpected did happen.

'We were at Waterloo station [in the Northern Territory] bull-catchin'. We might have been camped there two or three days, I reckon. Anyway, we got home after dark and I didn't have a torch. Had a wash and a feed, and I threw my swag back and oh the stink, geez it stunk. I thought, What the bloody hell is goin' on here? I used to carry a little 12-volt light on my bull buggy so whenever I was workin' on it I just hooked the light up to the battery. I used to park my Toyota right beside me swag and I'd hang my towel and dirty clothes on it. I hooked this light up on the front of the motor car and had a look in my swag and here it is: an 8-foot bloody king brown with ticks all over him. Oh, a big stinkin' bastard it was, right in my swag, eh. I must have killed him, got rid of him, I forget what I did. From that day on I have always rolled me swag. Every mornin' you know, and put your straps around it. He was a big snake. Geez, if he had bitten me it would have been the end of me.'

While at Waterloo, Milton also caught about 50 wild camels. The process was the same as bull-catching, apart from when Milton urged a worker to leap from the bull buggy onto the back of a galloping male.

'I reckon we were doin' about 30 kay an hour when he jumped on him, and I reckon by the time he jumped off him we was doin' about 60,' said Milton laughing. 'He was just hooked onto his hump like a monkey. Geez, that old camel got pace. Bloody hell, and this bastard couldn't get off and he was howlin'. I'll tell you what, it pulled some skin off when he landed.'

The camels were taken to Coolibah where Milton hoped their browsing habits would 'clean up the Parkinsonia.' It worked. Today, the highly invasive prickly bush doesn't exist on the station, but some of the camels still roam. Others were broken in by Stan, who by then was living in Katherine. The Jones patriarch had 'mucked around' with camels at Gordon Downs and had used them to pull fire ploughs. He was delighted to wind back the clock and with a growing tobacco-crackle in his voice order his new batch of cantankerous animals to 'Whoosh!' (get down) or 'Gyeeee!' (get up). They were later sold to tourist operators. One remained as a pet; Milton named him Cecil after Stan's favourite camel from nearly 40 years earlier.

Coolibah was to have another unusual pet at around the same time. After seeing a 'big old fella buffalo' near the homestead, Milton applied the bull-catching technique again and knocked down the 800-kilogram animal with a buggy. He tied it up on a long rope for about a month. After this the beast seemed nearly tame enough to eat out of Milton's hand. Nevertheless, although he didn't know much about buffalos Milton knew enough to realise his new addition wasn't to be trusted. He let it go and waited to see what would happen. A few days later, Milton was on horseback bringing up a mob of cattle when the buffalo came 'flat, sideways out of the grass.' It broke through two fences before a bullet stopped it.

Such experiences ensured every day was a mix of both the new and familiar for Milton. Work remained the centre of everything. While his BTEC jobs had slowed down substantially by 1990, his bull-catching, and increasingly his contract mustering, led him to be as 'flat strap' as ever. Despite soaring interest rates – a standard variable home loan rate in early 1990 was 17 per cent – Milton managed not only to repay his debts but continue expanding his business. However, it came at the expense of some of his fellow cattlemen who surrendered their land to receivers when the interest rates battered them beyond recovery. Milton was contracted by Elders to 'clean up the paddocks' at some of the sinking stations. Among the early stations he worked on were Limbunya and Fitzroy, both owned by Don Hoare in the Victoria River district. Their paths would cross again in the not too distant future, in unfortunate circumstances.

Amid his tough existence, Milton was led, or led himself, into situations to learn from, laugh about, and store in the memory to be recalled from time to time, often as a yarn around a campfire. Sometimes the campfire itself could be the story, as it was when Milton was bull-catching with Kurt Hammer at Limbunya.

'We must have lit a fire and cooked a feed there and we didn't put the fire out and we come back and there's nothin' left. Burnt the lot: swags; tucker box; the handles off the butcher knives; all the tins had blown up; a wooden box was gone, just the hinges left. We had a bit of tea in one thing and we were tryin' to drink this burnt sugar and geez it was horrible. It was cold. Christ, no swag, nothin', just the buckles left on the straps. We rolled ourselves up and camped in hessian for two nights. Then we said: "No this is it, we're gone!" Lots of things like that happened over the years; I gotta jog me memory to think of 'em all,' said Milton.

Limbunya was also the scene of harmless pranks that could so easily have gone wrong. Milton, Kurt and some Aboriginal workers were walking some cattle from one bore to another when they came across a buffalo track on the road. Milton immediately made up a story that the marks must have belonged to a beast that a stock inspector had injured with some misdirected shots earlier in the day. This was enough to put those unaware of the twist of truth to be edgy.

'That night at the camp Kurt and I got a blanket and put it over our shoulders and heads. We got down and started singin' out *wa, wa*, a real flat sound,' said Milton. 'We broke a few bushes and next thing the blackfellas took a scatter this way and that way, and we heard this big thump on the ground next to us and I said to Kurt: "What was that?" He said: "A big fuckin' rock." Then we realised the rifle was in the Toyota and all the blackfellas had got in there too. Not good. So we had to start yellin' out and tellin' 'em we wasn't a buffalo. They all camped inside the yard that night, they were still a bit unsure, you know.'

Whether it was in the midst of silliness or seriousness, Milton loved his work. He was married to it: the calluses; Barcoo-rotted skin; constipation; breaks and bruises; breathtaking sweeps at 1000 feet; triple decks of bulls off to the meatworks; busted axles; burnt swags; a weekend blinder at a pub then back to bumping, strapping, skidding . . . what a way to live. And yet, he was missing something, or more particularly, someone. Neither Milton nor Dominique knows exactly when they 'tangled up' again, but it was likely to have been 1989 or '90. Kurt's sister had spent part of her time away from Milton in the remote settlement of Borroloola, in the Territory's east. When she returned to Katherine, she at first wasn't interested in renewing an old relationship, but was drawn in soon enough. She moved to Coolibah, and although it was a relative advance from a bull-catcher's stock camp, it was still a shock.

'It was unbelievable,' recalled Dominique. 'My God, it was terrible; it had been abandoned for a long time. The first wet season I was there we ended up sleeping outside because it was too damn hot in the house. It was just like an oven. The first Christmas, I was cooking dinner and it was 52 degrees in the kitchen.'

While trying to start again amidst the clutter of yester-year, Dominique had every reason to wonder if things would improve not only at the station but on the merry-go-round of a relationship with a work-obsessed man. It was time to hang on and see while Milton led her and his business in a new direction.

PART THREE

THE MAN FROM COOLIBAH

CHAPTER 9

MONSTERS OF THE TOP END

When interviewed for this book, Owen Pugh had grease on his hands. He'd taken time out from fixing a bore to walk through the early evening's stickiness, make a Soda Stream drink and sit down next to a churning fan in his home for a chat. He wore blue shorts and a blue shirt, his long legs were skinny and scarred, and his ginger moustache peppered with white straggled over a mouth that was missing a few teeth. The top joint of one of his fingers was missing, legacy of a machine accident. Adhering to the age-old Australian description for redheads, his nickname was 'Bluey'. He spoke slowly, with dry humour never far away, and his flat vowels belied a South African upbringing.

Bluey was a boy when he left Cape Town with his family in about 1960. After going to school in Melbourne he was lured to Alice Springs by a sense of adventure.

He became an apprentice diesel mechanic, but by the time he was eighteen he realised 'you get paid more for wrecking trucks than you do for fixing them,' so he took up carting cattle.

'I drove for all the tin-pot people, anybody that needed a steering wheel attendant. In them days there wasn't a whole lot of roads, so you couldn't really go wrong; as long as you had a good back and could dig your way over a hill or through a creek they'd put you behind a steering wheel.'

He moved from small operations to a formidable empire when he got a job with Buntine Roadways, established by Noel Buntine, a major player in the road-train industry. While working there, he met Milton, but can't remember when or where that was; it was just a case of 'You all sort of circulate in the same environment and sooner or later you bump into each other.'

The responsibilities of marriage and raising a young daughter eventually steered Bluey off the road and into a job managing a rival company owned by multi-millionaire Robert Holmes à Court. He didn't enjoy it, and he yearned to return to the road, but his acceptance that 'career transport drivers don't really stay married or have families' prompted him to seek work well away from grinding out long hours on bitumen and dust. Luck was on his side when he received a call from Noel Buntine's son, Dennis.

'He said: "I've just bought Yarrawonga Zoo near Darwin. Come and run it for me,"' recalled Bluey. 'I told him I didn't know shit about a zoo, but he said I'd pick it up. So I went and ran that for a while.'

And that is where he became a student of *Crocodylus johnstoni* and *Crocodylus porosus*, the freshwater and the infamous 'man-eating' saltwater crocodiles. Popular history in the Top End has long thrived on stories about deadly encounters with and lucky escapes from these descendants of the dinosaurs. US President Barack Obama even became crocodile publicity fodder when he visited Darwin in 2011 and was insured by the Northern Territory government against a crocodile attack. The newspaper archives offer all sorts of attention-grabbing articles. As much as any, one that appeared in *The Mail* newspaper in Adelaide in 1931 underlined a perception that remains common today:

> *Death Lurks in Crocodile Infested Waters*
> *LOATHSOME – cowardly – treacherous.*
> *The huge crocodiles that infest the waterways and lagoons of northern Australia are hated alike by man and beast. Floating hour after hour with only the tip of the nose and an eye showing above the water, they wait for whatever prey may come their way – fowl, fish, beast or man.*

Bluey preferred to learn about the creatures from personal experience, and as time passed he realised the often-described 'monsters' of the Northern Territory could potentially provide a profitable business. Their skins could be sold domestically and overseas, particularly through Asia and parts of Europe, to make handbags, belts, shoes, wallets, purses, knick-knacks . . . 'not a bad quid.'

Crocodiles had been killed for their skins in the Top End for many years. In his book *Hell West and Crooked* the jackeroo-cum-buffalo-hunter-cum-crocodile-shooter of the 1920s and '30s, Tom Cole, wrote of earning 'one shilling and sixpence an inch, measurement taken across the belly.' At the time crocodiles weren't only killed for their hides, but for public safety. Methods included: shooting, trapping, poisoning, and at least one hunter said he occasionally used dynamite. After World War II, hides were exported to Europe, but by the late 1960s crocodile numbers had plummeted to the extent that the Northern Territory government declared both species protected. Consequently numbers rose, and since then various conservation and education programs have created a greater awareness about the habits of these infamous Territory residents. In addition, a small number of farming licences have been granted, allowing the harvesting of particular wild crocodiles and eggs to be used for commercial, tourism and conservation purposes.

After doing his research, Bluey was so convinced money could be made that he mentioned a possible venture with Milton, whom he'd run into from time to time over the years. Milton agreed it was worth a try. He saw an opportunity.

'I sat back and looked at it and thought, Yeah, well, that could work. Crocodile farmin' wasn't somethin' I set out to do. It just happened. I could see potential. Not a lot of people knew a lot about it, but I thought it was a good idea and when you get to that stage you gotta put a lot into it, which I have with nearly everything I've done. There was a lot to do in the old Territory, and there's a lot to do yet.'

The initial steps involved developing business and conservation plans that were made in consultation with National Parks and Wildlife officials and Darwin-based crocodile expert Graham Webb. The centrepiece of these was a series of night-time surveys of numbers of both freshwater and saltwater species at three waterholes in the Victoria River district.

'We had to count 'em on logs, in the water, on the bank, and estimate their sizes. There were two full surveys, and then we were given a permit to go back and catch a certain amount out of each hole: 10 per cent from one, 20 per cent from the second and 30 per cent from the third. And they were the ones that helped start the croc farm. Then we had to go back the next year and count the populations again to see if our catchin' had an impact,' recalled Milton.

Their work led to the allocation of a licence for the Coolibah Crocodile Farm, which was built on a small block of land that Milton subdivided little more than a kilometre away from his homestead. It was 1990. Initially facilities consisted of two temperature-controlled tin sheds and later a house for Bluey and his family. It was agreed Bluey would conduct the day-to-day operations, while Milton would provide resources and finances for early operational costs and additional infrastructure. He spent about $150 000 on the farm in these early stages. When not away mustering or chasing bulls he would also be involved in the core process of the whole industry; the process that has helped romanticise the image of those involved in the Northern Territory crocodile industry: catching crocs.

At first concentrating on the smaller, less fearsome 'freshies', Milton and Bluey experimented with various catching methods, all of which were attempted at night when a spotlight skimming across the water could detect the telltale gleaming slits of eyes that betrayed lurking crocs. Catching was also only attempted in the dry season when the cooler conditions slowed the crocodiles down. At one waterhole the novice catchers were provided with a net by National Parks and Wildlife, but it wasn't successful; wherever and whenever Milton and Bluey launched their flat-bottomed dinghy at the spot, the hunted 'went to ground.' Milton reasoned the crocodiles had become shy from being shot at by Aborigines living in a nearby community. Elsewhere, harpoons were tried: one was fired from a modified sawn-off .243 rifle and the other was a pole; both ran out a high-strain nylon cord. They met with mixed success: even if the crocodile was caught there was still the matter of tiring it out, hauling it back and then into the boat. Harpooning, particularly with the pole, was judged to be 'too hard and too slow.' Eventually they trialled – and accepted – a riskier method: put on a wetsuit, strap a short-bladed knife to a forearm in case of emergency, and 'just jump over the front of the boat and grab 'em.'

'You gotta grab a crocodile on the back of the head and wrap your legs around him and lay on him, sit on him,' said Milton. 'If you jump on him in shallow water it's easy: you just take him to the bottom and he'll thrash around and then he'll knock up and you got him straight away, and you can hold him on the head with two hands. The freshie has only got a small snout, but if you grab hold of it and he does a bit of a roll with you, you gotta let go in a hurry. He'll tear you to pieces. They are real strong.

'The bigger the better; the bigger the skin the more money we thought we'd get. Everything from 1 metre to 2 metres; freshies only grow to about 6 foot or so. The bigger fellas would be 50 or 60 kilograms. They were hard to hang on to. One night I grabbed one; actually

Dominique pushed me, she was there with me. I'd jibbed because it was too big and she said: "Go on!" So I went with it. Anyway, I went down, I'd hooked onto it, it was a big crocodile, and it took me down that deep me ears popped. I hung onto it and come back up with it. It was about a 6- or 7-foot freshie, a big strong bastard. I hung on all the way. God, if I knew then what I know now I wouldn't be jumpin' over the front doin' that because a freshwater crocodile is a pretty good diet for a "saltie", you know what I mean? He'll eat the freshie and me at the same time. You're jumpin' on 'em and they're squealin' and thrashin' around. But we were tryin' to make a quid, and I'm still here.'

Once caught, each crocodile was tied by the legs and a 'big old mongrel knot' at the end of the rope was placed in its mouth before the snout was taped, thus allowing about an inch gap between the jaws; otherwise if these were firmly clamped down, the crocodile could regurgitate food and choke itself. The eyes of the reptile were also taped shut. They were then taken back to Coolibah on the back of a Toyota.

Both Milton and Bluey received the occasional 'chewing' of a hand or arm, but nothing alarming enough to deter them. The strongest pain came from the balance sheets which quickly showed the freshwater trade just wasn't viable for them. The logistics were also demanding, especially the acquisition of meat for 'feed-lotting'; for this,

Bluey and his wife, Janelle, received permits to shoot feral horses and cattle in the nearby Gregory National Park. Additional supplies came from 'busted pizzle bulls' that served no further use in a herd, and any feral donkeys and buffalo on Coolibah.

'It's something that you don't think about when you start farming: the amount of food you go through. Even today we're feeding a tonne-and-a-half every week,' acknowledged Bluey. (At the time of the interview, the Coolibah Crocodile Farm had about 3000 crocodiles at various stages of growth. All were raised from incubated eggs.)

Eventually Milton and Bluey 'swung the gate' on the freshwater crocodiles, and were granted licences to go after the bigger prize. On average, saltwater crocodiles grow to between 3 and 5 metres long, and the larger males can weigh about 500 kilograms. A further glance at any one of numerous websites may crowd the mind with statistics – a *C. porosus* has as many as 68 teeth and can bite down with 2.2 tonnes of pressure – but the full magnitude of the saltie's reputation as a predator becomes apparent in stories of close encounters. Several years after starting the crocodile farm, Milton was part of an almost unimaginable incident on Moroak station, north-east of Coolibah on the Roper River.

'An old yellafella, Johnny, he was a horse tailer [the person who looks after working horses on a station], come trottin' up one mornin' and he said: "Hey, somethin' big come down from that hill and grabbed one horse. It grabbed it by the throat and put his throat out. Somethin' big on the side of that hill." That's what he reckoned, somethin' big like a bear because that horse was back two mile off the river by then.

'I went down and jumped in the motor car. I still didn't know what it was, and I thought he must have galloped through the dump and hit a bit of steel or somethin'. It had just broken daylight, and when I saw the horse, Jesus Christ, he'd been hit so hard all the meat around the throat was busted and it pulled the windpipe right out. He was breathin' through his brisket [breast], and his two veins were filled up with blood and there wasn't enough flesh and skin to hold 'em, so they've dropped down. Here he is standin' up there with his two veins from his brisket just under his cheek. He hasn't cut the veins, see, they're just hangin' there. And I'm lookin' at that and thinkin', What's happened here?

'I had a gun on the dash and I shot the horse straight away. I had a look at him and there was this big print of a row of teeth, and I said: "Johnny, crocodile, big one." There were two old busted pizzle bulls that croc killed then. And a couple of poddy calves. He was killin' bloody everything. He was right at the house, killin' the lot.

'You know a crocodile, if he's smart, he'll fish, like he'll set a trap to get a bait: he'll kill a wallaby and he won't eat a lot off him and he'll put the rest of it on the bank, he'll just leave him half in the water and half out. He'll eat the turtles and everything around him, the catfish and all that. And then a dingo or a pig will come along, or a kite hawk, and he'll grab 'em. This big crocodile I couldn't trap the bastard; I kept settin' this trap and I could see his tracks. He'd come up beside the trap and go back. A big steel trap. I was catchin' plenty of little freshwater ones. We must have had the trap in there three or four months.

'Anyway, it rained and the river come up a bit, and this young fella come back and said: "Hey, big crocodile in the trap." I went down there and he [the croc] had no back legs, he must have been fightin' and had 'em bit off. He needed the water to come up before he was able to swim into the trap. So yeah, we got rid of him. Big horrible bastard.'

Similar incidents all lay ahead for Milton as he and Bluey redirected their business. The vicinity around Coolibah had pockets of *C. porosus* habitat, particularly boat ramps, and where cattle drank. The bigger crocodiles were trapped, the smaller ones were harpooned. Soon, Milton and Bluey spread their operations further afield and surveyed areas by boat or helicopter south, east and west of Katherine, anywhere that didn't infringe on the catchments of their competitors, who were all based in the Darwin area. Conservation was a critical component of their operations, but it came at a cost.

'We used to take them from everywhere, but the conservation guys wouldn't let us kill 'em there and then. You know you can't really do anything with a 14-foot-plus crocodile unless you put him in a display somewhere in a zoo, and you can only have so many of 'em. The deal was, we had to bring 'em to the croc farm in the back of a Toyota, hold onto 'em for six months, and then we could sell the skin, shoot 'em. They just took up space and cost money and feed, so it wasn't a good exercise,' admitted Milton.

Once again they refined their business. They built incubators and prepared for the wet season, which was when crocodiles nested. When it arrived they did more aerial surveys, this time specifically making note of the locations of nests, which were usually near permanent water and sometimes on plant-pads that stretched out from the river bank. The nests were distinctive: oval-shaped mounds that were two or more metres long, nearly a metre high, and made from soil and plants. After finding the nests, Milton and Bluey launched into trial-and-error expeditions of collecting eggs which were then taken to the farm where they planned to rear hatchlings all the way to the commercially viable age, generally between two and three years. It was a bold undertaking for two men who were learning as they went. Bluey acknowledged, 'There were no books written on any of this, and certainly the farms in Darwin weren't going to assist us in any way.'

While searching for nests required patience, collecting eggs needed courage. Where possible, the best method was by air. Milton discovered that females would 'nine times out of ten run off the nest and go underwater and hide' when a helicopter hovered above them. Before or after this, depending on the location, Bluey would be dropped off at a landing point as close to the nest as possible. Once he'd clambered over often rough or boggy terrain to reach the nest, he then had no more than five minutes to collect the eggs – a good return was 50 or more – and carefully place them upright in an Esky before the mother had recovered from the initial fright and returned. In the meantime, Milton would remain nearby and keep watch for any unexpected arrival. If that happened, hurried escapes with or without the Esky were the only priority.

The western coastline near the mouth of the Victoria River was one of the early spots they ventured to. It was a place of haunting loneliness where secluded springs and windswept trees were like landscapes from the beginning of time. Few people had ever been there. Few people will ever go there. But it suited nesting crocodiles, and as a result . . .

'One day I was in a nest there,' recalled Bluey. 'Milton very rarely used to come into the jungle with me because he was busy flying. It was his job; it was *his* job to know where the crocodile was, it was *his* job to know where the next nest was, and it was *his* job to organise things. I just did the pack-mule work.

'I've got my head in a nest and my arse up, but this day when we were in the jungle I fell into some quicksand; I know that people don't think there's any quicksand in Australia, but there is. No one would have ever found me. And Milton was there, it was a tight spot and he'd come in to give me a hand. He used to carry a pump-action shotgun and I went down and he found me in there and pulled me out by the barrel of the shotgun. A good thing his finger wasn't on the end of the trigger. Anyway, he may or may not regret that manoeuvre now. The female croc was probably about 10 or 12 foot away, lying watching me, and I had no way of getting away; she could have just come in and grabbed me at any stage. I went down to me belly button. That was an interesting day.'

When reminded of this story, Milton laughed before he said: 'I had a good mind to leave the bastard there, too!'

At times the two business partners had their differences, but Bluey never lost respect for Milton's ability in the air – 'I can tell you I've not flown with a better pilot, and I've flown with a hell of a lot' – and it was this that enabled the pair to access seemingly impregnable places. Risks were taken that initially outweighed the returns but Milton and Bluey persevered, believing they could make the operation work. This led to much thought about how they could improve what they did. Bluey's recollection of their most daring *and* influential decision is today underlined with a wit that twenty years ago surrendered to disbelief.

'Milton started saying: "Hey, what happens if we get an old parachute harness and then I can pick you up with a chain Bluey and we'll drop you right on the nest?" What a wonderful idea!'

But it worked. It was called 'slinging'. As Bluey adapted to being a human tea-bag, he and Milton discovered their new technique saved time and money. When only dropped close to a nest, Bluey could take an hour or more to struggle through the 'jungle' to get to his destination and back again. Add to that the minutes needed for collection, and the quarter of an hour to pencil the eggs for identification, and it all added up to the completion of just one nest in an hour and a half. Of course there were areas where nests were close to each other, but the initial slinging-in still cut out the walk-in time.

While Bluey accompanied Milton on most of the early expeditions, other people were also employed at various times. As with bull-catching, Milton has forgotten some of the names over time, but his recollections of events remain clear. In the early days when he only had R-22 helicopters, he once worked with two young men along the Roper River. With Milton as the eye-in-the-sky, he was able to direct his helpers to various nests via two-way radio. From his position, he was also a prime spectator.

'We've found this crocodile nest on Kangaroo Island, I think it was. When the tide goes out, it's 10 or 12 foot of just sheer banks, mud banks. And there wasn't a place I could land anywhere; it was just thick scrub. Anyway, I see a nest and the crocodile there, and everything is fine, so I'm flyin' round lookin' for more. And I've told these fellas just to tie up there on a pad and follow the pad in and there's the nest. They've tied this boat up high, and this crocodile, it's bloody out of there! She has gone straight out where she thinks it's safe. Straight out the pad and landed in the boat with these two blokes! No rope or nothin' on this bastard, she's straight off the nest.

'When she goes in, she hits the floor hard and her nose gets wedged under the seat. This one fella has grabbed for the mangrove tree above him, and with it bein' all mud and everything, he's hangin' on to it with his two hands and two feet but he's slowly gettin' lower and lower over the boat. It didn't break off, it was just bendin' down in the mud. The other bloke, well, he's jumped straight in the river and he's hangin' on the side of the boat lookin' in. The crocodile, it's thrashin' itself around – as it would, you know what I mean – and oh, I'm just about fallin' out of the helicopter with laughter. Finally this thing has got its head out and it took off again in the bottom of the boat and it couldn't get out. Every time it would try to get out, its nose would hit the lip of the boat. Finally, the crocodile got out and jumped in the river and this fella jumped out of the river into the boat and the fella falls from the tree into the boat too. Straight away they reckon, "No more, no more crocodiles!" Ohhh, I laughed.'

Whenever there was a raid on crocodile nests, anyone involved could rightfully choose to count their blessings as well as their eggs. But for Milton and Bluey the risks were worth it, as gradually their crocodile farm returned a profit. In hindsight, an episode in the farm's fledgling days could have been considered a bad omen. At Coolibah, 1991 will always be remembered for a force of nature much mightier than the crunch of a saltie's jaws.

CHAPTER 10

THE BIG WET

When Cyclone Tracy devastated Darwin in 1974, Milton was living at Mountain Valley station with his father, brother Randall and sister, Terry. He remembers the heavy rains that hammered on the roof and cascaded down the external walls of the donga in which fragments of his broken family were staying. At times he could do little more than read comics on his bed. On a trip into Katherine he was amazed at the truckloads of tarpaulins and building materials being prepared to go to the Territory's capital. Then, about a month or so after the disaster he went to Darwin with Stan. One of his strongest memories was the lack of trees; those that were standing were stripped of leaves and there were few birds.

The 1974–75 'big wet' had record rainfalls and floods. Sixteen years later, the gauges spilled over with even greater numbers as a result of unusually long and intense monsoonal activity across northern Australia. In February

1991, the rain was relentless. Upstream of Coolibah, stations recorded falls of hundreds of millimetres in just a matter of days. In particular Milton had heard there'd been 'huge rain' about 50 kilometres away on Delamere station. Although Coolibah had received much smaller dumps, Milton knew there could be 'a bit of a flood' and his homestead was likely to be isolated for a few days. But that was nothing to worry about; it was just part of the wet season cycle. Then, about mid-morning, on 9 February, he received an emergency flood call via radio from Victoria River Crossing, just 17 kilometres by road from Coolibah.

Milton immediately flew with his pilot, Tim Anderson, to the area. They arrived to find that the most prominent building, the roadhouse, situated just a few hundred metres back from the river, was becoming an island surrounded by rapidly rising waters. Other buildings at the Wayside Inn behind the roadhouse were also being swamped. The police ordered an evacuation. A truck was parked close to the building, enabling everyone to climb up it, and then onto the roof of the roadhouse. From there, Tim and Milton shuttled about five people across the brown, cranky swell to where vehicles were waiting on the dry, higher side. Once they completed that, Milton, ever the opportunist, took a moment to look after his own interests.

'I said to Tim: "Well, it's gonna be a while before this goes down, I better grab some supplies." By this time

Tim's sittin' on the roof hoverin', and I shimmied down a pole. The owner of the pub, old Don Hoare – we used to have a few blues. I did the receiver work when he lost Fitzroy and Limbunya – he saw my helicopter, then me come out of the pub with a mailbag of bloody whisky under my shoulder, well, they reckon he near chewed the seat out of the aeroplane he was flyin' around in.'

Next, Tim and Milton flew to surrounding paddocks where some mixed stock, mostly cattle and horses, were standing along fence-lines. Tim hovered above the gates while Milton jumped out into shallow water and opened as many as he could. Using the helicopter they then hunted all but one of the animals to higher ground.

'This one horse. He only had one eye, the poor old bastard. He must have got a fright from the chopper, and he took off. So I went with him,' said Milton. 'We got in a bit of fast water, it would have been about 20 foot deep. I'm tryin' to hit him on the head and flog him up to try and turn him; because he was nearly blind he couldn't see he was goin' back in the river, the poor old bastard. I knew the old horse too, he was a good old horse. Anyway I'm tryin' to belt him across and I'm goin' with him in the floodwater, tryin' to hunt him out onto high ground. When I hit him the silly old bastard turned and he started strikin' me and belted me all down the shoulder. Lucky he didn't hit me in the head; he would have knocked me out. Anyway, not a good idea this one, so I left the horse and hit the main road where Tim picked me up.'

Back at Coolibah, Dominique and Bluey were busy lifting everything in the homestead as high above the floor as they could. They even took off the lounge-room doors. Dominique had also slaved in the kitchen, cooking corn meat and potatoes because 'We just didn't know what to expect.' Kurt Hammer, who was also staying on the station, rounded up about 30 horses and brought them close to the house. They would later be stood up on a slab of concrete that had a little more elevation than the flat surrounds of the valley.

Milton returned and instructed a second pilot, Jim Ryan, to find a suitable place to land and set up camp on the top of a nearby escarpment.

Dominique recalled: 'By about four o'clock the water was just coming over the helicopter skids on the pad near the back of the house. And Milton said: "We've got to start getting out of here." I had a three-legged blue heeler dog, and two pet kangaroos, little ones. Milton sent me up onto the hill. There was also Bluey, Jim, and Pete Vandenberg, another bloke who used to work at the croc farm. I had a mosquito net and my swag. I put the dog and the kangaroos in there as well. We all fought with each other the whole night.'

Milton and Kurt decided they would stay behind. At some point before darkness Milton swam about a kilometre to bring a boat that was tied near the bank back to the homestead. The waters were calmer than he'd imagined. They weren't furious, but they were still rising. By then, he and Kurt had skidded up the station's main generator onto the back of a truck, and had tossed some tyres onto a 40-foot trailer. They planned to burn these throughout the night in the hope that the light would settle the horses, some of which were spooking at the sensation of feeling their hocks covered in water.

'We kept burnin' them tyres, and we kept the horses there, ended up tyin' up three or four and settled 'em down,' remembered Milton. 'Anyway, it turned about ten o'clock at night and [the water] started recedin' and oh, we were happy because it was comin' and comin' and comin'. We didn't have a torch or nothin', just a mob of candles. We opened all the doors to the house and there were wallabies, centipedes, snakes, a bloody buffalo bull! The whole lot. The water was about 18 inches in places. And when we come into the old house she's dark and I said to Kurt: "We'll get on top of the roof and camp up there, chuck a mattress up there."

'We've done that and we've got all the doors in the house open. Anyway, Kurt comes walkin' round a corner and he's got no shirt on; he's just got a pair of shorts or trousers on. And he's got this big candle that's on a plate with all this hot wax. I'm comin' the other way . . . I must have startled this big river wallaby and it has hit the candle and plate full of wax and has gone straight over Kurt's brisket and burnt the shit out of him. I heard the thump when it hit him and he's "*Oohh*." He's tryin' to punch it and this wallaby has just scratched him, torn meat off him everywhere. He didn't know what had hold of him there for a while.'

Today, that memory prompts laughter, but that belies the emotions Milton rode when he wondered if his livelihood would be swept away.

'I remember that afternoon Milton went down the end of the house, he sat there and cried and just said: "We're going to lose everything,"' said Dominique.

After a sleepless night on the rooftop, and little better on the escarpment, everyone rose to see almost the entire valley underwater. Soon after first light they reunited at the homestead to inspect the damage. The old station hands' building, which is now the kitchen, had over a metre of water in it. It would take Dominique three days to clear the mud out. Elsewhere, water lapped at ankle to shin height in sheds and yards. The homestead was least affected, leaving Milton to wonder if those who'd built it nearly half a century earlier had known they'd picked the highest spot in the valley, or was it pure luck?

A more thorough assessment of the damage only came after an aerial inspection of the entire station. It revealed that some equipment had been destroyed, and kilometres of fences lay like cheap necklaces ripped apart and hurled aside after a partygoer's wild night. The temperature sheds at the crocodile farm had also been partially damaged, but thankfully they held little stock at the time; if the flood had happened just a few weeks later 750 hatchlings could have been added to the losses. Some horses couldn't be accounted for, and it would take Milton several days to estimate how many cattle he'd lost. He had a herd of only 1200. By the time he'd seen all too many bloated carcasses, some of which had been swept many kilometres downstream onto the neighbouring Bradshaw station, he initially believed he'd lost about 300. The final count was between 600 and 700, or on paper, assets worth hundreds of thousands of dollars.

The scene at Victoria River Crossing was also devastating. Demountable buildings and vehicles had tumbled downstream, petrol bowsers were wrecked, and the roadhouse was layered in mud after water had reached the counter. If one feature alone symbolised the destruction, it was the one-eyed horse that Milton had tried to save.

'I went there about three days later when the water was down,' said Milton. 'The horse was only about 500 metres from where I left him, and he had his head caught in the fork of a tree, and he drowned there, the poor old fella. I reckon he hung there for months. I often think that could have been me.'

After rising 17 metres at Coolibah in less than a day the Victoria River took its own weary time to subside.

The morning after it peaked, it had fallen back enough for Milton, Dominique and the others to begin mopping up close to the homestead. In the following days, the member of parliament for the Northern Territory seat of Katherine, Mike Reed, who was also Minister for Correctional Services, organised an unusual work party to help: a small group of supervised low-security prisoners from Gunn Point near Darwin.

'They sent us about five or eight of 'em and the biggest job was feedin' the bastards because we had no tucker or nothin' here. You know, we were still all hemmed in from the Wet,' said Milton. 'They had a warden here with 'em, camped here. We had 'em here for about a week. They didn't do much. We couldn't move, we couldn't get around. They were here too early.'

It was a challenging time where even the simplest of tasks could prove problematic. With bore pumps and pipes broken, Dominique sourced water from 'a creek which was right at the front door.' While boiling the water was an expected part of the post-flood procedure, the amount of swimming snakes encountered was an altogether different proposition. One evening when resting in the house, Milton heard a rustling sound on the verandah. He walked out to find an 8-foot king brown slithering towards him. In flood times, shovels have more uses than just for scraping up mud.

After the flood, Milton saw no option but to re-stock his station and start again. The money earned from bull-catching and mustering still promised to lend a healthy hand, but in the brutal ways of the bush some of it came from another's misfortune. At the same time that Milton and Dominique were rebuilding Coolibah, a prominent family in the area had begun a desperate legal fight to cling onto its land. And it was a fight that Milton was to be drawn into.

In 1962, Bill Tapp had paid a Territory record of £90 000 for Killarney station, about 100 kilometres south-east of Coolibah. In the following two decades he expanded his holdings to include the Roper Valley and Maryfield stations, which were north near Mountain Valley. But by the 1980s his ill health – it was no secret that he drank heavily – affected the running of his once-flourishing empire, and the debts mounted. In January 1991, Elders served receivership papers on Killarney, and the legal dramas began.

Milton became involved when the court-appointed receiver, called public tenders for the mustering of the three properties and the turn-off of cattle for sale. This included a BTEC muster on Killarney. The process was fraught with emotions after Bill Tapp's sons offered the lowest price to conduct the muster themselves. Milton's offer was $2.30 higher per head, but the lowest offer outside the Tapps' tenders. Milton was awarded the contract.

This shattered the friendships Milton had with Bill's five sons, Sam, Joe, Ben, William and Daniel. He had known them since his fist-flinging, drinking days at local rodeos when he'd competed against them, and occasionally brawled with them. It also left Terry Jones in an uncomfortable position because she considered the Tapp boys to be honorary brothers to whom she was bonded because of their mutual love of horses.

'It was sad when it all happened,' said Terry. 'I've never told Milton this, but when this Killarney thing was going on – oh that was ugly – all the Tapp boys came and had a meeting at my place in Katherine. They discussed all their business and I said: "I don't want to hear anything about it." Then they left and Milton came the next day with other people and they were talking about it, and I thought, Shit, I'm the meat in the sandwich, but I've got to be loyal, Milton is my brother. I didn't want to hear about anything the Tapps had done. I remember old June coming in to my salon once and Milton was there and man, did she feed it to him. She called him every name under the sun.'

June was Bill Tapp's former wife. They'd divorced in 1985, but June returned to support Bill and the family throughout the drama. Such was the strength of her feelings she staged a protest against Elders down the main street of Katherine. She had a banner that read: 'They stole his cattle, they stole his land, and they stole his work.'

The Tapps sought to stop the muster by seeking an injunction in the Northern Territory's Supreme Court. In refusing the application Chief Justice Martin noted: '. . . the proceedings thus far between the Tapp interests and the Elders interests have been bitterly fought at every stage. Each side distrusts the other in everything . . .'

It was against this backdrop that Milton conducted the musters, working closely with Elders. While they accepted the job at hand, it was Dominique who was often closer to reminders of the simmering discontent.

'I went that year to Killarney and I was book-keeping, and cooking for about 48 because we had all the security guards. We're still not sure who they were actually protecting: us or the Tapps. I don't know who was supposed to be attacking who. There were maybe eight security guards there, who'd all come from Sydney, I might add. This would all cost a fortune. That was a huge thing at the time. It was in all the newspapers. We were the bad guys going in there doing the job for Elders.'

An observer sympathetic to the debt-ridden would perhaps view Milton's actions as ruthless. But Milton took the view that: 'It's a fact of life. If I don't do it, someone else will.' For some it seemed heartless, for others it was an opportunity and a sound financial decision.

'That was a lot of excitin' times,' said Milton. 'Big jobs when you sit down and think about it now, you know thousands of cattle, and lots of emotions. So yeah, you've gotta cover all of that.'

A settlement between the Tapps and Elders was eventually reached. The Tapps were forced to relinquish Killarney and Maryfield, but retained Roper Valley station, which they later subdivided into five smaller properties for each of the sons. Bill Tapp didn't live to see that happen.

Today, Terry maintains a close relationship with the Tapp brothers: 'I love those boys. I can talk fondly of them, just like I can of Milton.'

Milton reflected on the whole episode as 'water under the bridge.'

'There are no problems between us [Milton and the Tapps] now. We get along good and see each other from time to time at campdrafts and shows. It's just somethin' that happened. You can't change it.'

At the time of the dramas, the early 1990s, the ownership of land had become a central theme in Milton's life. As more properties sank into receivership, opportunities arose for a man who'd begun to think that Coolibah was only the beginning.

CHAPTER 11

THE PEOPLE YOU MEET

No matter what happens to Milton in the future, it could be argued the most extraordinary connection in his life has already been and gone. To most readers the name Walter Umphrey means nothing, but to members of the American legal fraternity it belongs to a man whose deeds are legendary. In 1986, his firm, Provost Umphrey, played the main role in the first successful class action in the USA for asbestos exposure victims. It was estimated about US$150 million was paid out collectively to more than 700 plaintiffs. Walter represented 539 of them. Ten years later, he was one of five trial lawyers to be employed by the state of Texas to sue a number of large tobacco companies for offences including fraud and racketeering. The case was settled for US$17.3 billion. According to media reports the lawyers, who became known as 'The Tobacco Five', split the legal bill of US$3.3 billion.

By that stage Milton had already developed a strong relationship with the middle-aged Walter. Their link had been established through Kip Glasscock, the Beaumont attorney Milton had met on his initial trip to the USA.

'At one time Walter was actually a neighbour of mine,' said Kip. 'One of the well-known attorneys in the United States. A real big deal. I didn't have a part in the tobacco case. Darn it, darn it, darn it!'

After Kip returned home from his bull-catching trip with Milton in the Ord region, he spoke with Walter about his adventures and the opportunity to buy land in Australia. Walter decided he had to see for himself.

'So he come here to Coolibah, and we went fishin' and we got on with each other,' recalled Milton. 'I'm talkin' about a man who goes five-star everywhere. Anyway Walter said: "Well, let's get into business and buy a place here because it is so cheap." The land was cheap! You know, we could buy it for a dollar an acre. He was a man who'd travelled all over the world, and his words were: "You speak English, you're not shootin' at each other and the land's worth a dollar an acre and there's so much water, it's gotta go through the roof." He had the foresight to see that where a lot of people up here didn't.'

Milton liked what he heard and saw. He trusted Walter on the strength of a handshake; it was the way he liked to do business, although in the years ahead he'd meet others 'that weren't the same on the other side of the fence.'

As had happened with Killarney station, another person's misfortune aided Milton when Moroak station, 50 kilometres east of Mataranka, went into receivership. Milton and Walter pounced. They bought the pastoral lease through Walter's company, Tejas Land and Cattle. Soon afterwards they also secured Moroak's neighbour, Goondooloo. Together, the stockless stations totalled 2300 square kilometres: a sizeable start to a new business relationship. It was a stroke of incredible good fortune for Milton. To those in the Jones family it was further proof that the youngest member made the most of his opportunities. As sister Jenny mentioned with good nature: 'Milton had a habit of throwing up a dollar and seeing it come down as a hundred.'

Milton remembers he and Tejas paid about $450 000 for Moroak, and a little less for Goondooloo. Immediately, they began improving ageing infrastructure: fences, water supplies, yards; not much money was spent on this, but a considerable amount was used to buy cattle. Above all, the most overwhelming investment was in man-hours, and over the next few years Milton invested more time in Moroak than he did at Coolibah.

With his growing interests, he needed more workers. While there wasn't a shortage of come-and-go contractors for various jobs, he sought some permanent staff. He eventually ended up with a few men who had ridden life as though it were a saddle-bronc and they didn't care how many times they were unseated.

'Old Buckley' was the cornerstone of the characters. He drove graders and bulldozers. Somewhere, most likely along a road he'd built, he met Milton. They formed a mateship that led to Buckley putting in roads for Milton for years: on stations; for bull-catching; the placement of portable yards; trucking of crocodiles . . .

'That old fella, you could put him up in a helicopter and show him where you wanted a road. And he'd get back on the bulldozer and put the bastard exactly where you flew him. Not 100 yards, I'm talkin' 10 or 20 mile,' said Milton. 'God, he was a tough bugger. He'd sit down and pull his own teeth out with a pair of pliers. Drunken old bastard though, he was drinkin' all the time. I've seen him jump out of a Toyota once. We were goin' somewhere and he said: "I'll get a beer." I said: "No, come on, you're right, let's go!" But he wanted to go. I reckon I was doin' 60 kay an hour down the big gravel airstrip at Moroak, and there was a mailbag in the back, and Buckley just grabbed it, pulled it over one shoulder, jumped straight out of the Toyota and slid. He skidded to a halt, stood up, shook himself, shook the bag, threw it back over his shoulder and started walkin' back to the station to get a beer. Once, he jumped into crocodile-infested water and started swimmin' home. Another time he was on a motorbike, and we've started chainin' with the dozer [clearing vegetation with a heavy chain linked between two bulldozers] and he's gone over the chain on the bike and fallen off and this scrub chain has gone straight over the top of him. It didn't hurt him, just took a bit of skin off him. It pulled all the pegs and everything off the motorbike. I didn't see him until next lap around we found him there. A silly old bugger.

'One more I remember, he's there at Moroak and he used to keep the kitchen a bit clean, old Buckley. Anyway, I went away and come back and the place was in a hell of a mess. I'd been egg-collectin' and had a shotgun there and I said: "You dirty old bastard, get in here and clean this place up." There's pots and pans, a friggin' mess. Anyway he's got a broom and he's sweepin' it out and he's abusin' me: "You fat bastard, comin' home and tellin' me what to do!" He has kicked this old door open and he's got the broom and is sweepin' everything outside and I've blew the end of the broom off with the shotgun. I was standin' up behind the wall. I said to him: "I told you not to sweep it outside; pick it up, you dirty old bastard." God, didn't he go off. He took off backwards with this broom handle; it looked like a cocky had chewed the end of the bloody thing off. Good old Buckley.'

Years later, Milton showed his affection for his dozer driver when he gave him one of the blocks of land he'd originally bought in Mataranka. He also built a house on it for him. Buckley is no longer alive. His ashes were spread along the Limmen Bight River in the Territory's east, and Milton was made executor of his will. Today, the dozer driver's Toyota and a flatbed of possessions remain in the helicopter hangar at Coolibah.

Old Buckley introduced Milton to another hardened bloke who began at Moroak, and who today is as much a part of Coolibah as the dust on his eternally shoeless feet. 'Lurch' occasionally made an appearance on the television program *Keeping Up with the Joneses*. With a hunchback, bony legs, a patchy beard and a sun-weathered face he needn't utter a word to make it clear he has endured his times of hard living. Any harder, and Milton's run in to Mataranka to initially find him may have had an unfortunate ending.

'I was lookin' for a gardener at Moroak and Buckley had told me about this fella Lurch, so I went in and found him. He had a high house there with no steps on it. He had a ladder in there. Hadn't finished buildin' the house. Old Lurchy was in there like a mangy dog. It was just full of beer cans, the whole house was beer cans and cigarettes. I picked him up and I just told him: "Come on, get in." Buckley told him too. Well, we had to. He would have died if he'd stayed in town; he would've drunk himself to death. He's a good old fella, Lurchy, he wouldn't hurt a fly. Kind-hearted old fella. Since I've known him he's never had a shoe on; he might have had a thong on once when he went to town, I reckon. I slung some fuel into

Moroak one time when Lurchy was caretakin' there over the Wet [season]. He had the drums on the back of his Toyota and has dropped one off and it has landed on his toe. I didn't see him for another two weeks and I come back and he's got his foot wrapped up with a bandage. He didn't worry about a doctor or nothin'. One toe now sits out to the side. He's pretty easy to track.'

The third worker to join Milton at about the same time was 'Dooley', a Queenslander who'd worked on oilfields and as a ringer before he spent more than twenty years looking at the Territory's landscape through the windscreens of the cattle trucks he drove. Nowadays, he too lives at Coolibah. His face is littered with skin cancers. He has a grey beard and his eyebrows are surely wiry enough to make a barb or two. Dirt thrives under his fingernails. Before being interviewed for this book, he sat down on a stool outside the Coolibah kitchen and rolled some tobacco with the outside of his right hand into the palm of his left. Both were stained yellow. He began by saying he had 'that disease Northern Territory fellas get, the one that makes it hard to hold onto memories.' Sadly, his short-term recollections are confused, yet his long-term ones remain sharp. He said he was born in 1937, although he didn't know how old he was. Dooley is his surname, Jim his first.

'If someone called me Jim I'd take no notice of them,' he said, threading his words with smoke before adding incongruously, 'I'm not big-notin' myself. A lot of people I love aren't here anymore.'

Dooley spoke mostly about trucking in the days when roads were gravel and dirt, potholes and corrugations. Once, he was first through to Timber Creek, about 50 kilometres south-west of Coolibah, to pick up cattle after the wet season. The whole town 'went off its brain, and clapped and cheered.' He also told of the times that trucks would shunt and pull each other through rivers and up muddy banks.

'All them drivers were like brothers. If someone died we'd gather at the spot and cry. They were family,' he said.

When he entered the family of hard men at Moroak, he became a bore mechanic. He was to perform the same job on other stations Milton would buy. He was also responsible for one of the 'roughest feeds' Milton has ever had: 'some meat cut into three pieces, a couple of potatoes sliced in half, an onion, 5 litres of water and with the shit boiled out of it all for three hours.'

In the early days of working at Moroak, Dooley was on hand when Milton had one of his many escapes from disaster.

'Old Jim and I were doin' some floodgates on the Roper River. The water was brisket deep. I've gone in there while Jim is sittin' on the bank boilin' the billy can; we were havin' a bit of hop [tea and food], you know. He's got the fire goin' and I'm pullin' this wire across and passin' it to him, and he's holdin' it. I've got one wire across and gone back for the next one. Anyway, I see this thing move in this dirty bit of water, runnin' water it was. This bastard crocodile must have been just downstream and he come up to have a look to see what was goin' on. He must have been waitin' there to grab a beast because there was cattle pulled up there.

'The next thing it's poked its head up next to me. I had a pair of pliers in my hand, and that's all that saved me; I just whacked him straight across the head with the pliers as hard as I could, and he's just bangin' this way and that way. I've dropped the wire and gone but still held the pliers. Old Jim was watchin' on and all he could say was: "Oh gee, I reckon you might get outta there, young fella!" It doesn't get much closer than that, eh.'

The crocodile yarns at Moroak are some of the most vivid in Milton's collection. It was on this station that a horse had its throat ripped apart. The homestead was right next to the Roper River, 'just flick a stone with your thumb and you're there.' In floods, water could rush just a couple of feet away from it, sometimes 'runnin' hard with timber.' While this could be disconcerting, the presence of a huge male saltwater crocodile on the river's far bank was more so. When first alerted to it Milton put a chunk of meat on the end of a hook and looped it over the limb of a tree that overhung the river.

'As soon as that bait smacked the water, this croc come flat straight across,' recalled Milton. 'I pulled the meat and dropped it, pulled it and dropped it two or three times. All these blackfellas and I were there. And as soon as he saw us, he dived. Anyway, I sang out to 'em that I'd get me rifle and more rope because I was too close to the water and wanted to lengthen the rope. I was right on the water's edge, and a pretty bad spot. Anyway, we got a bit more rope and I joined it on and some blackfellas just pulled it up and dropped it. And I planted meself there, and the croc has come right along the water's edge and slid out near a paperbark tree, he's actually out of the water, not deep enough to swim, and *boom, boom, boom!* I shot him there, about 15 foot of him.'

Milton continued to have most of his crocodile experiences while egg-collecting, which posed countless variables. Firstly, there was encountering the wet season, 'the hardest flyin' you'll do.' Lashing rain, treacherous winds with mischievous gusts, at times cyclonic. Add the remoteness, the lack of access to fuel, and tiring days when Milton's bed was under the stars or in a deserted 'blackfella humpy' which was a sheet of iron against a tree. And then, there was the collecting itself. While Milton still mostly worked with Bluey on these jobs, he occasionally introduced new men. One was Sterling Buntine, another son of the trucking giant, Noel. Only in his early twenties, the Sydney private school–educated Sterling was a 'green pilot' who was learning his ways under Milton at Moroak. By that stage Milton saw the value in having two people who were able to fly the helicopter when collecting. It was good security in case things went wrong. And no matter how safe any situation seemed, a mere second or two could swing the fortunes wildly.

'We were up on the floodplain at Palumpa,' remembered Milton. 'It was all floatin' mat. You can't really walk on it, so you gotta pretty well hover on them with skids; we didn't have floats back then. Now, the way you do it is to come in and sit with a set of floats and collect the eggs off your floats. But it was different twenty years ago. I had this old Kawasaki helicopter, the Bell 47, and none of us could fly it real good. We used to put all the extra egg crates and extra fuel in it and park it, and then we'd use an R-22 to collect all the eggs and fly them back to the Kawasaki and load it up. Anyway, we're there and we're tryin' to hover the 22 on top of the nests and collect the eggs and it was very hard. I had Sterling with me, and he's on a nest and it started to sink and he's tryin' to throw this Esky in the front of the helicopter and I'm singin' out: "Come on, come on, get in!" I'm sittin' in the pilot's seat and there's not a lot of room in the front of the helicopter, and this Esky lands in and hits the collective [the lever which the pilot holds to control the pitch angle of the rotor blades, thus adjusting the amount of lift]. And I push the Esky back out and I'm singin' out to Sterling, but he couldn't hear me. He's got the Esky back in one hand and a pistol in the other and he's about knee-deep in water by this stage and goin' down. Not a good place to be because you're flat-out swimmin' out of there because of all the weeds; you'd have to go like a crocodile and stay on top of it.

'Anyway, then he just leaps straight over the bubble of the helicopter, and he's hangin' there like a green toilet frog. He's got one foot in the door and the other foot on the front of the skid. I don't know how he hung there. I thought he was gonna break the bubble. So, I've hovered from the nest over to the bank with Sterling spread over the front of the helicopter. That livened things up a bit.'

It wasn't the last frightening experience Milton and Sterling were to have together. Soon afterwards, they headed south across the Joseph Bonaparte Gulf between the mouths of the Fitzmaurice and Victoria rivers. To Milton, it was 'big, dirty black runnin' water . . . big tides' that was made even more unattractive by the lifeless needle on the helicopter's fuel gauge. They heard every 'fart and cough and rattle of pop-rivets' for twenty minutes until they were able to land and refuel at Legune station. Milton vowed he would never fly across that stretch again. And he never has.

Despite these misadventures, Milton and Sterling established a relationship that led to further expansion of Milton's business interests. In 1993 they launched

North Australian Helicopters (NAH), which they based in Katherine. At the time Milton had 'three or four helicopters' including a four-seater Robinson 44. With his burgeoning demands on his own stations, he had less hours to do as much contract mustering as he used to, but he was still determined to provide the helicopters. It was agreed Sterling would look after this.

There was one other partnership that was confirmed during this period, but amidst receiver work, buying properties and setting up new businesses, it had little chance of standing alone in an eternally hectic lifestyle.

'Milton and I got married in '93 in Katherine,' recalled Dominique. 'Milton's sister-in-law, Sue, organised the whole thing because we didn't have much time.'

The role of Dominique could never be over-estimated. Milton acknowledged she was the 'readin' and writin' side' of the relationship, and a sound counsel for him. However, from the earliest days there was a third partner in the marriage that was destined to present challenges. It was time itself. How much of it would Milton devote to his new wife?

ABOVE: Coolibah station. The road to the right of the Victoria River leads off the station, meaning the homestead can often be cut off during a big Wet.

BELOW: Outback stations are isolated places. Coolibah is 550 kilometres from Darwin. The surrounding country is a tourist brochure's dream.

ABOVE: Having a crack. Beau Jones practising his technique at Coolibah's own impromptu rodeo.

BELOW: Little Milton, with his mum Cristina leading him, is more than old enough to begin his equine education.

ABOVE: Little Milton and Alex down near the river.

BELOW: One mighty swimming pool in the backyard. The Joneses often cool down here in the river, with one eye scanning for crocs.

ABOVE: It can be isolating living on a remote cattle station, so campdrafting is a social outlet for Cristina and the family. (PHOTO JAMES KNIGHT)

BELOW: The two Miltons in an R22.

ABOVE: Yidumduma Bill Harney and Milton. (PHOTO JAMES KNIGHT)

LEFT: Trevor Easton doing his chores. Looks like a good drying day!

BOTTOM LEFT: Trevor the butcher. At times he has to cater for about thirty people living and working at Coolibah; he has his work cut out for him feeding them all.

BELOW: Jim Dooley casts his eye across the country in a pose every bushman knows well. (JAMES KNIGHT)

ABOVE: Muster time at Coolibah.

BELOW: Noise and position ... the two keys of working cattle in a helicopter.

ABOVE: Everything old is new again. In recent times Milton has followed his father Stan's lead and is now a racehorse owner.

BELOW: Not many kids get this close to a crocodile every day!

Living and growing up on an outback cattle station is a unique way of life. ABOVE: Beau, Little Milton, Cristina, Milton and Alex. RIGHT: Cristina, Jack, Milton and Little Milton.

CHAPTER 12

THE NEW GENERATION

It is a story worthy of a children's picture book. That is, if the ending could be changed. Milton was somewhere 'over west' contracting when he flew near a wedge-tailed eagle's nest. As he hovered above for a look, a chick fell out. Milton landed and picked up the stunned bird. It was fluffy, so soft in his hands. He put it under the seat of his helicopter then resumed working, and soon forgot about his passenger. He camped that night, and the next morning he heard chirping.

'So I brought him back to Coolibah and grew him up. Eddie the eagle he was,' said Milton. 'We used to mix the meat for the crocodiles near the yard. We had a mincer there: a lot of chicken heads and horse meat, a good brew of tucker for him, and we used to feed him on that. He used to hang there all the time. He was too young to fly, so he hopped around everywhere. Then he got to flyin' and I put a perch on a tank-stand and he sat up on that. I'd take off in the chopper and he'd fly along behind me to about the airstrip then he'd come back and sit on the tank-stand. He did that for a bloody season, eight months or so. I was frightened I was gonna run into the bloody thing. When I'd come back he'd whistle around and land, then soon as I'd take off again away he'd go behind me.

'Anyway, we had a dog that had pups. There was food around all the time for Eddie, so I think he was just inquisitive when he grabbed a pup. The old bull terrier bitch flew out and shook him, broke his wing and his leg and that was the end of him. We took him into the vet, but he ended up dyin' there, poor fella.'

Perhaps the thought of Milton nursing a bird seems incongruous. After all, his hands were the diary of a vigorous existence. When opened they told of scruffing cattle [forcing a beast to the ground and holding it on its side], tying crocodile claws, bending barbed wire . . . these hands were not meant to be cradles. However, on 16 January 1995, they were, and for the most important reason in life: they held the next generation of their own flesh and blood.

The lead-up to the birth of Beau Jones was coloured with an unusual Christmas hangover. Milton and Dominique had hosted a party for about 35 people at Coolibah, and then were advised by their doctor to move into Katherine to be close to medical facilities before the birth.

In preparation, Milton made a stew of all the festive leftovers: cherries, ham, puddings, everything into the one pot. Even a cup fell in and was left there. Milton thickened the mix with flour, then boiled it, cooled it, packed it into little containers, froze it and took it into town. The first time it was sampled was also the last. Soon after the stew was thrown out, Beau arrived.

While there is some sense of romanticism about living in Australia's remote bush areas, there is also vulnerability. And this is never more apparent than at times of illness. Beau was only a couple of weeks old when he started vomiting. Dominique was alone with him at the Coolibah homestead, Milton was away working, and the Victoria River was in flood. Dominique asked Bluey at the croc farm for help. He took the worried mother and baby across the water in a boat, and then watched them drive off for Katherine, two hours away. The doctor's diagnosis was reflux, but over the following few weeks Beau's condition worsened.

'About twice a week I was inclined to come over the flooded river and into town,' said Dominique. 'I kept a diary, and for three weeks Beau and I didn't sleep more than twenty minutes at a time. Milton was away working. Anyway, we came into hospital and they put a drip into Beau; they wanted to do a lumbar puncture, which I bailed on. While we're in there Kurt rings Milton and says: "I think you should get there, this baby's not real good." So Milton comes in. He was nursing Beau, and he's got tears because he thinks the baby's going to die, and it's the last time he'll see him.'

Milton then returned to work, leaving Dominique to take Beau to Darwin, then Brisbane. The newest Jones underwent surgery for pyloric stenosis, a condition in which the stomach's opening to the small intestine narrows, causing severe vomiting. He spent about three weeks in hospital.

In the aftermath of this, Dominique realised she would be on her own at other testing times in the future. It was the way Milton was. In 1997, he was also absent soon after baby daughter Alex was born and was taken to Darwin hospital, suffering from a serious bronchial virus. She remained there for about ten days. The pattern had been set: throughout the childhoods of Alex and Beau, Milton was a father from a distance.

'I actually didn't see a lot of them,' he admitted. 'I was always flat out, like everywhere, and they were at home, and in town and at school, and I was on the go all the time. I regret that now, but that's what you gotta do to make a quid sometimes.'

After Beau recovered from his illness, he was soon introduced to a home away from home. Two neighbouring stations north-west of Halls Creek in the Kimberley region had gone into receivership. Milton did the clean-out for Elders, and then bought the leases: Bedford Downs and Lansdowne added another 10 000 square kilometres to the Jones portfolio. Bedford also became the base for the family for about four months.

Despite all that he'd experienced, Milton was to encounter new situations on his latest stations that again underlined the unpredictability and danger of his work. His years of being around trucks and cattle ensured he'd had his 'close shaves', including falling into a crate full of bulls. He avoided injury by clambering up the slats, the pace of his feet and hands only matched by that of his heartbeat. His deadpan assessment: 'Yeah, that wasn't good.' But this was barely worth a mention when compared with the position he put himself in on the end of a Bedford loading ramp.

'We'd just had a storm. It was about five in the mornin', and I'd just loaded some bulls on a truck, some herd bulls. Old Jim [Dooley] was drivin' it. It had three trailers. Anyway, I've crawled over the fence and grabbed a sheet of half mesh and it touched a power pole, and she was alive. This mesh has burnt the wires at the top of the pole, and I'm hooked onto the mesh until the wires shorted out: 240 volts. I've tried pushin' myself off with a foot and obviously it's burnt out at the same time, and I've thrown meself backwards off the end of the loadin' ramp. My head went into a wheel of the truck, one of the studs drove into the back of it. I remember the wheel rollin' me over. I sort of did a full roll with me head in the wheel as the truck was takin' off.

'The truck changed gears and he was gone, and I took off up to the house. I had blood runnin' out of me everywhere. I'd just been near fried. I fell arse-over-head at the grid, I actually went through it tryin' to get to the house. What an ordeal! Dominique was there and her parents, Ken and Jackie. I just went in and swept everything off the table and started howlin! I thought I was gone. Geez, it give me a fright. That was a close one.'

The accident happened not long after Milton had been spectator to another potentially serious mishap. Round-yards that are often used for breaking in horses sometimes have their posts and rails covered in some sort of material to help prevent injuries, and stop the horse being distracted. Such a yard at Bedford was surrounded by rubber belting about 8 feet high: 'You can't see in, you can't see out.' It may have been a safety set-up for horse-breaking, but when combined with a 'bastard of a catch' on a gate, it created a challenging theatre for another particular purpose. These days, the process of branding cattle commonly requires a portable furnace that can be attached to a gas bottle. One or more branding irons are then heated in the furnace before they're pressed firmly for several seconds onto the hide of a beast that has been scruffed. It is a quick but sometimes unpredictable activity, as it was when Milton asked some of his station hands to mark about 30 calves.

'There are these three or four blackfellas in the yard, and they've brought out the gas bottle and the brandin' furnace with 'em because with the rubber beltin' they had no way of gettin' the brand through a rail anywhere. I poked me head over the top to see how they're goin' and they're into 'em. I'm goin' back over to the house for a drink of tea, but the next minute I hear this roar. They'd knocked the gas bottle over and the bottle caught on fire at the top. And these blackfellas, they're tryin' to get out and they're yellin': "Look out, it gonna blow up, it gonna blow up", which I thought it was. Anyway, they couldn't get out of this round-yard. They're tryin' to get over the top and they were buggered, and this gas is just roarin' its head off. Geez, I laughed.'

However, seeing the lighter side wasn't always usual. Milton's relationship with his workers, both Aboriginal and white, was founded on tough authority: 'I used to get behind 'em a fair bit.' But Milton never expected anyone to do something that he couldn't do. In those formative years, he was much more impatient than he is nowadays; it was, and still is, a case of 'get the job done.' There were high expectations, and if these weren't met, the repercussions could be harsh.

'You don't muck around if they get cheeky with you,' said Milton. 'Knock 'em arse over head. You get fellas gettin' cruel with cattle and floggin' em around the head, and I won't stand for that. You know they have an accident or wreck a car or somethin', well, you can understand that, but bein' cruel to cattle or stealin' . . . We had one fella steal a heap of stuff off us once, the bastard. He went through everyone's gear. What do you do with someone like that? Give 'em a hidin'! That's what he got. You know some fellas, you liven 'em up a bit. You tell 'em: "Go straight to the round-yard, pull your boots and shirt off, roll your jeans up and I'll be there in a minute." Then we're into it. One blackfella there I taught how to fight. He was in jail more times than he was out. Anyway, he stole a motor car from Halls Creek and he done time for it. I caught up with him after, and give him a bit of a towellin' and brought him back. He ended up a good boy, a good worker. I used to have a few beers and say: "Righto, come on in the round-yard", and he used to get a few hits on me too, the bastard, he was gettin' too good for me. He ended up gettin' a good one on me one day and blacked both me eyes. I was too embarrassed to let anyone know a blackfella had hit me in the nose so I went bush for about two weeks up at Moroak. That's about the only time I've ever run from anything; I went and hid there. Most of the time we'd start off havin' a bit of fun and then it would get a bit serious but that didn't hurt. It kept everyone on their toes. You gotta make your own fun in the bush.'

While Milton applied his own laws of the land, his operations were attracting the attention of very different enforcers. At around the time of purchasing Bedford and Lansdowne he also took a quarter-share in a small meatworks at Mistake Creek in the Northern Territory. He and his three business partners later decided to move the operations across the border to Kununurra but according to Milton 'were mucked around a lot by the government.' This turned out to be the least of Milton's worries.

CHAPTER 13
A BIT OF STRIFE

There is a saying among northern Australian cattle people: 'You always go next door to eat your own beef.' (Or, in wool-growing areas, 'your own mutton.') While this old line is often dusted off to bring a laugh, there is no denying it rings with some truth. Cattle theft, or 'duffing' or 'shaking', has always been part of pastoral life. Some thieves have grown into legends, none more famous than Harry Redford, who was believed to have inspired the character of Captain Starlight in one of the great Australian colonial novels, *Robbery Under Arms*. In 1870, in a bold crime – and also an incredible feat of droving – Redford and a small band of associates stole about 1000 head of cattle in central Queensland, and overlanded them through the Channel Country and Strzelecki Desert for sale in South Australia. Redford eventually stood trial in Roma, Queensland, but was acquitted by a sympathetic jury.

Milton was no Captain Starlight, but he had done enough to be in a 'bit of strife' with the Western Australia Police Stock Squad. At the centre of their case were allegations that Milton had gone bull-catching on the government-owned Ord River station without a signed contract of authorisation. This occurred the year immediately after his official three-year contract had expired. This was true, although Milton argued a verbal agreement had been reached to continue working.

'I didn't deny bein' there because I thought everything was straight up and down. We mustered a heap of the paddocks that the station couldn't afford to muster and sold the cattle. Most of the cattle we got went to Broome [meatworks] that was still killin' at that time. We got a lot. Huge.'

There were also separate allegations of fraud concerning the relocation from Mistake Creek to Kununurra of the meatworks that Milton owned with his three partners. He acknowledged the business was a 'target for everyone to talk', and rumours and accusations swirled through the region.

Police conducted searches and scrutinised paperwork on all of Milton's stations, interviews took place and charges were laid. In a reflection of the seriousness of the allegations, Milton had his passport confiscated and, since he was living in the Territory, he was also subject to an extradition process. Faced with an increasingly complicated situation that he 'didn't know how to handle' he contacted someone who'd supported him through legal dramas before, albeit in a courtroom on the other side of the world.

'I remember coming over, getting involved and talking to the local lawyers in Darwin and Perth,' recalled Texan attorney Kip Glasscock. 'I believed Milton hadn't done anything bad but somebody needed to be able to articulate that. I wondered why he was caught up in it because I obviously had great faith in him.'

Kip arranged Milton's legal representation, including high-profile West Australian Queen's Counsel, Malcolm McCusker (currently the Governor of Western Australia). Elsewhere, others defended Milton in different ways. In Darwin, Jenny Jones was working at a 24-hour diner after separating from her husband, Gavin. When a man who'd been spreading rumours about Milton walked in, Jenny told him: 'You can turn around and walk right outta here because I don't want your custom. I'm Milton Jones's sister, and you're dirt as far as I'm concerned.'

Milton was aboard the legal roundabout for about twelve months in what was 'a very stressful period.' But eventually relief overwhelmed anxiety when the case was dropped before it went to court in Broome.

However, this wasn't the end of the drama. In a complicated scenario that was affected by separate legal proceedings involving two other partners in the meatworks,

Milton assumed sole financial responsibility for the business when he bought out all his partners. Debts totalling more than a million dollars hung over the meatworks, and they became an increasingly heavy burden for Milton at a time when most of his other interests were flourishing. He took the view that the meatworks were worthless if they were closed, so it was best to try to keep them open and work a way to trade out of the mess. He sent his own stock to be slaughtered, primarily 'rubbish cattle.' Kurt Hammer also sent beasts from where he was chasing bulls in the Kimberley region near Gibb River Road. It was a small operation: about 60 kills a day.

This also drew the attention of the Stock Squad at a time when Milton knew he was under close scrutiny and 'the pressure was put on.' He didn't hold back when he felt he needed to defend himself. Kurt, who was also facing accusations of cattle theft, remembered one particular incident at Milton's meatworks during the short period when cheek brands were used as a form of identification on Territory cattle.

'The Stock Squad were gonna do everything they could to catch us pinchin' cattle. So the detectives are down there at the meatworks. And all the heads and guts and that were thrown in the gut pit, this big open pit. You know, it's just rotten with beef and maggots and everything else in there. When you kill the cattle at the meatworks all the hides are stacked up, so the detectives were there and they were goin' through the hides and they find one without a brand. "Aah, what about this, Mr Jones? Got you." And Milton said: "What for?" Milton reckoned they should just finish goin' through all the hides first to see if they could get him for any more. And they only found this one. And then they said: "Right, you're gonna have to get charged over this." And Milton, cool and calm as anything, said: "No, we're not finished the job yet. Bring that hide and come with me." And he goes over to the gut pit, and he says: "That animal comes from the Territory and it has a cheek brand on it and its head is in that pit. Now don't you need to get in there and look for it?" The detective bloke says: "I'm not gettin' in there." It was the last we saw of 'em.'

Milton's bigger problem remained the meatworks itself. What to do with a business that was draining him of money?

'You gotta be hands-on to run a meatworks and it was too big a job for me,' admitted Milton. 'Anyway, Ken Hammer [Dominique and Kurt's father] gave me a hand there with it and we devised this little plan. We'd store this meat up and then put it on the market. We had a big heap of beef in cold storage in Perth and Darwin. Every time I'd go to sell it, the prices would go down. If I could have exported it to Indonesia it would have been beautiful, but they wouldn't give the meatworks an export licence, so we had to try and sell it in Sydney, Melbourne,

Adelaide, the local market. Anyway, they were knockin' me back, knockin' me back, knockin' me back, so I dropped the price another twenty cents, or about that. There was a couple of hundred tonne of meat. I quit a bit of it but not the lot of it.

'And then everyone fired in and wanted to buy. Well, did it put the shit in the fan! These fellas from Western Meatpackers [a significant Western Australian business] they wanted to know, "Where's all this beef comin' from?" They swung straight up in their jet and we had a heap of cattle in the yard at the time. I made sure of that. A heap of feral cattle, cheap cattle. And old Rod Russell from Western Meatpackers took one look round and I said: "There's your deal, she's yours. I'll give you five years to pay for it." He couldn't knock that back. I think it was two butcher shops, and all the meat that we had in cold storage, and the abattoirs itself, so it worked out I got my money back plus a little bit more. It worked out pretty good. They only operated for about twelve months and then they shut it.'

Throughout the 1990s, Milton became well used to the fluctuations of his businesses. After about six years of involvement with the croc farm, he 'wanted out' and sold his share 'for a pretty good lift' to a new partner Bluey had met. Despite that change, Milton and Bluey still worked together collecting eggs; Milton recognised this was the most lucrative part of the crocodile industry because of the charge rates for helicopter hire.

Contract mustering remained the greatest user of the helicopters. By the mid-1990s the numbers of live export cattle being sold, particularly to South-East Asia, had risen sharply, thus ensuring North Australian Helicopters was in demand as stations sought to capitalise. However, after a record year in 1997, numbers and dollars slumped in '98 when the full effects of the debilitating Asian economic crisis took hold of the industry. Yet again though, Milton found an opportunity. In Indonesia, as elsewhere across the region, the crisis caused a collapse in parts of the country's beef industry. Feedlots closed, herd numbers slipped, and as per capita incomes fell, so did beef sales. The consumption of buffalo meat was a cheaper alternative, but this prompted the killing of working buffalo. In a bid to bolster their stock again, Indonesia turned to Australia as a source.

Milton gained permission from the appropriate Aboriginal authorities to catch buffalos in various parts of Arnhem Land. From there they were carted to Katherine and sold to an exporter who arranged for shipping from Darwin. The sizes of the orders varied over a few dry seasons. On average about 5000 were caught. They were mostly bulls that separated from the females before reuniting for mating at the beginning of the Wet. The catching process involved Milton and other drivers manning buggies, but as opposed to the 'bump 'em over' style of bull-catching, they used a 'bionic arm'. This was a piece of equipment that was attached to a buggy and could be controlled by a driver to extend over the neck of a running buffalo. Milton had previously tried this precise method successfully on cattle.

'When you're pushin' em over you need to run 'em around a little bit. But when you're catchin' 'em with a bionic arm you want to get 'em quick. The quicker the better. You only get one chance at 'em with an arm. As soon as you get beside 'em, if they duck off you've got trouble. You just sort of sheepdog 'em to where you want 'em; like head 'em straight for the creek where they want to go and just line 'em and get 'em before they get there. You just gotta go hard, flat out, and read your animal.

'There are big differences between catchin' cattle and buffalos. A buffalo will pull, just like they're pullin' a plough in Indonesia. When you arm a buffalo with a bionic arm you can knock your car into neutral and the buffalo will take you. You can run him right out on the road, take him a long way. But a red bull, as soon as you arm him, you've gotta turn straight off him real hard because the first thing he'll do is prop, and if he puts that front foot forward you'll run over his hock and break his ankle. As you're armin' him you gotta turn off him at the same time. And that'll pull him off balance and he won't bog them two hind legs in; if you get a big heavy fella you'll break his neck, just pull his hindquarters in half when he props. So pull him on the one leg and he won't prop as hard, and then you just go round the circle with him and then put him straight on the blitz or onto a tree.

'After you catch 'em you gotta handle buffalo different too. You gotta water 'em down all the time, otherwise they'll dehydrate real quick. They gotta wallow. Basically you catch a buffalo and put him straight on the truck, try not to head-rope him. Believe it or not, they have real sensitive skin; they have a lot of blood near the surface of their skin. You get a red bull and scratch him with a bit of wire and it won't hurt him, but it will a buffalo. So you just grab the buffalo with the bull buggy, and straight onto the truck with him. Most of 'em will stand up all right.'

The areas Milton and his teams worked in included 'Numbulwar country' on the Gulf of Carpentaria near the floodplains of the Phelp River, and further north at Ramingining on the edge of the Arafura Swamp. Their biggest job was in central Arnhem Land near Snowdrop Creek, a name that belied its pandanus-filled surrounds yet fittingly also told of the Northern Territory character. On his 1844–45 expedition through northern Australia, Prussian explorer Ludwig Leichhardt and his team followed the creek and stopped on its 'grassy and open' banks to kill a bullock that they'd called Snowdrop. In his journal Leichhardt described a scene of: 'Low sandstone ranges

[that] bounded its valley to the southward and south-east; stony ridges with stunted trees and Cypress-pine extended to the north-west.' To Milton it was 'bloody hard country but good for buffalo.' Buffalos can be more efficient eaters than cattle. They have wider mouths that enable them to pick up greater volumes of grass, and thus use less energy. Despite the BTEC campaign, they were still prevalent in the Top End, and were worth the money and logistics Milton needed to catch them.

'We had two or three graders and front-end loaders to put in about 270 kay of road: hard goin' some bulldust country, a big operation, huge. We set up a yard and a water tank and trough too. It was a huge job gettin' in and gettin' out. It was a long way to cart 'em: 270 kay of dirt, and another 100 kay or so on top of that to Katherine. The deal was the horns had to be within the ear-length, so we had to de-horn all these buffalo. We done 'em with little Stihl chainsaws. I think we delivered two road trains; we could only get two trailers in there, we couldn't get three. I just forget the number; it would be 300 I'd imagine.

'After we trucked 'em to Katherine, the way it worked was that they'd come off the truck and over the weigh-bridge and get weighed, and then they belong to the exporter. So, we've unloaded these bloody things at the Katherine Dairy, and they've come off the truck and by the time we've hit the bitumen to leave they're goin' across it too. The people there have blown the lot. They had some useless bastard in there; they'd weighed 'em and let 'em all in the one yard, and the buffalo have piled up in the corner and busted the gate and the fence. Here we are drivin' off and here are these bastards headin' down the road. We kept goin', changin' gears and got out of there!

'They wouldn't have ever got 'em all back. They would've got some back, but them buffalo come from Arnhem Land and the bastards were goin' back there too! We got paid. It was their blue. It would have cost 'em a quid, pushin' up to a couple of hundred grand's worth. We were gettin' about 500 bucks a head, I'd reckon.'

As with bull-catching, buffalo-catching is dangerous. Although Milton had a relatively accident-free run in Arnhem Land, he still had 'moments,' including one near the Mann River where metre-high grasses made the going slippery and uncertain.

'I had my young niece Georgie with me, Terry's daughter. I wheeled around the corner bendin' this buffalo and I went to arm this fella and he just shouldered me. I touched the brakes a little bit, which is the worst thing to do; I always had baldy tyres because you don't pick up as many stakes that way, you don't get as many flats. Anyway, this buffalo just skidded me flat, straight into this tree that was a couple of metres round. *Bang!* It was a dead tree and all I could think of was all them limbs fallin' down, so I just chucked meself straight on top of

Georgie and threw her on the floor, and all you could hear were little branches crackin'. I was waitin' for the big one but nothin' come down.'

The buggy wasn't in good shape. Literally. Milton had a mechanic, Errol Blakely, on site, and after an examination they found two pieces of the riveted chassis that usually fitted together like a puzzle had been bumped apart, forcing the bonnet to be a couple of inches out of alignment on one side. The initial prognosis was: 'It's buggered, can't fix it.' Adhering to the best unconventional practices of bush mechanics, Milton found a tree that leaned away from him, lined his buggy up, drove several metres away from the trunk, and then 'reversed her back flat.' The result: 'Bloody perfect.'

The buffalo-catching introduced Milton to new places in Arnhem Land, and in the following years more crocodile ventures would enable him to know 'every inch of the bastard,' from the open floodplains to the swamplands, tall messmate timber country, mangroves, pandanus, paperbarks, bulldust . . . an often harsh yet alluring environment. While he became well-versed in reading the country, the people within it provided an unpredictable element.

'On the Numbulwar Road there's a blackfella cemetery there and half a dozen graves,' said Milton. 'These two old bull buffalo must have been eatin' a bit of green grass around the graves there, you know. So we grabbed 'em, put 'em on a tree and we were gonna come back later to pick 'em up. Next day we've come back and there's no bloody buffalo there. There's just a head-rope, a head and bones. The blackfellas had been there and boned 'em all out, pulled the skin and beef off.'

It was just another revealing story about the Northern Territory. Whether or not he realised it, Milton had become a privileged observer of people and events that the rest of Australia either knew nothing or little about in its haste to reach the twenty-first century. Of course Milton was also a participant in this extraordinarily different way of life. The period that saw him walk a fine line with the law, buy into and sell an abattoir, and extend an arm in business over buffalos was crowded with other experiences. Milton was only in his mid-thirties but he hadn't stopped growing. And nor had the ebbs and flows of his life become any less extreme.

CHAPTER 14

THE BIG CATCH

Eighty thousand dollars in machine parts from the United States: 'Gone. Lost the lot.' Nine thousand litres of Avgas in a tank: 'Washed the bloody stuff away.' Six helicopters in the hangar: 'The whole lot went under.' The sight at the NAH base may have been depressing, but it was a mere microcosm of a scene that stretched throughout Katherine and beyond.

The foundations for the disaster in late January 1998 began when the Category 2 Cyclone Les developed in the Gulf of Carpentaria, and as it changed into a tropical depression across the Top End, it dumped more than 400 millimetres of rain in just two days in parts of the Katherine catchment. Katherine itself received only slightly smaller falls.

The result was a record flood. Three people were killed, 30 injured and 5000 – about half the town's population – were evacuated from their homes. More than 1000 houses were damaged. Aerial photos from the period show the roofs of some residences resembling tiny mats amid an ocean of brown. The business district succumbed to between 1 and 3 metres of water, including small waves that wrought havoc. Large chunks of roads were swept away, drainage systems were destroyed, and power grids, transmitters and phone lines all went down. In the angry currents that carried cars, gates, toys, timber and all sorts of other debris, a crocodile was spotted. On the surrounding farms and stations, there were significant losses of cattle, crops, machinery and infrastructure as the waters spread out over 1000 square kilometres.

'Gosh, that was a scary time,' recalled Terry Jones. 'Mum was living near me in a unit, and she came up to our place. I was living on the Vic [Victoria Highway] and I was watching the water getting higher and higher. I remember looking up and there was a road train that had pulled up and it started going underwater. Hell! I moved my car up onto higher ground and I moved Mum's little car up a bit higher.

'At four o'clock in the morning we got up again and here it was: the cars were bobbing, and oh, my saddle. I duck-dived and got it and my girls' saddles and put them on a top rail. I was in a two-storey building and the water came about a metre into it. At least it wasn't rushing as hard as in other places. Outside there was stuff going past everywhere: tyres, Eskies, a lounge. I said to my kids: "We might have to jump on one of those and tie ourselves to it." Mum had a little dog and I told her she might have to let it go, but she said: "I will never do that!"

'The rescue people came along and I told them to take a lady in a unit opposite us. She had nothing, poor thing, and a little child. Anyway they saved them, and then a friend came along and saved us. We would have been right, but at the time we didn't know that.'

Terry now jokes that she didn't see Milton much during the disaster because 'he forgot about me.' At one point Milton dropped off some food supplies to his sister, but for the rest of the time he and his friends and workmates, including Kurt Hammer, were kept busy helping others. In the aftermath, there was an outbreak of gastroenteritis, and supplies of clean water and food were limited. While he did some official government task work, Milton primarily conducted his own operations. These were appreciated by the recipients, but didn't always follow the letter of the law.

'I was away at the time of the peak, and only got there when it was startin' to go down,' said Milton. 'We went round to a haulage place, and there was a big heap of bully beef [tinned meat] there, cartons of it. So we've kicked the wall in and loaded it all and a big heap of fresh water bottles in the back of this little truck. We got some more stuff at Elders. I had a big set of bullock horns hangin' up in there and I demanded the key to get 'em, and we just went in there and got some more food and a big heap of beer. Lucky we did because the army came in there later with front-end loaders and dug the whole lot out and dumped it because it had dog food and grain; they wanted to get rid of it all because it was gonna get contaminated or whatever.

'Anyway, we got that little truck and it had a little refrigerator van on the top. Then we got a fuel truck that was full of diesel and oil and had an air compressor. I didn't even know who owned 'em. We had nothin' ourselves, didn't even have a Toyota . . . all under water. We sent a helicopter straight out and knocked a fat bullock and cut him up and brought him back and hung him up in this cool room, and then we're right: beef, fire, we're away.

'Then lots of people come to NAH. We fed and watered, ooh it must have been 300 people for a few days, maybe longer. About three days after the water started goin' down everything hit me. I was openin' this tin of bully beef out on the helicopter pad with an old mate of mine and I told him: "It isn't real bloody flash here." I slowed down a bit and started thinkin'. I'd been goin' on adrenalin. It was bloody all go. It was a real kick in the teeth to the business. People were bringin' back machine parts to us eighteen months after the flood. They found bits and pieces in all sorts of places. That 80 grand's worth was our very first order to Robinson. The things you go through.'

Nowadays, NAH has a mezzanine floor to contain all the machine parts well above flood level. According to figures from the federal Attorney-General's department, the financial cost of the whole disaster was $70 million, and 'it was estimated that 2000 people left Katherine during the floods & many would never return.'

Despite its dangerous side, water is the lifeblood of the bush. And to Milton, it provides an escape. When he can, he finds time to go fishing with his mates and they cook their catches over campfires, complete with rum to fuel and embellish yarns long into the night. His memories include the landing of a 10-foot tiger shark in the mouth of the Mary River; its jaws are now hanging from the tip of a buffalo horn in the station hands' kitchen at Coolibah. And along the Limmen, he once hauled in a groper that was 'the length of the back of the Toyota.' He said he would have let it go, but the 'hook had buggered the poor fella up in the gills.' So he froze it and took it back to Moroak where he gave it to some Aborigines who'd been camping in a yard while tailing a mob of cattle. The groper's head hung on a post for months.

There was also the time Milton and Kurt Hammer were on an old jetty on the Roper River. Kurt had a 'gut feeling' they were going to land something sizeable, and after setting a strong hook and line, he was proved right.

'Somethin' jumped on and started pullin' Kurt into the water,' recalled Milton. 'Geez, it was heavy, he mucked around with it for a good 30 or 40 minutes. It's murky water down there and there was a couple of lumps of steel, big girders runnin' into the water, and Kurt is halfway out on one of those and I said to him: "You don't want to go there, you might slip in." He said: "You get a gun and shoot it when it pokes its head up." So, righto I was ready, and Kurt is playin' this big bloody thing and next thing you know it poked its head up and I let one bloody shot go and dropped the gun and took off. I thought, If that's his head I'm not hangin' round to see the rest of it. It turned out to be a stingray, as big as the bonnet of the Toyota. He was used for crab bait, cut him up and put him in the crab pot. Big bastard.'

In mid-1998, Milton prepared to reel in a much more rewarding catch when he walked into a room in a Darwin hotel and met representatives of the Malaysian company Desa International, owned by the Sultan of Sarawak. Desa had been affected by the Asian financial crisis, and was selling its two stations, Camfield and the neighbouring Montejinni, about 120 kilometres south-east of Coolibah. Both had once been part of the enormous Victoria River Downs (VRD) that in its heyday was the largest cattle station in the world, spanning about 21 000 square kilometres. In his colourful book *Frontier Country*, author Glenville Pike noted that, 'Old timers in the Territory outback used to speak nostalgically of the early days on

V.R.D. when it was possible to ride a month in a direct line without reaching the station's boundaries.'

After World War II, 'The Big Run' was carved into smaller blocks and these days is about a third the size of its gigantic past.

Camfield and Montejinni, which consisted of both an 'East' and 'West' station, totalled 5862 square kilometres. Milton considered the land to be 'good country, a lot of open country.' With well-developed infrastructure and the Victoria River, the blocks were an attractive proposition. Milton couldn't afford to make an offer by himself, but with Texan attorney Walter Umphrey keen to add to his Australian cattle portfolio, the multi-million-dollar commitment was within reach. After submitting a tender on behalf of Tejas, Milton went to a local restaurant to 'have a few wines and a feed' while he waited for a decision, which he was told would be made quickly. When he was summoned back to the hotel with his lawyer, he was hopeful.

'These little Malaysian fellas had a plane to catch at six o'clock. It was about 4.30, I reckon. Anyway, we went in there and they said: "More money, we need more money." They wanted another $2 million, but I said: "I'll give you $200 000 more." They just wanted to haggle, and said they would go home and decide. I told 'em I had just as far to go, and if they walked out of the room without makin' a decision my offer was finished. "You walk your way, and I'll walk mine," you know what I mean. My lawyer went downstairs for a smoke, and I went and sat right outside the room. Next, the Malaysians' Australian secretary walked out and got in the lift and I jumped in beside her. She said: "Oh well, I suppose I'll have to find another job." And I knew that meant they'd accepted the offer and were out of Australia. Anyway, they called us back in and accepted. You know when a fella's in a hurry he rolls his swag and leaves all the blankets hangin' out one end of it? Well, that's how these fellas packed their bags. I noticed that when I was in the room. They were out of there, and we got the deal: almost $14 million we paid for 'em.'

They paid $6.2 million for Camfield and $7.5 million for Montejinni. Milton borrowed money from Elders to help finance the deal.

With the added responsibilities Milton became even busier. He moved from station to station – a week here, a fortnight there – while also managing to contract muster, catch bulls and buffalos and collect crocodile eggs. He saw little of his family. By then, Dominique, who spent nearly all her time at Coolibah, had a nanny to help her look after three-year-old Beau and twelve-month-old Alex. While this partially eased the workload, Dominique still searched for the hours needed to manage the paperwork for all seven stations: Coolibah, Moroak,

Goondooloo, Bedford Downs, Lansdowne, Camfield and Montejinni.

About a year after buying his two latest stations, Milton decided to move with his family to Camfield, a more central base to monitor all his operations. It proved a critical moment in a marriage that was starting to break apart. Dominique didn't want to go, and a heavy load soon weighed her down. At first she was parenting, cooking, gardening and doing the office work. A cook was eventually employed to help her, but she still found herself 'going to bed at eleven o'clock and getting up at four. It was killing me.' Worries over the start of her son's education added to the pressure.

'Beau needed to be at pre-school but we couldn't keep anyone on the station to do it,' recalled Dominique. 'I said to Milton that we had to sort something out. We then decided to open an office in Katherine to look after administration work. We'd been at Camfield about a year, and I decided that I'd come and live with the kids at a house we bought in town. I'd get Beau into school and run everything from in there. Then we'd go out to Camfield on the weekends. That wasn't ideal either. Milton was still here, there and everywhere. And between us things just fell to pieces.'

Milton believed his considerable time away – often for weeks on end – was 'probably half the reason why we split up.' Broken marriages are extremely personal affairs and there is no need to dwell on this one here. In a direct manner Milton acknowledged: 'Dominique has been a big part of my life. It's straightforward. I was married, had a couple of kids. Dominique obviously wanted a bit better life, didn't want to be in the bush all the time, so she wanted to go to town. That's what she got. She went to town and I kept goin' out here. No good me sittin' in town. I didn't want to be in town. So that's basically how it happened.'

Despite a situation that could have caused him to take sides, Kurt Hammer maintained strong relationships both with his sister and his best mate. In the months that followed he knew questions would be posed, particularly about Milton.

'I think everyone thought he wasn't gonna do any good because they all thought Dominique had been the brains,' recalled Kurt. 'But I knew he'd be right. He just kept goin' ahead in leaps and bounds. He has always had good ideas and foresight. He can tell you what's gonna happen, especially in the cattle industry.'

The cattle industry was what drove Milton, and even after his marriage broke down, he was able to maintain his focus. He established his own road trains, wholly for private use, to transport stock between the stations. He was handling about 80 000 head of cattle. Although he had developed good herds at Coolibah and Moroak/Goondooloo, he recognised Camfield had the potential to provide greater returns. He also felt he had a 'point to prove.'

'When we bought Camfield and Montejinni everyone sort of said: "Oh, that young fella, he won't know how to do this, and he doesn't know the country." Well, I knew the country, but they just sort of classed me as a rough, tough bull-catcher with not much idea. Pound for pound you won't find anything better than Camfield. For cost of runnin' I'm sure there are other places. You know, Wave Hill is beautiful in good seasons; it's huge and can run about 80 000 head of cattle. Camfield is small but can still run a lot of cattle, about 30 000. And the homestead is right dead smack in the middle. A lot of these places you gotta go 100 mile that way to a paddock because your house is right at the other end. It's that sweet a block, Camfield. When it's right, it does the job.'

So Milton set to work. He capitalised on a bitumen road that already ran through the middle of the station by adding an extra 2-kilometre sealed stretch to the main yards, enabling easier transport and all-season access. He also put in a double loading ramp to increase the speed and efficiency at which cattle could be sent on their way, and to the surprise of some, he built a weighbridge that allowed cattle to be weighed on station, as opposed to in Katherine or Darwin, by which time the beasts would have lost some condition and valuable dollars in weight.

'Havin' the weighbridge right there meant the cattle were full of feed, full of water, loaded and sold. We paid for the weighbridge with the very first load of cattle,' said Milton.

Further station improvements included the repairing of bores, all of which had broken windmills. After doing most of the work himself – 'I don't mind muckin' round with 'em' – Milton boasted there was one season where 'We never had to start a diesel motor, and if we did, it was just start the bastard for the day and that was it, finished.'

Most of the work was more about rolling up the sleeves than unfolding the dollars. However, in the midst of smart business operations there was still a place for mischief.

'We were there at Montejinni. A cold mornin' it was, and I'm in a chopper,' recalled Milton. 'We must have had a couple of thousand head of cattle strung out along the fence. We were on the VRD boundary: Lucky Strike I think the name of that bore was. From Lucky Strike goin' back to Ogden's yard. We've got ten or twelve men mounted up there, and this one bit of a useless bastard, he's on the tail there, and the horse didn't know much about man and man didn't know much about horse, you know what I mean? This bastard's all hands and heels and elbows. But the cattle are goin' good and I'm hangin' right off 'em way back in the chopper. Then I see this big old king brown there. So I got out and I shot him with my squirt [pistol; also know as 'squirter']. He was on a red claypan. I blew his head clean off. It's the best shot. You could never ever do it again as long as you lived. I would have been 50 foot off the ground, not real high. And he was, geez he must have been 7 or 8 foot, a big snake. I went down and picked him up and sat on his tail, and that's how I could hold him and fly.

'So I'm sittin' on him and he's all hangin' outside with blood goin' everywhere. I get back to where the cattle are and I'm thinkin', I'm gonna drop him on this fella, this useless bastard. Liven him up a bit. So I cocked me arse to one side when I thought it was about right and released the snake. And this snake's come down and you couldn't have done it better if you were standin' beside the horse, I'm tellin' you. The horse has took off and propped and this fella has gone right up in the irons and bloody nearly over the head of this horse and at the same time this snake's gone underneath the cantle-line [the back end of the saddle that slopes upwards] of the saddle, and he's pretty well dead even, three or four feet either side of the horse under the saddle. And the fella is sittin' back down now, and I've turned around and took off.

'The horse knew there was a snake but the useless bastard didn't. So this old horse is just gatherin' country up, he's just flat. And this snake's flappin' like bird's wings. They've gone through a mob of cattle and over the fence. Cattle are startin' to go everywhere, and I was killin' meself laughin'. And this fella found this big king brown slappin' this horse under the guts: well, he just threw one leg straight over the pummel of the saddle and dismounted. God, it rolled him up on his arse and the horse has gone hell for leather, and the snake's come out. About two hours later we've got all the cattle back together and got things settled down and they picked this fella up. He went back, got into the motor car, went to the station, got into a mail truck and he went to bloody town. That's the last we ever seen of the bastard.'

It seemed Milton never missed a chance to raise merry hell. Sometimes though, he played the lead role without meaning to.

CHAPTER 15
EMPIRE BUILDING

It was around Christmas time in 2001, and the USA was still coming to terms with the horror of the 9/11 attacks that had shocked the world only a few months earlier. Milton stepped off a plane at Los Angeles airport and waited in the immigration line with his travelling partner, Eric Webb, who ran an aviation business in Queensland. They were going to attend a helicopter convention, and Milton also planned to catch up for a mix of business and pleasure with Kip and Walter, whom he hadn't seen for a few years.

Milton had a new passport but mistakenly he'd had the necessary tourist visa stamped in his old one, which he'd 'thrown on the dash of the Toyota and forgotten about.' He didn't think about it until he reached the counter at the head of the line. The immigration officer was immediately concerned. Milton further complicated his predicament by marking on his official entry card that his purpose of visit was 'vacation'. He was holding a carry-on duffle bag, the only luggage he had brought with him. It was confiscated. Then he was told to follow a red line to an area where he met another customs official behind a counter. The questioning intensified.

'He asked me what I did, and I told him I operated helicopters and cattle. So he said I was goin' on business. I told him it was half business, half vacation, and that wasn't good enough for him. The big fella called me a liar, and I got me hackles up.'

Milton's biggest problem, though, was his lack of visa. After further questioning he was taken into a room that had several bench seats where there were some passengers from other flights.

'There were a couple of Asian women there,' said Milton. 'One had a wok . . . And that was quite funny because she said she was goin' on a holiday, and the official was askin': "Well, what are you bringin' all the cookin' gear with you for?" There was another two fellas there, they were dressed identical with leather vests on, and they had identical haircuts, and the same coloured hair. South Americans, I think. And they'd been caught tryin' to use the same passport. One had whisked it back behind him, the bugger.'

Any amusement Milton might have felt at what he saw was quashed when another official came in and asked him questions about his night in Jefferson County Jail sixteen years earlier, and he was also quizzed about the Ord River cattle-stealing allegations. Milton knew it all led to one conclusion: 'They thought I was a bad bugger.' The lack of visa alone made the result inevitable: Milton was going to be put on the next plane back to Australia.

'The only ticket I could buy was a first-class ticket. It cost me a lot of money; I probably should have bailed on that and they might have left me there. Jesus, I didn't like that. Anyway, I got me duffle bag back, and I was the first on the plane. They took me round the back way to put me on it. They actually escorted me on and then a security guard sat outside. I told him: "This is bullshit!" And he said: "I know it is, but this is what we gotta do."

'Then the hostess came and saw me – I reckon the staff must have been drummed up – and she asked: "What would you like?" I said: "I'll tell you what. I want the biggest three-course meal you got and a double rum, and I want the double rum right now. On ice." She said she couldn't do that until we were in the air, but I told her I didn't care and she should go and get the captain, and "tell him to bring a bottle of rum. If I'm flyin' first class and I've been waiting in a room for eighteen hours, I want a drink right now." Anyway, the old captain come across and he got the hostess to give me a double rum. I had one, and then I was right. I had duck for dinner. Christ, what an ordeal. It was pretty embarrassing.'

When he arrived in Sydney, Milton left his naivety about international travel at the airport and returned to familiar ways, including the knack of knowing when to buy and sell. His most unusual purchase at around this time was the hotel at Top Springs, which was little more than a roadhouse settlement next to Montejinni station, 300 kilometres south of Katherine.

How Milton came to be a publican was preceded by an incident in which all the details may never be known. It can be assumed, though, that Milton hadn't endeared himself to the previous owner. The altercation between them happened after Milton had trucked some cattle from Camfield to Montejinni, and had gone to the pub with a few workers. It was raining, and the nearby Armstrong River was in flood.

'A big heap of blackfellas were there, and they were all starvin',' recalled Milton. 'They said, "Bring us beef, bring us beef." You always give 'em beef, otherwise they might go and shoot one and take the front leg off, you know. Anyway, I dropped a bit of beef off there and this old bloody publican, oh dear did she go off. She didn't want us to feed 'em because it could affect her business. One thing led to another and we had a few drinks and told her where to go and what not to do. Anyway, when we took off, the blackfellas were camped there and all their dogs were there trottin' down the road, and it was on Montejinni. A pack of dogs can go after a beast, so I pulled the gun out and was into 'em. The blackfellas must have got a bit frightened and they all ran back to the pub, and the old girl, she's rung the coppers and reckoned I was shootin' at the blackfellas.

'The coppers met us halfway to town, and I was told to get into the back of the paddy wagon. We got back to the cop house and it was late. I was in the cell and out in the mornin'. There were stories that I'd caused a riot and shot people, and [the] medivac [plane] had been out there. What happened was that one gin has given birth to a piccaninny while they're all there in the floodwater, and that's what the medivac was for. And they reckon it was me shootin', and it was just a big bullshit story. Nothin' ever came of it.'

Except that Milton was barred by the publican from patronising the hotel. His response was: 'If I'm not goin' back, not one employee of mine is goin' there either.' Milton had about 70 staff. He told them if they took just one step into the Top Springs pub, they could be walking out of a job. He then set up recreation areas on his stations where alcohol could be bought by his workers at cost price. Whether this affected the bottom line at the Top Springs Hotel is open to conjecture; however, the business was eventually put up for sale, and . . . Milton put an offer in. It was rejected, and the local Aboriginal authority bought it for a lower price. When takings began sliding, the hotel was again put on the market, and Milton again put in an offer. This time it was for about half as much as his initial offer; nevertheless, it was accepted.

'They had the whole bar shut, and they had meshed it up,' said Milton. 'It was a fortress. So we pulled all the mesh off it and spent a lot of money on tidyin' it up, and we've still got it today. We've got a good relationship with everyone, and it works good. A good buy.'

Land and leases remained the centrepieces of Milton's portfolio. In 2002, he and Tejas bought the 3003 square kilometre Delamere station for $15.2 million; it was only separated from Coolibah by the Gregory National Park. By then, Milton had virtually paid off all the debts on Camfield and Montejinni. In a region where some of the biggest cattle players were huge corporations – representing the interests of such intimidating magnates as Kerry Packer and the Holmes à Court family – Milton had established his own considerable empire: three stations outright, and a further five with his Texan associates. In all, they represented 110 000 head of cattle spread out across several million acres.

This, however, was as big as it would be as Milton went through a period of reshuffling his pieces in his very own outback version of Monopoly. He sold Bedford and Lansdowne to his NAH partner Sterling Buntine, and in return he bought Sterling's half-share in the helicopter company. It proved a win for both men. Milton would expand NAH, while Sterling was on his way to becoming one of Australia's leading cattle barons whose personal worth, according to the *BRW* Rich List, has at times pushed beyond $300 million.

Milton also shuffled himself around. He moved to Moroak from Camfield, and then placed managers on Camfield, Montejinni and Delamere. Most of his cattle work revolved around these four stations, with Camfield as the 'factory', the hub for his stock movements in the course of strategic selling, building up herds and the boosting of the stations' values.

'We sold a lot of cattle out of Camfield hard and fast,' said Milton. 'My plan was to put the breeders off there and onto the other places. So we just used it for dry cattle [cattle without calves]. I had heifers on one side and steers on the other, then it was straight down the bitumen. Anything we could sell with a bit of weight: 400 kilograms was a good-sized steer to sell . . . 380 to 400 kilo was your mark to sell, and at $2.10 [per kilo] for an animal like that, ooh, good money. We just had first-, second- and third-year cattle. It worked beautifully. Muster a paddock and pretty well straight onto the bitumen.

'With the double loadin' ramp we could load a truck every twelve minutes. You know, export cattle. As long as you got all your truckies. You got fifteen to eighteen trucks there to load, all the truck drivers get on the crates and the gates and a couple of fellas move 'em and one fella will be drivin' the truck forward, and you just run the cattle up and as soon as fifteen or sixteen are up there he shuts the gate and then there's the next fifteen or sixteen. The whole operation was a good set-up, perfect. Muster with two or three young fellas on the tail and a couple on the lead and away you go, you'd have 'em home in half a day. Then through the yard and onto a truck and gone. Make a lot of money with not a lot of people.'

The success of Milton's strategies wasn't only seen in dollars per kilogram, but also dollars per acre. In 2003, Moroak and Goondooloo, which both benefited from Camfield cattle, were sold at a sizeable profit. Only a year earlier, live export sales had reached a record peak.

'When it all fired and this export business got bigger and land went through the roof I was the first cab off the rank to sell. We had ten million on it [Moroak/Goondooloo], just put a ridiculous price on it, and Tony Davis, a private landholder said: "I'll give you nine and a half for it," and I said: "Done!" That gave the investment the Americans had put into Australia straight back and it filled my pocket. I moved back to Coolibah, and here we are with Camfield, Montejinni and Delamere, the three best places with about 60 000 or 70 000 head of cattle, and the bloody export lined up.'

The export markets would dip between 2003 and 2005, but the prices of land remained high, and provided Milton and Tejas with an opportunity in which one thought loomed large: windfall. In late 2004, they entered negotiations with pastoral giant, Australian Agricultural Company (AAco), over the possible sale of Camfield, Montejinni and Delamere, including approximately 50 000 head of cattle. As expected with a deal of this size, there were intricacies and complexities, and it was reported in the media that AAco undertook 'extensive investigations into the portfolio.' Milton wanted to step back from being a front man because he was wary that even a slight concern from AAco could affect an arrangement he already had in place with the company. As part of the expansion of his helicopter business (NAH), Milton had bought a base in Mount Isa, Queensland, and also purchased some AAco machines. He capped off negotiations by signing a five-year contract to provide services to AAco.

'I didn't want 'em comin back and sayin': "Oh, there aren't cattle there" or "That bore doesn't work," or anything like that,' said Milton.

He needn't have worried. The sale went ahead for about $80 million. Milton and Tejas had previously bought the stations, which at the time had significantly less stock, for a total close to $29 million.

If Milton had been placed in a corporate city office full of pinstripe suits he would have been as out of place as a tin of bully beef at a Bondi brunch. However, he had shown himself to be an astute businessman who needn't wear a suit to play the game of dollars. Milton knew when to buy and he knew when to sell. It was part knowledge, part gut instinct. However, during this period, his gains and losses weren't only on balance sheets. Milton also discovered the price of being human.

CHAPTER 16

FAREWELL AND HELLO

Stan Jones lived in a unit in Katherine. At one point his good mate Normy, an old Territorian who'd endured his rounds with the bottle, moved in with him. The host was going deaf, the guest was going blind. They reckoned they made a good pair. Then Normy died, and Stan felt a gap widen in his life. He yearned for company. His children visited him at different times. Milton was too preoccupied with his work to go often.

Among the inevitable signs that tell us yesterday can never return, the knock on Stan's door from a Meals on Wheels volunteer was one of the most depressing moments for Jenny Jones. It was recognition that a proud man whose resourcefulness was the foundation of his life would never again be able to look after himself. Jenny used to drive down regularly from Darwin to 'clean, wash, iron and cook' for her father. She vowed: 'When you're ready, I'll look after you, I'll never put you in a home.'

Stan eventually moved to Darwin to be with his eldest child.

'I took Dad to a psychiatrist because he was starting to rip his clothes off and they told me he was getting dementia. Just symptoms, starting to lose his memory,' said Jenny.

There were other health problems too: a sensitive stomach, and a heart that was under strain.

Stan was in and out of hospital. Then in March 2003, his arrival at Emergency heralded admission for something more serious.

Jenny rang family members. Milton, who was in Darwin at the time, came while Stan was still in Emergency.

'When I went and saw him he said: "Oh, I'm crook, I'm not good. Tell the bastards don't put any more needles in me,"' recalled Milton. 'So I told the doctor: "Don't keep jabbin' him. Just whatever you're puttin' in him I don't care but he doesn't like needles. Just give him tablets or whatever."'

Father and son spoke for a short time. Milton promised Stan that once all was well again they would go for a helicopter flight over Gordon Downs. It was a pleasure they'd discussed before. They spoke about Milton's work, and they passed a few comments about cattle. Then, Milton felt it was time to go.

He recalled: 'Stan said: "Turn that bloody light out. On your way out tell 'em to turn that light out. I want that light out." And that was his way of tellin' me he was gone, eh. I asked him if he was sure, and he said: "Turn it out." That was his last words to me.'

Over the following three days every other Jones offspring visited their father. Jenny maintained a bedside vigil.

Stan died on 26 March 2003. He was 84. Not long before his death he'd asked Jenny if she could do him a favour 'because I'd appreciate it.' She was able to do him that favour: Stan was buried in Katherine cemetery in the plot next to Normy.

'He'd slowed down a lot, he was pretty steady, the old fella,' said Milton, speaking quietly. 'He was a big man, Dad. Big up top. He sort of fell to pieces in the old legs, he had broken legs and a bit crippled up he was . . . yeah . . . the old heart just sort of slowed down and stopped, his veins collapsed. Anyway, he was ready to go.'

Jenny, Randall, Llawrence, Terry and Milton all had their own ways of coping with the death. For Milton, it was a case of returning to work. In the unpredictable twists that life brings, he was at the time in the 'getting to know you' stage of a new relationship.

Cristina Mundell is twelve years younger than Milton. She is slight and sinewy, with brown hair and intense blue eyes. Born in Dalby, Queensland, she'd grown up on farms, firstly near Condamine, then Toowoomba. Cattle, wheat, sorghum, horses and open spaces were the backdrop to her childhood. After finishing high school she worked in Brisbane for a while as a hotel banquet waitress. Wearing crisp black-and-whites was not a good fit, metaphorically, for someone who preferred dust on denim.

'I didn't really go much on that,' she said, laughing.

She moved south to the New South Wales central tablelands, where she studied agricultural commerce at the Orange Agricultural College. She gained her piece of paper, but still felt the need to be educated, albeit in an environment that no lecture theatre could provide. Much to her mother's concern, she headed to the Northern Territory where her older brother Angus had been working; her younger brother Hamish was also in the bush in north Queensland, so there was some sense of inevitability that Cristina would follow the family leads.

Her first job was as a ringer on Bunda station, about 250 kilometres south-west of Coolibah, and close to the Western Australia border. To get there, she 'belted' down the roads in her 308 Monaro, 'a really good car, easy to fix' – the assessment of someone who didn't consider herself an 'A-grade mechanic' yet knew the basics. The following season she upgraded to a LandCruiser Prado because she 'was sick of no air-conditioning and the dog breathing down my neck.' She arrived at Bunda's neighbour, Birrindudu, which flanked the north-western edge of the Tanami Desert. Was fate playing some role? This was the area Stan Jones introduced his family to in his Gordon Downs days.

'On Bunda I did the stud work and the mustering with the boys,' recalled Cristina. 'At Birrindudu I did the same thing in the stock camp and a bit of bookwork because I had a shoulder reconstruction after I had an accident off a horse. We were chasing cattle, the horse tripped and fell over end-on-end and my left shoulder was the first point of contact with the ground. But even with an accident like that, I still loved what I was doing.

'The places were extremely isolated. There was a lot to do on horseback. They were big days too. One place, we walked the cattle from one of the yards at Birrindudu right through to Nicholson station. It took us about three days. There were no choppers or anything there. They were dry cattle too, no calves. At other jobs, the choppers would put the cattle on the bore and then we'd walk them 20 or 30 kilometres back to wherever the yard was. Long, hot days. It would go until late at night, until we got there. We'd be very thirsty. I still actually don't drink enough water during the day now because I always think if I get stuck without water somewhere I'll be conditioned to it.'

Cristina also did contract fencing, but after two years of dust and endless skies, she sought a change of scenery and lifestyle. She found what she was looking for in sweeps of brilliant yellow canola fields, snow-capped mountains and clear streams. High River, Canada, was a small town on the doorstep of Calgary, the city famous for its 'Stampede' rodeo. Cristina got a job working with horses and cattle at a feedlot. Again, she loved what she did, but she didn't enjoy the sub-zero winter which gave a woman who thrived on the outdoors a new appreciation of the indoors.

'It was the prettiest place. It was so nice but just too cold. It was freezing, awful.'

After a year, Cristina returned to Australia where the call of Northern Territory life was too strong to ignore. The roads again led to the remote Birrindudu before Cristina's boyfriend at the time was offered a job looking after the stock at Coolibah. Cristina went too, and about a month after her arrival, she met Milton for the first time.

'We met at Camfield while Milton was still living at Moroak,' recalled Cristina. 'I'd heard about him because of the stations he'd bought. To tell you the truth, I really didn't like him. I thought he was a bit arrogant but I didn't really think about it much. It was sort of: "How ya going?" between us and that was about it. When I met him, it was probably around when his marriage had just split up, and the subconscious alarm bells ring and you think, Poor bastard, stay away from him!'

And that remained her view after she broke up with her boyfriend, moved into Katherine and accepted Milton's offer to work in his office. A few months later, she received a phone call from her boss that had nothing to do with sorting papers: he invited her to dinner. More getting-to-know-you occasions followed over several months.

'I started to know him pretty well over that time. But I'm not a big one for change,' said Cristina with a gentle laugh. 'I think persistence probably got Milton over the line.'

The most decisive moment came about a year into the relationship after Milton had sold Moroak. He rang Cristina and said: 'I'm gonna come back and live at Coolibah. Why don't you come out there?' Cristina mulled over the decision before she accepted that she was ready – or at the very least, willing – to begin a new stage of her life. Now, she looks back at the period by mixing carefully chosen sentences with enthusiastic bursts.

'You know how a memory triggers something, and you laugh so much?' she asked. 'I think it was the second day I was at Coolibah – the house wasn't air-conditioned back then – and I was going in to clean things up. There was a bar where our bedroom is now. And there was an old pine cabinet there that I opened up. There were a heap of bottles of wine, and on top of them, you could hardly even see it because it was entangled in the bottles, would have been a 7-foot brown snake. Huge! I just shut the cabinet again. No one was there with me, and I didn't have a gun or anything. I raced up to the croc farm and got Bluey and said: "I've got a snake in the cupboard and if it's not there when I get back I'm not sleeping in that house." I didn't know where it could have gone. Anyway, it was there, and Bluey who's really good with that sort of thing, got it out. He held it up and it was longer than him. It was just the most repulsive thing; I could smell it for months afterwards. We had heaps of those sorts of snakes. The overgrown gardens were a haven for them. When the house was eventually done up, they pulled a big one out of the wall. It had been dead in there for however long.'

Being a station owner's partner posed some challenges for Cristina. At the head of them all was building a relationship with a man who was away more often than he was home.

'I think there was a turning point for me with Milton,' acknowledged Cristina. 'I went out about six or seven one morning to check the bores. You didn't need to check them every day, but I used to worry if there was no water, because then you'd perish your cattle. Milton was away, but I was expecting him home either that day or the next. So, I was out doing the bores, and from memory I think it was a tail-shaft that fell out of the Toyota. There was nothing I could particularly do about it and I was a long way from home.

'Milton got back and when I wasn't there he went out looking for me. I'd stayed in the same spot all day, and then I heard the chopper and Milton started calling me on the radio because he'd been following my tracks. That's when I said to him: "I didn't think I'd ever be that excited to hear your voice." I didn't know how long I was going to be there; it wasn't going to be weeks or anything. It was only about 10 kilometres back to the main road, but I didn't want to walk there because there were some weird things going on around the place. Someone had even tied a noose to a tree over the river, and those sorts of things play on your mind. We never found out who it was.'

Despite such a worrying mystery, Cristina cherished the isolated lifestyle. It was: 'Being able to see as far as you can see, and doing your own thing.' She was comfortable. She was content. And, two years after moving to Coolibah, she was happy to say, 'Yes.' It was June 2005.

'We got married in Darwin, in the Botanical Gardens,' said Milton. 'Had a horse and buggy cart us down the street, and I thought the horse was gonna take off too. This old sheila and her daughter had these two horses and anyway this one horse was as green as grass, it was. I tell you, I just about had the bride under one arm jumpin' out of the buggy there at one part. It got to the [traffic] lights and it wouldn't bloody move. Everyone was yackin' and cooeein' on the main street and the horse started playin' up, rearin' up and carryin' on. I thought, There's gonna be a hat go under this bastard. This thing is just gonna bolt. But she was right, the woman held him.

'Cristina got pretty crook after that, she got the bloody flu. She was crook there for about three days, and so was

I from the rum. We just booked into the Crowne Plaza and got the penthouse upstairs for a week and people came and people went, and then we all came home again.'

They returned to the homestead they'd recently redesigned and renovated without losing the original features including the walls made from stones that had been carted from the nearby Victoria River. Back in the 1940s, Olive Underwood, the then de facto wife of Coolibah's owner Tom Quilty, was actively involved in the construction of the building and the general operations on the station. Sixty years later, it was Cristina's turn. In addition to the physical work that she never shirked from, she assumed many of the administrative responsibilities for a continually changing stable of business interests run by a man who could give the impression he was in perpetual motion. Milton may have become a married man again, but he wasn't yet ready to settle down. His life was to remain unpredictable, and sadly this included unforeseen tragedies.

CHAPTER 17

THINGS ADD UP

On 21 February 2006, an NAH Robinson 44 helicopter took off from the remote Gunpowder airstrip about 100 kilometres north-west of Mount Isa. It was a scorching afternoon, 38 degrees Celsius. The pilot, 28-year-old Vita Stott, had three passengers, all technicians who were surveying potential routes for power lines and water pipelines as part of a feasibility study into the development of a copper processing plant on a mining tenement. Three survey flights of the area had already been conducted by Vita that day.

The helicopter didn't arrive at an organised rendezvous site, concerns were raised, and by early evening the national search and rescue organisation, AusSAR, was alerted. There had been no reports of distress calls or activation of an EPIRB (emergency position-indicating radio beacon). A night-time operation was undertaken in a fixed-wing aircraft that had infra-red imaging equipment. It found nothing.

The next day a rescue helicopter joined the search. By late morning, the burnt wreckage of the NAH helicopter was discovered on a hill in steep, rocky terrain near the Mount Gordon mine. There were no survivors.

Three and a half years later the findings from a Queensland coronial inquest stated:

> *The precise cause of the crash has not been ascertained. There is no evidence of any mechanical failure. Ms Stott's lack of experience in this type of flying and the overloading of the aircraft may have contributed.*

The tragedy was the second of three accidents in a difficult period for Milton and NAH. About two years earlier, a North Australian Helicopters pilot, Harry Wardale, was killed after he hit a power line near Mount Isa, and in September 2007 Christian 'Stumpy' Stenhouse, father of two and a good mate of Milton's, died after the R-22 he was flying crashed and burst into flames on Doongan station in the Kimberley region.

When being interviewed for this book Milton didn't wish to speak in detail about the accidents or how they made him feel. Too painful. He elaborated most about Stumpy.

'Big Kurt was in with him. And they smelled a bit of rubber burnin' and landed. Stumpy, silly thing . . . Kurt got out of the helicopter and said: "I'm not gettin' back in it, leave it here." They had a satellite phone under the seat. Anyway, they were the best thing you could buy at the time. You know, I had twenty of them, one in every aircraft. And old mate [Stumpy] sat there for about two hours tryin' to get a signal but he couldn't. So he said: "I'll get home with it," you know. And he didn't,' said Milton who took a deep breath before continuing. 'Yeah, bloody belt blew off and rolled up and . . .'

'After that, we took care of all his family's cattle. Dalgety's put a price on 'em and I bought 'em all. That way they had some money comin' in.'

Milton was shopping in Brisbane's Queen Street Mall when he received the phone call about Stumpy's death.

'He just about collapsed and basically lost it,' remembered Cristina. 'He handled all the accidents pretty well, but it was impossible not to be affected and show the emotions. I suppose I carried Milton a bit. We couldn't both fall in a heap.'

During her early days as a ringer in the Northern Territory, Cristina presumed she would graduate to flying helicopters at some stage, but once she knew a few people who'd died in accidents, her thinking changed. The list included one of her uncles, who was a passenger when a JetRanger crashed near Gove in the Territory's north-east. She would later lose a friend who'd become engaged not long before his accident.

When Cristina married Milton, she accepted she was teaming up with a man who was never going to be comfortable in an air-conditioned office shifting paper around a desk and counting the hours until his lunch break. To this day, Milton's reliance on helicopters is something Cristina battles with.

'It does worry me every time he flies off, and I often have dreams about him crashing. If we ever have conflict I hate him going off flying because there'd be nothing worse if that was that and he didn't come back. And I worry about my brother Angus flying, too. Choppers, they're a means to an end. I'll still fly with Milton, but I don't particularly like it anymore. You definitely need choppers but you have to treat them with respect.'

Because of the nature of his work Milton had endured his share of hazardous times. However, it was the commonplace procedures that often provided some of the biggest surprises. In his early years as a pilot Milton had once taken off in a Bell 47 only to feel his machine 'hangin' down on one side.' A quick look out the window told him a pump and drum had hooked around a skid after they'd been used for refuelling. Milton responded by working his helicopter sideways, and lowering it until he could 'gently rub' the pieces onto the ground. On another occasion he pulled a spark plug out of an engine, but it was so hot he tossed it away without thinking, only to hear it hit the main rotor blade of a machine that was turned off and running down. The momentary lapse cost him $40 000.

All his experiences have taught him how to improve his operations, which he continues to fine-tune today, especially in relation to heli-mustering.

'About nine o'clock in the mornin' is your first fuel up, three hours after startin'. A lot of the accidents I've known have been about nine o'clock, believe it or not,' said Milton. 'That was due to runnin' out of fuel and young fellas not bein' able to find the fuel or bein' too far away. It's about judgement and havin' enough fuel reserves to get back there. One of the things I've noticed is you might get a fella who's a new pilot and new to the country. And he'll take three or four drums of fuel out and he'll put the bastards a few hundred metres off the road. Well, you should put the fuel right in the middle of the road on a station so the pilots can find it. You can miss it easy if it's sittin' off to the side. I've heard it on the radio lots of times: "Where's the fuel?"

'The other thing is, fuel in the middle of the road makes it easy to pick up when fellas are goin' back home. Otherwise the drums will stay in the bush there for bloody two years and someone will pick 'em up later and put 'em back in the heat. And they've got water in 'em and the paint is fallin' off the inside of 'em. And then they fill 'em up again and you have dirty fuel in the chopper. So put 'em in the middle of the road where you actually have to drive around 'em. That has stopped a lot of accidents, you know.'

Mustering is tough on the machinery. Low flying, dust, frequent turning, and the pilot's adrenalin can all affect wear and tear. Milton gets regular reports from his engineers who can tell when particular pilots are 'knockin' the choppers around.' Each helicopter is serviced every 100 hours of flying time. The type most widely used by NAH, and indeed throughout Northern Australia, is the Robinson 22. The current Beta II model has a four-cylinder 145-horsepower engine. In comparison, a popular Australian suburban car, the Volkswagen Golf TDI, has four cylinders and 140 horsepower.

'In the twenty years I've been operatin' there've probably been eighteen choppers we've crashed or lost,' acknowledged Milton. 'It's a fair bit. But then you look at how many hours we've done and the type of work we do and it's pretty safe, really. When you do a lot of hours you gotta expect a few accidents. As long as someone doesn't get hurt it doesn't worry me much.'

In 2009, Milton increased his fleet to about 40, mostly R-22s, when he bought the Darwin-based company Albatross Helicopters, which had twelve machines. This led to an even greater demand for pilots, who over the years have been recruited from throughout Australia and overseas. The three fatal accidents Milton has been associated with through his company are reminders of his responsibilities to nurture the careers of primarily young men.

'When they start flyin' with us, I like to bring a fair percentage of 'em here to Coolibah for twelve months and see if they want to stay. I like to have a good look at 'em. I put 'em through a few hard yards. If they can look after a tractor, a horse and the cattle then they'll look after your helicopter and themselves. It works good because you know the fella you're sendin' out then. The deal is, they gotta know how to strain a fence and cut a killer up. I tell 'em that until they can bone a killer out they haven't got a musterin' endorsement, so that makes 'em keen to get on a knife.

'It's true. You send a young fella to a property, he's gotta know all that sorta stuff, otherwise he's no good. When I was learnin', the chopper pilot had to go and get the beef; he goes and shoots a bullock you can't get in a yard, or a fat cow he left behind somewhere. It's about knowin' the country, the people you're workin' with, your machinery and yourself too. You gotta respect 'em all. That won't make you become a good pilot but it will help. It's all about what you learn along the way.

'I've had a lot of good young fellas go through here. We must have employed a couple of hundred pilots over the years. People ring from everywhere wantin' to come and work here. We just try to pick out a few. I talk to 'em on the phone first, and then I ask 'em a few questions and I can work it out pretty quick whether they're any value. And I tell 'em to send a photo of themselves and a resumé. I might tell 'em to, "Ring me in a week at this time." If they ring me early or late, well they're out, basically. If they can't do that right . . . well, you know what I mean. When someone comes out here, whether they're wantin' to be pilots or workin' with cattle, you put 'em in a yard and tell 'em what to do. If he doesn't listen to you, you'd tell him again. If he doesn't listen a third time you'd give him a hit under the ear. And fourth time hunt him out of the yard, put him on a truck and back to town. Gone!

'You get a fella with a bit of a nasty streak in him, it doesn't come out. You know he might be floggin' cattle with a stick. You can't take that. It's the same with the helicopter. That happens a lot. If a young fella gets angry when he's flyin', well he could kill himself. And it could be just because there's a vehicle parked in the wrong place, or he's asked for a gate to be opened but no one does it.'

Among those who have advanced through this tough school is South Australian Matt Wright, who'd been employed by the NAH managing director, John Logan, as a junior pilot. He did some early work at Moroak before moving to Coolibah for about twelve months during which time he was thrown into a 'big learning curve.'

'He [Milton] didn't know my name for the first six months. It was, "Oi you, get up and do this!"' acknowledged

Matt, speaking via phone from an office in Derby, Western Australia. 'He was a hard man, that's for sure. He expected work. It was five a.m. to seven p.m., you work your arse off, and try to get to the top and work your way into a machine. If he sees you've got some sort of potential he'll keep you moving up. I had nothing else going at the time. I couldn't go anywhere else, so I had to knuckle in and get the work done. You definitely had to earn your stripes. It was a good job and good experience.'

Helicopter work had taught Milton that 'little things can add up to big things.' This not only applied to the safety of the pilots and the machines, but the reasons for flying to begin with. And none was more poignant than when Milton assisted in a search for a little boy who went missing near Larrimah, about 200 kilometres east of Coolibah.

'He'd gone off from his mother late in the afternoon,' remembered Milton. 'I got a call that night, and was over there just on daylight the next day. I wanted to get there early because it was stinkin' hot, near the end of the year. If we didn't get him by lunchtime he'd be dead, or just about, in the heat, so we had to go quick. There was a couple of yellafellas who come out there from Larrimah and Mataranka, and I knew one of them. I said to him: "You pick his track up and don't leave it."

'And that's exactly what he did. It was spinifex and sand country. He'd draw a ring around the track for me so I could see where he was. He was foot walkin', and I just stayed with him, workin' either side. The key was to keep to the track. If you lose it, pull up and get another fella to go wide, or drive a stick in the ground so you know where you are and then go round wide until you find the track and go again. Don't pull up and start thinkin' he's gone this way or that way.

'Anyway, the boy was only about four years old and he'd probably gone about 5 kilometres parallel to the main road where he'd gone off from his mother. And I reckon the moon come up and he walked straight towards the moon, then he heard motor cars and cut out towards the road, and he went right across the road, and that yellafella stayed on his track all the way. And he found the boy near a fence. That's where he pulled up. It must have been about one o'clock, I reckon.'

But in an unforgiving part of Australia, Milton had learnt not every search ended with tears of relief. The helicopter accident at Mount Gordon was a dreadful confirmation of this. At that time, Cristina was pregnant. A month later, on 27 March 2006, another Milton Jones entered the world, born at Wesley Hospital in Brisbane. In a touch of synchronicity, just a matter of minutes' drive away was the suburb of Milton.

'Big' Milton had his third child. And 'Little' Milton had a father unlike any other.

CHAPTER 18
RITE OF PASSAGE

The lines are among thousands penned and sung by Australian country music greats Slim Dusty and his wife, Joy McKean.

> *Where the land is big and wide, and tall dark ringers ride*
> *On the plains of Peppimenarti, where the old Moyle River flows.*

While the song 'Plains of Peppimenarti' tells of kangaroos, tough men, stock camps, chasing bulls and catching barramundi, Milton came to know the area for its crocodiles. The broad expanse of floodplains 120 kilometres north-west of Coolibah and a short drive to the coast near Joseph Bonaparte Gulf was one of the main sources for Milton's egg-collecting, which remained a highly profitable part of his business a decade after he'd pulled out of his farming partnership with Bluey. And as he continued his missions for 'white gold', he again found himself in precarious positions.

'This'll take a bit of swallowin',' said Milton. 'I was on a crocodile nest once and the crocodile jumped up and pulled the passenger seat out of the Robinson 22. I was hoverin' there on this floatin' nest and just havin' a look and she's reared straight up, grabbed the bottom of the seat and pulled it clean out. Jumped up about a metre. I ended up shootin' that bastard. Bad crocodile. That was on the Moyle River.'

Cristina went on a few collection runs, but didn't enjoy them, so chose to stay at Coolibah. Instead, Milton ventured out with numerous others, some of whom were experienced, others raw and wide-eyed. The latter would consider any job from which they returned unscathed was successful, regardless of the number of eggs gathered.

'Once I went in to check this nest out and it was full of eggs,' recalled Milton. 'And I said to this fella, a yellafella he was, "I'll go back and get the box. You wait here." I've come back and the fella said: "Hey Milton, that crocodile right here!" He's up the tree, this fella, he's heard the crocodile and he's gone straight up the tree, and she's come back to the nest. I'm puffin and pantin' and walkin' through all this grass. The next minute, wooh, she has taken a big snap at me. And the fella says: "I told you that crocodile is right here!" I've took off and I've got all this cane grass under me fingernails, and oh, talk about pain when I was scratchin' and grabbin' tryin' to get out of there. The croc had just sat there and let me come in, the bastard.'

The Peppimenarti area, together with the Fitzmaurice and Victoria rivers, weren't the only collection areas for Milton. From about 2000 onwards, and certainly in the last six or so years, the Arafura Swamp in the far north of Arnhem Land became an important catching location at different times. Spreading across 700 square kilometres, it is part of the floodplain for the Goyder and Gulbuwangay rivers, and also sits next to a coastal plain affected by tides. In places it is heavily wooded with paperbarks, and mats of grasses and weeds hinder easy movement for humans, but make it a haven for bird life.

During his earliest trips, which all needed permission from the appropriate Aboriginal authorities, Milton and others built a rudimentary pad from cut timber that was slung in by helicopter. It was sturdy enough to hold a drum of fuel and support people to collate details on the eggs that had been collected. In an area where there were few landing spots, the construction showed Milton's initiative, and contributed to gigantic hauls in both eggs and dollars.

'It was real valuable because there was nowhere to land for 10 to 20 kilometres,' said Milton. 'And the whole swamp takes about an hour and a half to fly round. Collectin' was all helicopter work. Fly in, fly out. We had quotas from different farms. To supply the helicopter and do the whole lot was up to 42 bucks a viable egg. It was good money. We certainly made a good quid out of it.'

Egg-collecting wasn't Milton's only earner in the area. At various times he was also contracted to catch crocodiles. The dangers of his working environment were underlined by one particular observation he made of the Territory's survival-of-the-fittest brutality.

'There was a little island in Arafura Swamp, probably covered about ten acres,' said Milton. 'There was about twenty head of cattle and about twenty or thirty head of buffalo. They were starvin', bloody dyin' poor. In the middle of this island there was a real dark green patch, and the cattle were right up in there, and that's where all the crocodiles were too. I'm tellin' you, there would have been 150 crocodiles on this island as well. Just surrounded the island. I landed this helicopter and I had a fella with me. I was gettin' out with a gun to shoot these cattle, poor bastards were blind from starvin', and next thing about ten or fifteen crocodiles – they were wantin' to get back in the water, all 12 or 13 foot, I suppose – come from the centre of the island all [going] flat [out] for the water. But a crocodile can only go so far because he has to pull up and settle himself down. And they pulled up right around the helicopter and this fella thought he was gonna get eaten. He didn't know what was goin' on, he thought the crocodiles were all comin' to get him. That was somethin' different, I've never seen that before.

'Anyhow, what was happenin', these cattle were goin' down and the crocodiles were hookin' into 'em. A crocodile won't eat rotten food. He wants fresh tucker all the time. There was a heifer there, buffalo, I reckon just lookin' at her head she would've been about four years old. When you get a buffalo head and try to cut its horn off with an axe or smash it, it's bloody tough. And the crocodiles had killed this thing the night before and smashed one horn off it and the only thing that was recognisable was its rump. It had all the hocks chewed off, the shoulders and head were all smashed, the guts were gone, and it just had its hips and its two buttocks, the two biggest parts of the meat. That's all that was there. To smash that horn off, you know, terrific power. The bottom jaw was all pulled out of the head. Jesus Christ! Just twisted it. It was dead fresh, the meat wasn't stinkin'.'

One of Milton's largest jobs involved catching females that were to be used for breeding at the Darwin Crocodile Farm. Over several weeks Milton worked with various teams. His preference generally was to have no more than two other people with him. On one trip he reunited with Kim Walker, the first man to give him a bull-catching job in the west.

Each operation began with the aerial surveying of billabongs. Any considered suitable would be at least 'eight or ten mile long, big enough to poke in all night.' Essential equipment – a 14-foot dinghy with a 15-horsepower engine, a small Honda generator, a fluoro light, and a tent – was then 'slung in' by helicopter to a campsite.

The catching itself was a well-drilled night operation conducted by spotlight. Unlike his early days of catching, when Milton discovered harpoons weren't efficient for hauling in freshwater crocodiles, the need for safety with the more dangerous salties demanded a return to old ways. While one person drove the boat, the other manned a harpoon; this was an aluminium pole about 12 feet long with a small brass head that had two triangular-shaped prongs about 2 centimetres long.

'We used to do two or three nights and then we'd have to pull up and grab a couple of hours' sleep here or there because you couldn't sleep in the middle of the day, it was too bloody hot,' said Milton. 'You'd try to get the harpoon in the [croc's] neck in a soft spot just behind the head, and away from a little hard piece of armour platin'. The big trouble was a lot of the weed; when you'd harpoon 'em they'd go under the weed and you'd have to pull out. But once you got 'em in a good spot, you'd hold 'em on your string and get 'em to the top as quick as you could, like soon as you hit 'em you pull 'em! You'd have gloves on because the string could go out real fast and cut your hands to bits.

'Anyway, you get the crocodile to the surface as quick as you can, then put a nose rope and some duct tape on it. Power on your boat a little bit, and the crocodile would come up beside you, then you put your hand over and vent it [check its sex by feeling for a vent in the abdomen]. If he's male, just cut the rope and tape and drop him. It's just a bow-line on the end of your rope. We'd tried splicin' the ropes and havin' all these bloody fancy tie-up knots, but in the end the quickest way was the safest too.

'If it was female we'd just go straight to a tree and a bit of bank and just tie her up, and then we'd just chuck a bit of tape over the tree. Usually if you got one you'd get a few more there close. They make a bit of noise and the bastards get inquisitive and come up. Nobody gets into that country much, no boats get in there, so they don't know what to expect. So we'd keep goin' like that all night, tyin' 'em up just like bull-catchin'. Then we'd come along next mornin' and either bundle 'em all up in the boat, or put 'em on a long sling from the chopper. If you had three of you for that part it was good. With only two, that's me in the air and another on the ground, it was pretty hard to get the crocodiles off the tree and hook 'em onto the chopper.

'I'd pick 'em all up by the nose and sling 'em back somewhere close where I could put a big belly-net under 'em. Then I'd take about five or six at a time and sling 'em back ten or fifteen minutes to a cattle crate truck and drop 'em straight in there. We didn't head-tie 'em. We just let 'em move around. Just tape their eyes and their noses and put the rope knots in their mouths to keep 'em open a bit and stop 'em chokin' if they regurgitated. And we put some hay and a few broken bushes on the floor that they could get under. Then a fella would cart 'em back to Darwin, and stop along the way to water 'em.

'We made a good quid out of that too. We lost one or two out of the whole exercise from start to finish. One of the real interestin' things was that we trapped a few too. But only the harpooned ones have been successful breeders. They just pumped out the eggs like you wouldn't believe. I just told the farm they were good and quiet and had been broken in properly.'

The environment in which Milton worked would almost certainly provoke a strong sense of vulnerability in the everyday suburbanite. After all, it isn't too dramatic to suggest that with a mere step the wrong way you can cross the line between relative calm and a fight for survival. All it takes is the snap of a jaw, the strike of a fang-bearing head or the stab of a horn. Because of this, Milton wore a 'squirter' on his hip, a 10-millimetre semi-automatic Glock which had recoil that could pound even the strongest of hands. A powerful weapon and a comforting travel companion.

'One time there, we'd been harpoonin' these crocodiles all bloody night. It must have been about three or four in the mornin' and I said to the others with me: "We'll close our eyes for an hour." I think it was Marcus, and Nick Robinson from Darwin Croc Farm. Pretty big fellas, whitefellas. And we've got a two-man tent. You always take a tent in the Top End to stop your arse bein' chewed out by mosquitoes.

'Anyway, we've got mud and shit all over us and we're hot and we're lyin' in this tent. Nick's snorin' and Marcus is snorin', and I'm there awake, no way in the world I could sleep. We had this little petrol generator, and it's makin' a little *brrrrrr* noise right beside us, and the fluoro light is on. We wouldn't have been in there for fifteen minutes and the generator has run out of fuel because it has been goin' all night. I'm lyin' there and that was the worst because I could hear all the mosquitoes. I could hear everything, and suddenly this bloody bull buffalo was right there too, and he's sort of *annnn snort* . . . that's how they sing out. And oh Christ, we're in a tent, three of us, and this buffalo's here and it's gonna whale us, you know what I mean.

'Have you ever tried to get out of a tent without undoin' the zip? I'm tellin' you, it's hard. Anyway, I sleep with my pistol on me hip. And I'm inside this tent and I've just come out firin' and these two fellas have come awake, and you could imagine this tent with three of us in there goin' every which way, and I reckon the buffalo's been given a hell of a start and it's gone. We could hear the timber crashin' where it went. Bugger that. We got out of the friggin' tent and back in the boat; that was the safest place to be.

'Another time we were catchin' them big crocodiles there on the Arafura. We had to land the helicopter about a kilometre away from the boat we were usin'. Anyway, that's no problem. We've landed, and there's a big crocodile in the trap and the boat's there. Away we go and we've got this bit of a walk in, and I've got a squirter. We've got about ten steps away from the trap, and the fella with me said: "What about that bastard? What are you gonna do with him?" And I said: "What's that?" I turned around and here's this bull buffalo right on top of us. The fella knew it was dead serious when I just dropped the gear and went for the tree. He didn't even look around. He went up a pandanus tree. You know those coconut crackers who run up the coconut trees? Well that's how he went up it. And I went to about the second fork in this other tree. Lucky, because there are big ones up there that have got big thorns up 'em. There was one of them bastards right there; lucky we didn't try to go up it. It was hot and dry and all burnt ground.

'Anyway, this buffalo is round me tree and beltin' it, tryin' to hook me. I pulled my squirt out and drove about three straight into his back, and he took off. It didn't kill him but away he went. Then I got a bit frightened, I thought he might have gone back to the chopper. But he didn't, he pissed off. Here we were breezin' about a crocodile, and a buffalo near runs over us. He must have been on season. Generally they're pretty myall buffalo there; they don't see anybody much in the middle of that swamp.

'One more I remember. It was at a big spring that runs from the Goyder into the Arafura Swamp, and it just goes out into fingers everywhere. It's sandy and all beautiful couch grass, buffalo keep it all short, and it's not far to the water; if you're quick enough there you can put a snare on a crocodile. And we'd made up a steel pole with a wire snare on it. Anyway, we shot a bloody bullock there and put a bit of bait where we wanted the old crocodile to go. We ended up catchin' about seven or eight that way.

'The first one we got, we're gonna fly out of there to a truck. And we've got litters on either side of the chopper, one of these R-44s. We got the old crocodile nose-roped and all laced up with stretchies [octopus straps] and whatever else we had there to tie the bastard on, his head is pointin' forwards and we reckoned it was all secure.

'Next thing, this old helicopter started wrigglin' and the fella I had beside me looked at me. I've looked out at the crocodile and at the same time it's come straight in the door and wedged itself down where the pedals are.

It's still got its nose-rope on, like it was safe. I'm sittin' in the helicopter and I'm "Bloody Jesus Christ!" We're goin' along and this thing is tryin' to come in the front seat with us. It has got halfway in, and I'm tryin' to kick it out and anyway we got it out and it had a flight down from a thousand feet. So yeah, just booted it straight out. So whenever you're flyin' a crocodile on a litter, always point him backwards. That's the lesson.'

These stories all became lessons to be passed down to the people Milton worked with. By the time junior helicopter pilot Matt Wright started with Milton, he'd already clocked countless miles of adventures. He spent his early years in Mount Compass, a small dairy and market gardening area 50 kilometres south of Adelaide. During a somewhat nomadic childhood, he also lived with his family for a while in Cairns before he was led by his stepfather on a dream to sail around the world. The journey began from Taipei where a yacht was picked up, but fate soon flung a storm into its path, and both a vessel and a dream were broken.

'We ended up for about nine months in PNG [Papua New Guinea] after that,' recalled Matt. 'I enjoyed it, I didn't mind. Mum absolutely hated it. She had two kids and we were living in a little shanty over there near a plantation on a beach, I think near Rabaul. I was only young. I've just got a few memories of going to school with the local kids, and mucking around spear-fishing. It was good times.'

Matt and the family returned to Australia and retraced their steps from Cairns to Mount Compass. All the while Matt found the outdoors to be his master educator. While others his age caught footballs, Matt preferred catching reptiles and healing sick animals. He was encouraged by his mother, although the sight of snakes, including poisonous browns, in the house was undoubtedly more worrying than muddy clothes tossed in a corner.

After finishing high school, Matt became another in a guild spanning generations of those drawn to the Northern Territory, the 'last frontier'. He bounced from job to job and across borders as he compiled a resumé of the diverse: work on a Victorian ski resort and a New South Wales cattle property, and three years' service in Australia's Army Reserve. He then joined a team drilling water bores all across the Territory, and it was at this stage that he made a life-changing decision.

'The choice was whether to continue on the drilling and go across onto the oil rigs, or go and fly helicopters, so I saved the money and went and did my chopper licence.'

His journey eventually led him to Coolibah where he was introduced to egg-collecting, partly due to the reason that 'No other pilot would go out because everyone thought it was madness.' But Matt 'loved it' despite experiencing 'a lot of interesting calls.' One such moment was along the Goyder River where, like in the Arafura Swamp, there were few places to land. Matt had been going from nest to nest in a harness at the end of about 100 feet of rope, long enough to clear the tallest paperbark trees that crowded the area.

'I had a crate of eggs and I'd just come down onto a bit of flat,' said Matt. 'And as I put the crate down, I was about to unhook, and I look up and this buffalo is coming flat! And I'm running. I'm out of there, but I was still hooked on to the line. And Milton's looked down and seen what's going on.'

Milton chuckled when recalling the moment.

'So I've just *whoosh*, pulled the chopper up again and jerked Matty off the ground, and he's gone one way, and of course he's got a swing up on the hook. And just as I've jerked him back his legs have run straight across the top of this buffalo. This buffalo is up him, gonna nail him. It's cheeky, that bastard, it's swearin' and swingin' and hookin'. And I've got Matty up above him and I'm thinkin', Matty are you gonna be cheeky to me anymore? I'll put you on him if you're not careful. The buffalo took off into the water and away he went. And we landed there. That was a funny episode. Livened us up, eh, got a bit of action in the camp.'

It also 'put the wind up' Matt, who remembered several other times when he, Bluey and another collector, Jimmy King, were in the middle of trouble.

'We had a few crocodiles run over the top of us at different times,' said Matt. 'Not too long ago Milton put me on a nest, and I unhooked and was looking for a croc coming through one waterhole and it came from the opposite direction. I had to jump over the crocodile while at the same time I was hitting it on the snout as it launched up. Milton thought it was the funniest thing, but anyway we're still here to tell the tale.'

For Matt, the experiences were rungs on a remarkable climb. Now in his early thirties, Matt is host of the acclaimed international television series, *Outback Wrangler*, produced by Nat Geo Wild. He is dedicated to wildlife conservation.

While humour and understatement are common tools that are used when stories are told of the moments that so easily could have finished in tragedy, no amount of downplay could soften the recollection of an escape that Matt witnessed from afar. He and Milton were both flying machines on a 'one for one' collecting run along the Goyder. Bluey was in one harness, and his twenty-year-old daughter, Raine, was in the other.

'After we finished the business together, I still worked with Milton because he hired the choppers to me,' recalled Bluey. 'This time, Milton was flying me but he couldn't land, and that's the trouble, you're working in a landscape that people couldn't devise in their worst nightmare. We were working on floating mat, just a huge mat of floating vegetation over what could be 10 foot or 10 inches of water, you don't know. These females, they can come up through that floor at any point. They hear you there and the next minute they just spear up through the floor and you don't know where they're gonna come out. It's very exciting.

'Anyway, Milton put me on this nest – I had my harness on but I wasn't hooked – and the nest was starting to sink. So I had to spread the weight out more by going down on my shins, like kneeling. I was pretty low, and the next minute – I never even saw her coming . . . *bang!* I got hit and she's gone straight across my shoulder and chest and one arm's pinned to me and she's trying to pull me down through the floor.

'Milton probably got a bigger fright than I did because, well, he saw it all and I didn't see much. I was trying to stop myself getting sucked through the floor and possibly eaten. Anyway, Milton has come around and he was going to hit the crocodile with the tip of the skid on the chopper. And I was trying to get a handgun out. I was sort of flailing away madly. Eventually she must have thought I tasted like shit, let me go, and she just stood up on her tail, spun back and went down stern first like the *Bismarck*. She seemed pretty big at the time. I suppose she was 8 or 9 foot or so, bigger than me, anyway.

'Milton came down but he couldn't land; the world was just made of marshmallow. It was a good thing I wasn't really chewed up. So I got on my knees on the skid – I didn't trust my legs at that stage – and Milton just pulled me back over to hard ground. Then my daughter came along and she started getting up me. "What do you think you're doing?" She didn't see me get chewed up. They flew me into the clinic, and the nursing sister and her assistant stuck me that full of chemicals that I glowed in the dark.'

Bluey carries the memory in scars across his chest, but it hasn't stopped him from collecting eggs, which he continues to do to this day. And when possible, Raine still helps.

'She's been coming out with Milton and me since she was about fourteen,' said Bluey. 'We used to sit her underneath the chopper counting eggs, then we started taking her out onto the easy-to-get nests. I bought her a handgun for her sixteenth birthday, probably to keep all the boys away.'

Among the greatest gifts parents can give their children is the knowledge gained from experience. While Little Milton was taking his first steps in the world, Beau Jones was striding into adolescence. This meant he was ready for *his* education in the art of egg-collecting. After his parents separated, he lived with Dominique, and his sister, Alex, in Katherine but both Jones children from the first marriage were still able to spend time at Coolibah, primarily during school holidays.

'My earliest memory of Coolibah was when a snake coiled up in the air-conditioner outside the house. I remember Grandma [Dominique's mother] shooting the snake with a shotgun and she blew all the air-conditioner out,' recalled Beau. 'I started helping Dad when I was about twelve or so, just tagged around with him and did whatever he was doing. I was [in] Grade 7 when I started egg-collecting, so I would have been twelve. One of Dad's mates came out and filmed a little video of us going round collecting the eggs with Matty. That was my first real one, just going in there and getting the eggs, with Dad and Matty showing me how to do it. I was pretty scared because there were crocodiles everywhere and you didn't know what was behind you or what was next to you. You just got in there, did it, and got out.

'I actually claim saving Dad's life one time. There was this one nest we saw down in this gully. We had to land on top of a hill and we scaled down this big rock face, sort of slid because it was really steep, rocks falling down everywhere. Then we had to wade through this water that was about waist-deep. Got through there, then climbed through these mangroves, there was mud everywhere. Dad's got his head stuck down into the nest and I'm just holding on to him to give him a hand. Then I look at this bubble in the water, and this crocodile came out and I pulled Dad with all my strength, and he's jerked back and the crocodile just snapped around.

'We eventually hunted it away with a stick. We had only one fertile egg in the whole lot and we had to carry that all the way back up. I would have been about fourteen.'

Reflecting the view of many a worker who'd come under Milton's scrutiny, Beau discovered his father was a hard boss.

'I learnt to do what I was told. Mistakes can cost a lot of money, or people can get hurt. I made mistakes, not only with egg-collecting but other things too; like Dad told me to do something and I did it wrong or too early or too late. He was fair but pretty hard. You had to reward yourself. If he told you to do something, you did it and you could be happy for yourself. There was never any real reward from him. It was more like, done, finished.'

It was all part of the Jones rite of passage towards adulthood. For the man in charge, it was a piece of the greater picture that Slim Dusty told of in 'Plains of Peppimenarti'.

To a way of life you people love and prize

PART FOUR

A MAN OF THE LAND AND SKY

CHAPTER 19

KEEPING UP WITH THE JONESES

It was just a few days before Christmas 2009, and the three visitors from Melbourne sat drinking and chatting with their hosts late into the evening in the kitchen of the Coolibah homestead. Suddenly, the relaxed mood was broken by the arrival of an intruder.

'Milton, there's a snake!' said Cristina.

Milton reacted with a cursory look at the floor.

'Oh yeah, you're right,' he said.

'Well, come on, do something,' urged his wife.

The barefooted Milton casually grabbed a roll of Christmas paper and tried to shoo the intruder outside. His lack of haste was abruptly countered by the crack of a stock whip, wielded by his wife. The snake, a non-venomous keelback, was dead but destined to live on in the tales to be told by the three Melburnians.

They'd arrived only the night before to be greeted by Cristina, wearing shorts, a shirt, and wet-season mud. It had been an eventful day for her: she told the visitors that earlier she'd killed a taipan at the back door of the homestead. Later in the night Milton had walked in. He'd been to Katherine to pick up a few horses, but what should have been a relatively easy trip had turned into a drain on hours and patience when his truck became bogged on the drive home.

'He was quite subdued that first night I met him,' remembered Daryl Talbot. 'What Cristina didn't know was that he'd actually gone and bought some tinsel which he wanted to drape around one of the horses because it was Cristina's present. But he was disappointed that in the whole drama of the bogging and unloading of horses he wasn't able to reveal the present the way he'd hoped.'

It was Daryl's earliest insight into a husband and wife he would come to know well. Daryl was managing director of the independent television production company, WTFN. He and his colleagues Steve Oemcke and Damian Estall had gone to Coolibah to talk business. This followed their decision earlier in the year to research heli-mustering in outback Australia as a potential TV series that was similar to the successful American programs *Ice Road Truckers* and *Deadliest Catch* which respectively featured the lives of Alaskan truckies and fishermen in the treacherous Bering Sea.

'We were looking for something that compared in terms of scenery and that sense of wild frontier adventure,' said Daryl. 'After several months ringing around various cattle stations across Australia, our researchers eventually made contact with Milton and Cristina. Our team jumped on a plane, went up and filmed them for a week, and when they got back we knew we basically had what we would call "TV gold".'

They then began pitching the idea to various media organisations. Australia's Ten Network was the most enthusiastic. However, it wasn't interested in the 'adrenalin-filled, blokey version' that WTFN proposed, but was intrigued by the prospect of following the ebbs and flows of life on a remote station. Consequently, WTFN reworked their pilot program, Network Ten liked what it saw, and a series was one step closer. At that stage, WTFN had no formal arrangement with Milton and Cristina, so Daryl and his colleagues headed to Coolibah. They began discussions the morning after they arrived, going from LandCruiser to helicopter as they joined Milton on his station rounds, feeding pigs, checking on stock, and always finding one more job to do. It wasn't until beers spilled into the conversation at the end of the day that everyone loosened up, and Daryl felt 'a bit of a rapport' had been established.

'My impression was of a man who was focused on what he wanted to do. He wasn't easily persuaded and he was quite considered,' said Daryl. 'He said to me up front: "I'm not much for reading and writing, so when it comes to that, ultimately it will be Cristina." I had long discussions with Milton and Cristina about what we'd do and I kind of thought we'd reached an agreement, but then the next day we were sitting round having breakfast before we were due to leave and Milton turned to Cristina and said: "Well, it's now up to you. Do you want to do this?" I could see it was something that Milton wanted to do but if Cristina didn't want it to happen, that was it. That was a really telling moment; it told us a lot about the relationship between Cristina and Milton. Milton is the front man but Cristina is certainly his rock.'

Cristina's answer was confirmed by the arrival at Coolibah of a television production crew in February 2010. By then, Milton and his staff had constructed a number of demountables to be used as the crew's living and working quarters. Plumbing, electricity, phones and internet connections were also provided. For the following six months, as many as five people at any one time – cameraman, sound recordist, film producer, series producer, executive producer – helped document life on the station. The logistics and remoteness ensured the project was challenging, and in preparation WTFN went as far as arranging a psychologist to meet with the production team before filming began to discuss potential problems such as loneliness and close-quarters living.

Keeping Up with the Joneses was first broadcast as a one-hour program across Australia in October 2010. The following fifteen half-hour episodes spanned two series, and have since been shown in Europe, Africa, the Middle East and New Zealand. In this age where television has enabled people to peer into lives far beyond those on the other side of the backyard fence, the revelations of the day-to-day existence at Coolibah have created both an awareness of and fascination about Australian outback living.

'I thought the whole TV thing was a good idea,' said Milton. 'It didn't worry me if I got on bloody camera or not. I just thought it would be a good thing for the kids. And it has been. It's there on the shelf forever. The kids can see what it was like, and this is how it was. It's better than a diary. You couldn't get a better thing than that to keep for your family. It's the same thing with this book. A man could be dead tomorrow.

'I suppose it has made a difference. If you walk down a street in Darwin every bastard knows you. They all say g'day and I think, Who the hell is that? Where do I know you from? It's a bit of a laugh, it doesn't worry me much.'

Keeping Up with the Joneses was an apt title, as Milton and Cristina had shown they weren't only successful but were at the forefront of innovations and new ventures. With Milton indeed the front man and Cristina the chief consultant, adviser, administrator and joint decision-maker, the couple has, in recent years, consolidated some business interests and grown others. Their developments include the securing of an irrigation licence that has allowed them to draw water from the Victoria River, which they've used to grow commercial hay since 2009. This could easily be dismissed in a region that relies on natural grasses to feed stock, but Milton noticed the times were changing, especially during musters when cattle were yarded and waiting to be transported.

'I never wanted to be a farmer, no way, but just the need for hay, well, that's become a big thing. Basically a lot of these places [stations] don't have many staff anymore, so they don't tail the cattle as much as they used to. In twenty years handlin' cattle I never used a bale of hay. For my horses, yes, but not hay for cattle. I always had five or six fellas and we'd let the cattle out after musterin' until the trucks got there and then you put 'em back in. You'd save a couple of good little laneways or paddocks along the main road for it. But now people don't tail any cattle, so they gotta have hay. You might have to leave cattle waitin' for two days, so either they gotta let 'em out, get a helicopter to yard 'em again, or they buy the hay, road trains of hay. Hay and helicopters: for as long as the Territory is here they'll always be needed, I reckon.'

In 2011, Milton and Cristina sold nearly all of the 10 000 bales they produced. Using their own road trains to freight them, they made deliveries in a six-hour radius from Coolibah. In 2012, they bought two new trucks to enhance the operation. It was all part of Milton's general approach, not only to business but to life: 'You have a look at what is needed, and you do it.' Perhaps there was an element of risk when first starting, but Milton was backed by his own judgement.

'I've lived here long enough and I know it,' he said.

The NAH helicopter business has also grown, and now includes a tourism arm, Coolibah Air. In a melding of the old and the new, permission was granted from the Northern Territory government to base a helipad in Darwin for the tourism venture, in addition to helping in emergencies, and servicing the Territory's burgeoning oil and gas industry. In the early stages of seeking approval, Milton met with the man he once knew as 'schoolie', former Epenarra station teacher Gerry McCarthy, nowadays a government minister whose portfolios include Lands and Planning.

'In through the parliamentary office came Milton Jones, an older and larger version, but exactly the same as I remember from the bull-catching days,' said Gerry. 'We shook hands, and he had a bit of a giggle and said: "Doesn't life change people!"'

At the time of this book being written, the NAH fleet consists of 26 R-22s (two-seaters); ten R-44s (four-seaters); four Bell 206 JetRangers (five-seaters); and one Bell 206

LongRanger (seven-seater) – 41 machines. An R-22 costs about $300 000, a 44 is between $500 000 and $700 000, and the Bell 206 tops $1 million. The work they do is broad: heli-mustering; feral animal eradication; surveys; spraying; fire control; emergency response; search and rescue; the slinging of loads. Clients range from pastoralists to mining companies, government departments to councils and holiday-makers. A snapshot of activities may include monthly gas pipeline checks where a helicopter takes off and lands in short intervals, sometimes just hundreds of metres; on a recent project a new 260-kilometre road into a mining site had to be mapped out. In 2011, NAH also assisted in search and rescue during the Queensland flood disaster.

While the helicopter now overshadows work in the saddle, it might surprise some to learn that another recent Jones business venture has been the breeding of stock horses. Primarily Cristina's domain, this operation is still in its early stages but it is gaining considerable momentum. The stallions and surrogate mares are based in Tamworth, New South Wales. At a suitable age the progeny are transported to Coolibah, where they are raised.

No matter how the Joneses' business interests have developed, the core of them all remains the piece of marginal country 550 kilometres south of Darwin. When Milton first flew over it, he could never have imagined what it would come to mean to him: a 'rough, little block' that his accountant encouraged him to buy; a central spot from which to launch bull-catching trips; a cattle station; a crocodile farm; a poor cousin to other land bought; a stage for a television series – and a home.

CHAPTER 20

A KIND-HEARTED BUGGER

Several years ago Milton was running a yard near Gregory National Park when he stopped for a break at the Victoria River Roadhouse. In the distance, towards Coolibah, the sky was blackened by storm clouds. No sooner had Milton sat down than he got a call from Cristina.

'The roof's blown off,' she said.

'Oh yeah, you got me,' replied Milton.

'I'm telling you, the roof has blown off the whole house!'

'Jeeesus, has it?!'

Milton returned home immediately to find the roof had 'come off like a can-top' and hit a helicopter about 30 metres away. Air-conditioners that a technician had only finished installing earlier that day were also 'plucked out.' No other building was damaged, and no one was hurt. Neither Cristina nor Milton had seen a 'cock-eyed bob' (sudden storm) like it, but that didn't make it at all unusual. It was simply a moment that demanded an action – 'Yeah, we cleaned up and put the lid back on' – before moving on to the next happening in station life. The way they dealt with the incident was a reflection of the 'expect the unexpected' philosophy that Milton and Cristina adhere to. Over the years, surprises have abounded: an ammonia-like stench that led to the discovery of two king brown snakes mating under a bed; the comings and goings of a drifter known as 'the wheelbarrow man' who stole food from the cold room at night; the phone calls from city-living parents who believed their troubled children would benefit from some hard knocks in the bush; a mob of pigs attacking and eating a bogged cow while it was still alive; the Wets and Drys that defied the weather bureau forecasts; the fluctuations of the market . . . they've all helped to keep Milton and Cristina prepared.

Owning, living on and operating a cattle station is an enormous undertaking for a family at a time when many properties are controlled by corporate empires. In some ways, it's akin to a corner shop taking on Woolworths. A glimpse at everyday logistics on Coolibah gives some indication of the challenges. The electricity supply, depending on the station's demands – they are larger during mustering season when more people are on the property – requires either a 45 KVA or 80 KVA generator, the latter of which costs about $300 a day to run. The household water comes from three sources: rainwater, a river pump and a 120-foot-deep bore powered by a diesel motor that is started every morning and runs for about six hours a day. A typical order of fuel is 60 000 litres, and oil is bought in 1000-litre pods. A television signal is received via a satellite dish, and general communications, including phone, internet and UHF radio all work off a repeater tower that relies on solar power. Food is bought in bulk from a business in Katherine, and is delivered to the front gate every two weeks; in addition to the family's needs, as much as $2000 worth of groceries is ordered for the staff.

Milton and Cristina not only operate Coolibah, but run some cattle – about 14 000 head – on property leased from the Menngen and Wanimiyn Aboriginal Land Trusts, which own blocks that were formerly Innesvale and Fitzroy stations: in all, about 4856 square kilometres or 1.2 million acres.

'I've leased these places around us knowin' that I only want 'em for ten years or so,' said Milton. 'If I wanted more places I would have kept one, a big one. They are a lot of work, and a lot of responsibility. You know here at Coolibah, you can go away and do a bit of contractin', a bit of crocodile work, a bit of buffalo, muck around with a few horses. You're not sort of tied to it. If you've got 30 000 or 40 000 head of cattle she's all day every day. But here it's a good life; you can do a bit of this and a bit of that.'

As many as 30 people may work on the station when it's at its busiest during mustering, but these days the full-time staff comprise a head stockman, mechanic, bore-runner, gardener (Lurch), governess and cook. Amid the positions of necessity, there is room for sentiment and loyalty. Former truck driver, Jim Dooley, who has worked for Milton for more than twenty years but is now in declining health, is also kept on the books. He is still given jobs to do, and waits for them while drawing back slowly on his rollies at the station hands' quarters. When he tells Milton he's ready to work, his boss might reply: 'You got enough fight in you for a willie wagtail to beat an emu, I reckon, Jim.'

'You don't find those old fellas like Jim and Lurch anymore,' said Milton. 'They're good old men, good on machinery. You know they'll get the best out of everything you got. They don't wreck anything. You know, drive steady; that's what you want in the bush.'

While clichés suggest that the ruggedness of an outback character is moulded by a life in the outdoors, this isn't necessarily so. Traditionally, station cooks can be as tough and colourful as the people they feed. Through the years some have gone bush to escape a life, or patch one up. Perhaps they have gone to lose themselves *or* find themselves. Whatever the case, they inevitably come with recipes in their minds and spice in their stories. Trevor Easton has been the Coolibah cook for more than four years. His favourite dish is bacon-and-egg pie – 'I make me own pastry' – and his secret to a luscious mashed potato is half a carton of cream. But a search further back than Trevor's meals finds the miles of a man in his early sixties whose journey to the kitchen was via many a detour rather than a clear-cut path.

Trevor, the son of a butcher, was the youngest of nine children who grew up with working-class grit in Newcastle, northern England. He went to Brownrigg School in the rural setting of nearby Northumberland. This wasn't only a place of learning for students, but also for the administrators who were in charge of one of England's earliest co-educational boarding schools; in some quarters it was considered to be a sociological experiment.

'There were three barracks down the bottom for the males, and three barracks at the top for the girls. A big lawn separated them, but we learnt a lot about the birds and the bees at an early age,' said Trevor, laughing while he sat in his kitchen, a bottle of beer resting on the dining table in front of him. 'I learnt to cook at the school. Because I didn't like religion, I had a choice of switching to domestic science. I didn't know what it was but I said I'd give it a go. And I went into this classroom and it was full of girls. I had to learn to sew and knit as well. It was an interesting school. There were a lot of head-bangers there, used to come from bad upbringings.'

As much as he may have become familiar with saucepans, Trevor preferred holding reins. His father had cart-horses, which Trevor learnt to steer onto the Newcastle beaches to collect coal when he was just two years old. By the time he went to Brownrigg he was a competent rider, and joined the school's pony club for 'five bob a week extra.' One of his teachers, who was a keen fox-hunter and show-jumper, arranged for Trevor to work at a hunting stable. The early-morning duties of shovelling manure and mixing feeds gave the young Easton a greater feel for what he wanted to do for a full-time job, so when he left Brownrigg as a fourteen-year-old and 'six-stone wet through', he gained a jockey's apprenticeship. However, no amount of ambition and dedication could overcome his biggest rival in racing: the adolescent growth spurt. Within three years he was too heavy for the flats, and began going over the jumps, or 'joomps' as his accent styled them.

'I rode about 30 winners in England, flats and jumps, and had a few spills. I rode with some of the best, like old Scobie Breasley and Ron Hutchinson [Australian-born jockeys who achieved great success in Britain and Europe], but I was only a kid then. Old Scobie beat me one day at Salisbury on the flats. I thought, I'm going to get this – there was about 15 yards to go and I was about two, three lengths clear – but like an idiot, I had the lot chasing me and I had a quick look to the right-hand side to see where they were. Well, old Scobie was on the other side, wasn't he? He just went *boom*, and on the post he beat me by half an inch. I was disappointed in meself and I got a bollocking off the boss for looking around, but old Scobie came up, gave me a pat on the shoulder and said, "It happens to all of us, we've gotta learn somewhere. I knew I was going to get you because I saw you keep looking. That's why I went on the other side; you didn't have a clue where I was."'

By the time he was 21, Trevor had chosen to look only ahead when, at the encouragement of a mate, he decided to come to Australia: 'It cost me ten quid, the best ten quid I ever spent!' He first worked in Sydney as a labourer before his ability on the knife, a skill he'd learnt from his father, led him to a boning room and then a butcher's shop. The thought of better money soon lured him to Hobart, where he completed a blackjack course and became a croupier at Wrest Point Casino, and later in Launceston. While working his way up he'd also been a room service attendant: 'I even got a dollar off Roy Orbison one night.'

Throughout all this, he continued riding and shoeing horses. His highlight came when he was on board Stop and Think, 'the best jumper I ever had' on its way to winning the Tasmanian treble: the Hobart Cup Hurdle, the

Geoffrey Hardman Hurdle in Launceston and the National Steeplechase at Deloraine. It was a modest reward for someone who regularly went straight from dealing cards on night shift to saddling up for trackwork.

Marriage came, then the first three of four children. A move to the Gold Coast followed; the position as senior pit boss (a gaming supervisor) at Jupiter's Casino was irresistible. As time passed, the kids grew, the marriage faded and folded, and Trevor, by then in his mid-fifties, decided: 'I'll go further afield and see what I can find.' A friend he'd met through racing told him about opportunities on cattle stations. Trevor was interested, so began searching what he came to know as the 'bush bible for jobs', the *Queensland Country Life* newspaper. He worked on three stations over a two-year period before he went back to the bible and looked again.

'This ad said: "Cook and domestic duties wanted for privately owned property." I thought, Oh, they want a sheila. I waited about another week, and the ad was still in there, so I thought I had nothing to lose and just applied for it. Cristina answered the phone. I said: "I'm looking for a job, but I see you're after someone to do domestic duties, so you want a female?" Cristina said: "Oh no, we can find something else for you to do." I told her: "Well I'm a butcher and a farrier." Her ears pricked up and she said: "I'll ring you back when my husband comes in."

'Half an hour later the phone rang, and Cristina put me onto Milton. He was interested because they had their own butcher's shop there and thought I might be useful. So I came and he gave me a three-month trial. After that I asked him: "Did I pass the test?" And he said: "Oh, I think so." And that's the only compliment I've had off him since I've been here. He's pretty tough. He'll give you a bollocking, or he'll get up you a bit but half an hour later he'll come and have a beer with you. He doesn't worry about it after that. He doesn't hold a grudge.'

For a man who founded some of his greatest experiences on hands and heels, it's the knuckles and nose that tell much about Trevor: he has been in a few scraps in his time and is not one to shade a comment with diplomacy. But his summary of life on the station is positive overall.

'Coolibah is a good life. It has its moments. It's enjoyable. You wish you could get some female company instead of bloody helicopter pilots who aren't my favourite people. Ringers are the same. You get your good ones and your bad ones.'

Cattle may provide the meat, but people provide the backbone of station life. Each individual brings their own skills, ambitions, personality traits and experiences. There are those who are barely old enough to leave home, and those beyond caring where they find themselves and their swag. They all come together to work – men and women. Romances may bloom; lifelong mateships are formed; some threadbare relationships are held together by professional tolerance and bitten tongues; others are beyond repair. Milton has seen them all, been in charge of them all.

'I'm a kind-hearted bugger as a boss,' Milton said with a laugh. 'I've told you I get behind 'em a fair bit. But I set the pace. I don't ask 'em to do somethin' I can't do. You know, I'm gettin' a bit long in the tooth now but I still do a good day's work. I expect a lot from everyone. Well you gotta. You get the job done, and then get on to the next one. I'm gettin' more patience as I get older, I think. I never used to have much patience.'

Coolibah hosts a weekly barbecue, on either Friday or Saturday night, when the Jones family and staff cook a killer and relax with a few drinks. These get-togethers are notable social occasions because apart from the roadhouse 17 kilometres away there are few options for distractions. The nearest station, Willeroo, is about 100 kilometres 'up the road' and the closest settlement, Timber Creek, is a 70-kilometre drive. No one has reason to feel this isolation more than Cristina.

'I probably should go for a drive down to the roadhouse and socialise a little bit more than I do,' she said. 'The days can just go by and suddenly you think you haven't been anywhere for months. One of the reasons why I do campdrafting is to get to events, otherwise I probably wouldn't leave here all year, and I don't think that's a healthy way to live. There's eight or nine that I try and get to without having to go too far. Halls Creek is probably the furthest I'd go. Might be 600 kilometres. I've got to have an interest outside – well, it sort of blends in with Coolibah – but you've still got to do something for yourself.'

Perhaps an understanding of the isolation is best gained in the context of raising a family, where there are no simple comforts such as mothers' groups or child health centres. On 20 December 2010, again in Brisbane, Cristina gave birth to Jack, the first Jones child whose name was chosen by Milton. They returned to Coolibah only after Cristina had endured an extended stay in hospital because of a worryingly low heart rate.

'That was a very difficult time,' she remembered. 'Little Milton was nearly five, and that was quite a demanding age, especially when he hadn't had to share my time particularly with anyone. Milton was away working; he was away a lot early on. And Jack was a real screamer, he just wouldn't stop; I think he must have had reflux, and I was getting up two or three times a night. It was a full-on wet season too; I couldn't even go to Vic River [the Roadhouse] just for a drive. But what do you do? You just got to do it. I haven't really missed support groups; I haven't really thought about it much. It probably would be helpful, even now, but I probably wouldn't set the time aside to do it either. I just like doing my own thing.'

Because of his work, Milton isn't harnessed by the same isolation. Nevertheless, he doesn't feel the 'need to go out and listen to every bastard all the time.'

'But I appreciate Cristina can get frustrated,' he acknowledged. 'We try to get out of here when we can, especially during the wet season when it quietens down. Go away for a couple of weeks, a month or two, but by the end of it we're ready to come home. We go to Darwin a bit, book into a unit, go out to dinner and do some shoppin'. Sometimes to Brisbane too. Cristina's mother and stepfather are there. I don't like cities much – no, I don't like 'em at all. I don't mind Darwin. I know my way around Darwin, I can drive comfortably there, but I wouldn't even try to drive a car in Brisbane. I'd have an accident straight away. The city, there's not much for me.'

Cristina's views are similar.

'I don't mind going down to Brisbane or Sydney somewhere, just for a change and to see different restaurants. I get sick of cooking and thinking of things to cook: how to make the beef tonight. Again! But when we go away it takes me about two weeks to settle down because I just want to come home. I worry about things a lot at Coolibah when I'm away too. And then of course the phone never stops when we're away, so it's not much of a break, really. It's a change of scenery, I guess, but I love coming home.'

So, the bush has become the classroom for the latest generation of Joneses. Little Milton and Jack will both learn to tail weaners and care for their horses. Such basics are fading in the modern age, but to Cristina they provide the foundations for learning about station life. If in the future the boys follow their father's path and become helicopter pilots, they will already be ahead of many because they first understood the basics on the ground.

'Next year [Little] Milton will hopefully do a lot of riding; I've got him a new horse,' said Cristina. 'He's getting old enough now to start exploring and chasing cattle and that sort of thing. I think it's a huge part of his education. Going over to the yards, seeing what's happening, and there's the discipline too: knowing what to do and what not to do.'

Little Milton has begun his formal education through the School of the Air. Supervised by a governess, he sits in his own purpose-built schoolhouse near the homestead and follows lessons broadcast from the central base in Katherine. Unlike his dad, who struggled through correspondence sessions, Little Milton has the advantage of regular Skype tutorials. When considered old enough, he'll be sent away to boarding school in a capital city. It's a way that Jack will follow. And after that . . .

'I would like them to come back here and be involved somehow in the businesses but they need to be educated to do it too. But that's a long way off, I think,' said Cristina.

The growing up of all four Jones children has been an education not only for the youngsters, but their father too.

'I've learnt a bit over the years, I'd say,' admitted Milton. 'I'm havin' a lot of fun with Jack. He's the first one I've really been there to see walk for the first time. It's great. This is the first year [the 2011–12 wet season] I haven't been away egg-collectin'. I've done it for nearly twenty years, and the rest of the time you're away musterin', but now that I've stopped a bit I'm seein' more of Jack than the lot of 'em, really.

'It's nice to see Jack and Milton grow. Milton is learnin' the ways. There was a dead blood finch on his trampoline not long back. He brought it over to me in the kitchen. He was feelin' sad about it. It's all part of it.

'It's great fun with Beau. We don't see much of each other. [Beau and Alex both attend boarding schools at the Gold Coast and split their holidays between staying with Dominique in Katherine and visiting Coolibah.] Some stories I've forgotten about, he remembers. He's had a lot of excitin' times, Beau, he has been to a lot of places in helicopters with me and done a lot of egg-collectin' and shootin' killers. He's a bloody good shot, I'll give him that. Geez, he can shoot. He's as good a shot as I've seen, I reckon. That's honest. Out of an aircraft or on the run, he's a great shot. I think he's gonna be a lot like me. I just see him and he acts like me and thinks like me:

the way he moves and that, I've been watchin' him. He hooks in. He's a good little worker. Strong.

'When Alex comes to Coolibah she really puts in. She gets on a horse, she's good in the yard, she can drive a car good, helps Trevor do a bit of cooking. She likes the outdoors a lot more than inside. Her education is goin' well, she's rowing now. You look at all the kids and you see a bit of yourself in 'em. It makes you feel good, real good. I think Jack will be the one that'll be here. I don't know why, but I reckon he's the one that's gonna be on the land. I think all the others will get into somethin' else. It's what makes 'em happy, you know. I'm not one for dynasties or anythin' like that. I've seen a lot of that and you see what can happen. The first generation get it, the second generation work it and make the fortune, and the third generation lose it. You hear a lot of it. But anyway, that's all to come isn't it?'

And who knows where the Territory cattle industry will be by the time any of the Jones children are grown up? Once again, the maxim is 'expect the unexpected'. A basic understanding of how to run a station like Coolibah can be gleaned by examining the logistics of the yearly stock cycle. It must be noted that Milton has only Brahman and Brahman-cross cattle, while some stations still run the longer-haired Shorthorn.

'You have a look at a Shorthorn beast to a Brahman beast in the paddock,' said Milton. 'One is slab-sided and ribby, the other has got a bit of condition on him. Brahman are just a lot better do'ers. You get 'em to the market quicker, and ticks are a big thing. Shorthorn cattle, ticks suck 'em alive.'

At Coolibah, the cattle cycle gains momentum at the beginning of March when the staff numbers increase in preparation for the first muster. Phone calls are made and received months and weeks earlier to determine jobs and trials; since the *Keeping Up with the Joneses* television series there has been a noticeable increase in the number of hopefuls making contact from New Zealand. However, the overall search for employees has become more difficult because of competition from the much more lucrative mines across the Top End and in Western Australia.

'It's hard to keep people out here,' acknowledged Cristina. 'You can probably get a job with half the hours for twice the money, more benefits, whatever. Young fellas in the mines can earn 150 grand. How do you compete with that? I guess it's a certain type of person who comes here. It's not everyone's cup of tea. I think the first job I had on a station was $180 a week, and that was great money. When I got up to $360, I thought, Gee, that's good, that's really good. You basically had to save every cent to get home.'

Depending on the type of season, it's likely still very wet at Coolibah in March. The 'big rains' have gone, but the creeks are still flowing and there is plenty of surface water. One of the first jobs is to cut hay, both natural grasses and fertilised pastures. This four- to six-week period gives Milton a chance to cast his eyes over his new workers and determine 'Who I want and who I don't want. You put 'em on tractors, and see what they can do. It all comes down to who's got common sense and who doesn't.'

The grunts of a grader will also be heard, for as soon as it's dry enough, all the roads on the station that will be used during the muster are prepared for heavy vehicle use. Bores are also serviced and started, portable yards are built, floodgates are pulled up, and 'You get your choppers in and away you go.' The first-round muster begins in early April. Generally, the Fitzroy-leased area is the starting point because it's predominantly red soil and dries out the quickest, meaning easier access. However, this may vary from year to year. As is the way with most stations, there is no set routine. But there is usually a constant: 'one paddock at a time.'

Milton works on a success rate of mustering 70 to 80 per cent of all stock during the first round. The sale cattle are mostly weaners. They're separated and put on trucks back to the yards near the homestead for processing. The same happens to cleanskins to be culled. Calves are branded and 'put back onto mum', while joiner heifers (heifers about to join the herd as breeders) are placed in their own area before it's decided what paddocks need 'toppin' up with more cows.' Dry cattle, mostly steers and spay heifers, go into another paddock. There may also be a need for inoculations against botulism, and there's also the application of the 'law of the gun.'

'That's my motto,' said Milton. 'What's left behind, you go through with a gun and clean it out. Every year you shoot just one or two paddocks, big paddocks with a river system through 'em. Keeps it so much easier and tidy. You might see a cow and a little calf or a good cow here or there, and that's no worries, just leave 'em. But if you see them bastards hangin' in the corner of the paddock with horns and teeth and ears, clean 'em up. Finished, done. Put a bullet in 'em, one behind the shoulder and keep goin.' It's sensible management.'

After the first round ends in late May or June, general station maintenance takes place. During this two-month period the number of workers is cut back, and Milton may go away either bull-catching or contracting. Then the second round begins in September, and lasts another two months or more. A success rate here is about 90 per cent because conditions are drier, the land is more accessible, and the cattle come together more readily.

Activities slow down towards the end of the year when the wet season closes in. In the early weeks of the New Year, Milton and the family try to go away before thoughts of another muster come around all too quickly.

The cattle cycle is driven by dollars and sense. You need only look at the cost of servicing a herd to see the money add up, and the level of management needed.

'You'd want about 5 per cent of bulls to your cows if you could afford it,' said Milton. 'Depends on the country. Where you got windmills and bores, and you know your cattle are all on the one water it can be less, but we're on the river so you want plenty of bulls all over. As many as you can get. But they're expensive; 50 bulls to a thousand at about two and a half grand a pop. We've got about 8000 cows at the moment. We just buy paddock bulls now. Geez, they're dear, the bastards, you buy 'em and that's the end, you never see 'em again. You put 'em there and you might get $800 for 'em in five years' time. If you get five or six years out of 'em they're done. They're two years old when you get 'em, and seven or eight when they're done. Sometimes you gotta leave behind a few Mickeys [young cleanskin bulls] in that river country. You'll always miss a few of 'em anyway.'

As with the majority of Northern Territory stations, Coolibah provides only for the live export trade. Some areas closer to Queensland, particularly in the Territory's south-east, sell 'back inside', but the trucking costs for most pastoralists make this an unviable option. The growing of 'heavy beasts' is pointless because there is no market for them, unlike in other parts of Australia. Time is also a factor: in such marginal country it could take six or more years to 'grow a bullock out.' The priority is therefore on younger cattle, weighing from about 270 to 350 kilograms.

'A road train of export cattle, you're lookin' at $100 000 a load,' said Milton. 'Fifteen hundred to 1800 steers at $500 or $600 a head. I select 'em here, then we send 'em up to a little place I got out of Darwin, it's 14 square kays; we can run about 1500 to 2000 head of cattle on it at a good time. And they're sold from there. The agent and the buyer will come out, they'll run 'em through and say: "This one, this one, don't want that one, that one." They just about take everything because we pre-select here. So, there's no rubbish that we send up there, it's all straight ahead. We'll send up about 4000 over the year. That's the aim. We'll produce about 3500 here ourselves a year and probably buy in 500 or 1000. I buy cheap cattle wherever I can. And we'll bring 'em here and feed 'em, put 'em in the feedlot, and then I'll box 'em in with another hundred of mine, and then go just tradin'.

'One of the interestin' things is the demand for cattle in the Wet. You gotta keep up that supply. But what happens here, sometimes the roads are closed or affected because the government puts a weight limit on 'em; the big heavy road trains just wreck 'em, so you can't move cattle. You have 'em sort of half-loaded but that gets too expensive. There's quite a bit of floodplain country around Darwin. And now we've got our own block – we've only had it for a couple of years – we can take the cattle from here around first storm time, which is about September, and we'll hold 'em until about January and sell 'em. Then they're close and handy, right on the bitumen, and they're 20 kay from the ship.'

The mere mention of ships and cattle together has become a national polariser. In June 2011, the Gillard federal government suspended the export of live cattle to Indonesia, which represented about 60 per cent of Australia's international live export market. It followed the broadcasting of a report by ABC TV's *Four Corners* program in which horrific images were shown of the inhumane treatment and killing of stock in some Indonesian abattoirs. The ban, which coincided with the peak selling time during mustering season, lasted a month. Amid political debates, and media reports stating some pastoralists were faced with shooting stock, the cattle industry lost millions of dollars. Sales to Indonesia in 2011 fell by 21 per cent from 2010. After the ban was lifted, the federal government introduced a new Exporter Supply Chain Assurance System, which has increased the responsibilities on exporters before they are granted licences. At the time of writing, there are reports that the Indonesian government is considering changes to its import permits. In a volatile industry, there is continuing uncertainty.

Milton wasn't affected by the ban, and has had no problems since.

'We've been pretty fortunate because I got a good relationship with one of the biggest exporters, Suntory. And it was a relationship I earned. A while back I give 'em 12 000 head of cattle and 90 days to pay for 'em. They needed a hand, they were pushin' wind and they approached me and said: "You come over and we'll take all the cattle off you at this rate." It was good money, but they needed 90 days for it to work, and I agreed. No agent was involved. It was a big risk; you know 12 000 head of cattle offshore, you could be done and finished. They took me over to Indonesia and showed me their facilities and what they do and how they do it.

'Anyway, when this crisis hit they actually got in contact with me and said: "Milton, you got any cattle?" And I told 'em I did. So they said: "We'll take your cattle, same deal like before." We didn't argue or anything, it was a done deal. They put 'em on a floodplain straight away. When the export stopped it didn't affect me one inch. We just had to sell 'em a few smaller cattle where they'd make a quid out of 'em on the floodplain; we kept operatin' while a lot of other people were sittin' there chewin' the fat. It's a relationship that we earned. We give 'em credit that once, and they've come back and shown their appreciation.

'It's worked both ways. When Stumpy died in the helicopter crash, and I bought his cattle, about 1000 head, there was a certain amount that needed sellin' straight away. I didn't want to make anything out of it. I just told the Indonesians what had happened and the position the family was in – you know, they might have lost their block – and there were no worries. They were happy to handle it.

'As for the animal welfare, well that's a huge thing with cattle. It wasn't a good thing that they stopped the trade. I think it was very badly handled. We have to look after our cattle here. Our yards, our cattle handlin', our musterin', our truckin' facilities, our shippin' . . . it doesn't get any bloody better than we're doin' in the Territory. It's our livelihood, and it's a matter of pride and respect too for the beasts and the stations, you know. If you get cattle, and they're spooky and touchy and they run onto the truck and they hit their head or they hurt their legs, or if you have a fella mistreatin' 'em with a stick or you knock an eye out or somethin' like that, they reject 'em. If we send 'em to Darwin and they're not good and happy, the vet will say "no" to 'em, or they'll be in the feed yard wearin' my brand and the exporters will say: "No, we don't want any more of 'em." And that's not a good reputation to have. You can go into buyers' offices and they'll have all the names of the properties they're buyin' cattle off and they'll just class 'em with a star. Five stars back to one. Five is very good, buy as many as you can. That's what we want. That's what the industry wants.'

Typically, the cruellest handler of stock in northern Australia is the most uncontrollable: the weather. In 2009 and '10, Milton experienced two of the hardest dry seasons he'd ever seen when rain at Coolibah finished in March and didn't come again in healthy falls until Christmas time. The stock, particularly old cows were 'knocked around.' Whole road-train loads of hay were taken around and dropped at bores, but this didn't altogether stop the need to look at some cattle through a rifle sight.

'You just gotta do it,' acknowledged Milton. 'We'd go out and have a look all the time and you see an old cow there with a big weaner on her, and she can't get up or she's just about ready to go down, you're better off shootin' 'em than lettin' 'em die slow.'

Ironically, the rain became a killer too: water in creeks and gullies, mud on the banks, and cattle too weary to haul themselves through the bogs. No matter when the dry season ends, there is always the hope that an early fall isn't 'four or five inches in one hit' but a steady soaker that puts some feed on the ground, enabling the cattle to 'get their feet back under 'em.'

The weather dictates behaviour and fortunes: 'If you've got the rain you load up the numbers and buy a few in, but if you haven't got it, you sell. That's about how it works.' But there can be an element of rolling the dice. A poignant example is the conspiracy played by the recent dry seasons and the export trade. The weight limit on cattle sent to Indonesia is 350 kilograms. This means young cattle. In a bid to keep money coming in during the hard times some pastoralists gambled on selling heifers – or they had no financial choice – but in doing so they cut back on the potential breeding numbers in their herds. And when the dry seasons killed some of the older and less resilient cows, there were prospects of idle hands at branding time. Further down the line, old and depleted herds can lead to station owners swinging gates for the last time.

The hinges haven't rusted over at Coolibah. When assessing his and Cristina's success in operating a cattle station, Milton sat back, folded his arms behind his head, and said: 'It takes about a million bucks a year to live here and run it. A million to live here and a million in the bank, that's about the plan. You know, you gotta work your country how it will work for you. You can't change it. Jesus, think about it, it takes about a million bucks just to sit here.'

CHAPTER 21

A GOOD LIFE

Story-telling in the bush is an art. It has existed in various forms for thousands of years: some Aboriginal paintings sheltered in shade on a Coolibah rock face are testament to that. In the pastoral age, yarns that are true or false or embellished have long been heard from campfire to living room, fence-post to saddle. Life would be dull without them.

'We all try and tell stories of what's goin' on and where,' said Milton. 'I don't mind tellin' a story. What else you got to do in the bush, eh? I come through the era when there was no TV and we didn't have a lot of things, and all you did at night-time was sit around and tell stories. Some stick with you a bit, but no, I don't really have a favourite. One will hang around for twelve months, and you'll get another one and use it for twelve months and get another and use it. They tend to sort of fade out after a while.'

In the time spent digging into his memory for this book, Milton sidetracked onto many an anecdote. Some were mentioned as little more than asides, like the story of the bloke who was so afraid of the dark that every time he closed a gate at night he'd turn his vehicle around so the headlights lit every step of his way; or the myall fella who literally believed a 'black band' had been placed around a truck to stop it delivering cattle to a meatworks during an industrial dispute, or the one about the pack of dingoes swinging off a fully grown cow that was about to calve: 'had the ears pulled off her, the bastards'; or the five men who were fast asleep when Milton and Kurt tossed a 14-foot python onto them, and in panic one dashed away only to slam his head straight through a fibro wall.

Other recollections came wrapped in advice:

'If you lose a dog, pull your shirt straight off where you lost him and chuck it on the ground. Come back next day and he'll be layin' on your shirt, nine times out of ten. He'll stay there with your shirt, but if you don't he'll trot along lookin' for you. Or light a little fire, even better. Everything will come to fire, believe it or not. You light a fire and it's a homely thing, if you know what I mean. And you can smell fire from a long way. I know I can smell a fire for miles if you get the right mornin' or the breeze is goin' the right way. It's common sense in the bush.'

And then there were the conversations whose direction shifted mid-sentence, such as the time an observation about fat heifers turned from: 'Look good, don't they?' to . . .

'On the Roper, fishin'. We all went down there fishin', and we were all drunk on rum. So we got there and the mosquitoes! *Jeesus* Christ, you've never seen anything like it. They could eat you alive. We've got all these mud crabs and rum and we're sittin' down on the bank and you couldn't get out of the flame of the fire otherwise these mosquitoes would eat you alive. We're there and we've had this big feed of crab. Anyway, Kurt is gonna choke down [go to sleep] and I said: "Take them bloody trousers off before you go in there. You got crab and mud all over you, you bastard." You see, we had to share a swag because there wasn't enough room in the boat for both of us to take one. So he's lay down there in his swag and he's got no trousers on, must have had underpants on. And I just got that sheet and I pulled it back when he's choked down. The rest of us was all there still drinkin' rum. Anyway I pulled that sheet down and the mosquitoes just hit him. All over the arse they hit him. They near carried him away.

'The next mornin' we were just gonna run this bloody net and Kurt's in the boat and he couldn't sit still. And I said: "What's wrong with you?" He dropped his dacks and showed us, and Christ, I've cruelled him! They near ate him alive, chewed the piss out of him. He wouldn't have felt anything. The rum had him.'

Many of the stories represented mischief that spans both the past and present; Milton thrived on being in the middle of the actual happenings, and so many years later there was a boyish enthusiasm, at times a sense of cheeky wickedness, in reliving them. All the recollections, no matter what mood or theme they reflected, were a portrait of a man whose bush identity could never be mistaken. But when he was asked to describe himself . . .

'Me? Oh, I dunno. It's hard to look from inside out. You gotta look from outside, don't you?'

So, we do. Through his stories.

'Did I tell you that one where we were runnin' this yard? We had the crush and the loadin' ramp set up and bloody wings and we thought we were gonna get about 300 head of cattle. We got about 1100 I think it was, and we were a long way to cart 'em too: a rough road, we had to follow the swamp [Arafura] around all the way. Anyway, runnin' this big yard full of cattle, too many. We pulled the crush out and jammed 'em in this yard. They were all wild cattle, you couldn't let 'em out again. And we went two or three days and nights cartin' 'em. I had this front-end loader and I dug a hole – we were right beside this spring, a runnin' creek – to give 'em a drink. I'm there and I got home at about two or whatever time it was in the mornin' after I'd done a couple of loads in the truck and come back. And there was a pump we were waterin' the cattle with; I just left it tickin' over, fillin' the hole up and runnin' back in the creek to keep the water a bit clean for 'em.

'I'm standin' on this pallet with the hose over the top and I'm havin' a bogey [a wash]. It was dark. Moonlight night, that's all. And the buggy's right there, the trousers are on the front seat. Anyway, I got my towel and soap and I'm havin' a wash and next minute, wooh, right here beside me this crocodile has snapped at the bloody water and is hittin' the pallet where the hose is runnin' over.

'I've dived into the front of the motor car and shinned meself. I always carry a gun beside the seat, and I went there and there was no bloody gun. So I started howlin' out. There was about four or five of 'em in the camp and they come runnin' out. I'm yellin: "Where's the friggin' gun?" By that time this thing had turned around and gone back in the water. Bugger that! I cleaned meself up and I actually put me swag in the Toyota. I said to these fellas: "There's a crocodile right there and we're campin' about the same distance off the water. He could come and pull you out of your swag."

'I woke up in the mornin', had a feed, and was loadin' trucks and I see these cattle standin' back, they weren't drinkin'. They were just lookin' in the water. A man knows what's goin' on, and I said to a mob of blackfellas, young fellas: "Get that bit of poly pipe and poke in there, and get that gun." I have a look and I see his track where he's gone in and I knew he was still there, so we lifted him up, I shot him, and we pulled him out . . . about a 12-foot saltie. That was four or five years ago.

'I'll tell you one thing that happened to me the other day, only three or four months ago. I had this bull tied up to a tree at Mistake Creek, a big black Brahman bull he was. Anyway, I put the arm [mechanical] over him, untied him off the tree and pulled him over to the truck. He didn't know what was goin' on, this old bull, and this young fella has come out to put the wire rope on him to pull him in the truck, and the bull saw him and took off and took me round; it was on a bit of laterite, a pebbly ridge. He took me round three times in complete circles in the Toyota. I was sittin' there with the foot on the brake, and he lifted the front wheel right off the ground and the other front wheel was near off it. Three full circles before he stopped. Heavy bull. I thought the bastard was gonna roll me over . . . yeah bulls, I've been belted a few times by 'em.'

Of all the stories he told, it was one of the very last that perfectly portrayed Milton the man in his element: his resilience, his ability to expect the unexpected, turn adversity to opportunity and, most of all, to survive and thrive in an unforgiving land.

'One particular thing I remember, I was at Cherrabun, and there was a lot of big salt flats there and they were wet. Anyway, I tied this bull up, and I took off and got bogged to the arse in this Toyota, right in. I was about 20 metres away from the bull. I thought, Jesus Christ, how am I gonna get out of here? I slipped back and jumped around this bull and pulled him arse over head. He already had a back strap on him, but I scruffed him down and put a front one on too. Then I got all my head ropes – they're about 10 foot long – and I joined 'em together. I had enough rope to go from the Toyota to the bull, so I tied the bastard to the Toyota, then I slipped back and pulled the two straps off him. He hit the end of the rope and kept goin' and away we went. He pulled me out, I got over the other side and scruffed the bastard again, tied him up and kept goin.'

Throughout his life Milton has indeed needed others to help him, but it has been his own intuition and drive that have enabled him to succeed in a part of the world that shows no pity and offers no favours. From his earliest years Milton underwent an education which taught him that success – perhaps even survival – wouldn't come from neat handwriting and gold stars. When just a teenager he put down the pen after the hand that held it slugged authority in Kingaroy. From that moment on, he seemingly skipped his adolescence and hurried into manhood, albeit with a mischievous boyish streak. What followed was an adventurous existence that others, especially city-dwellers, might struggle to fathom. Milton is an authentic product of his environment. Among the dust that dulls the tip of the tongue, the risks to life and limbs, bullets fired at bone-weary beasts, and the myriad other elements that paint the picture of station life, there is a sense of belonging that only bush people, both black and white, truly know. To Milton, this belonging is at his very core. He may say he is best described by looking at him from the outside, but then again . . .

'I love the land, I know how to live off it, and I know my way around pretty well. When you burn a bit of country and you get a storm straight across it and that smell of rain on that burnt grass, well, it doesn't get any better than that. Put your nose in the air and walk through that any time. Or a cattle truck goes past you after you've been in Brisbane or America or somewhere and you smell that shit and piss in it. I reckon that's a bloody good one . . . yeah, not a bad life, eh.'

ACKNOWLEDGEMENTS

This book would never have happened if it wasn't for the enthusiasm and commitment of Milton and Cristina Jones. I thank them both for their hospitality at Coolibah and later during the Katherine campdraft when I returned to read the entire manuscript to Milton in the back of a gooseneck. (The sleeping cabin in the Kenworth was very comfortable!) I appreciate both of them being so forthright and constructive during the whole interview and writing process. A particular thank you to Milton: it's an immense undertaking to open your life up to public exposure. Hopefully, those who read the book, especially those from urban areas, may gain a better understanding and appreciation of remote bush life.

Many people kindly gave their time to be interviewed either in person or over the phone. They each contributed valuable insights into Milton, in addition to their own lives and the ways of the Territory. I am indebted to each of them: Jenny Jones; Terry Jones; Randall Jones; Dominique Jones; Beau Jones; Yindumduma Bill Harney; Robert van Kuijck; Robert Parkinson; Gerry McCarthy; Owen 'Bluey' Pugh; Kip Glasscock; Jim Dooley; Kurt Hammer; Tim Anderson; Matt Wright; Daryl Talbot; and Trevor Easton. A particular thank you to Jenny Jones for also providing some of the photos. My search for interview subjects was made easier at various times by the help of John Moriarty, Ted Egan, Kelly Parkes, and David Robertson.

I am neither a Territorian nor an historian, and therefore had to start from the very basics with research. I am grateful to Belinda Lee, who helped sift through some information and also conducted two interviews. Francoise Barr from the Northern Territory Archives Services was particularly friendly and tremendously helpful. I must also thank Gordon McIntyre from the NT Department of Lands and Planning for providing information about the various stations Milton has bought and sold. Darrell Lewis, whose books about the Territory are exceptional, was also helpful. Much of the information obtained for this book was gained through resources at the Northern Territory Library, the State Library of New South Wales, City of Sydney Library (Glebe), and the Macquarie University Library. My thanks also to Joy McKean for allowing the use of the lines from the Slim Dusty song, 'Plains of Peppimenarti'.

As with the writing of any non-fiction book, the paths of discovery may wind to many diverse places and people. I'm indebted to stock and station agent Bert Hewitt for guiding Milton around the Gunnedah saleyards. Furthermore, thank you to Tom Lyle for driving Milton throughout the district and explaining the intricacies of farm life, and to Hugh Simson for opening Milton's eyes to broad-acre machinery. I must also thank Angus Mundell for flying me in a helicopter from Darwin to Katherine en route to Coolibah.

A very big hug and thank you to Hachette Publisher, Vanessa Radnidge, whose idea it was to write this book. The whole process started with a meeting between Vanessa, Daryl Talbot and me at a Bondi cafe. Daryl was a wonderful 'middle man', and there's no doubt his enthusiasm paved the way for *The Man from Coolibah* to become a reality.

The publishing of a book requires an enormous team effort. In addition to Vanessa, whose enthusiasm over a number of years has kept me writing, I am deeply thankful of the work and support provided by the rest of the team at Hachette: Fiona Hazard, Matt Hoy, Jaki Arthur, Laura Hanly, Kate Flood and Isabel Staas. A special mention to Karen Ward, who did a wonderful editing job, and to Kate Ballard, who coordinated the project. Thanks also to the team at WTFN Entertainment, especially Daryl, Steve Oemcke, Lachlan Ryan and Jayne Pakinga. Thank you too to Jane Burridge for doing the business side that I so hate!

In the sheltered world that writers often plunge into, it's always great to have a few extra sets of eyes to read over the pages. All I can offer Duncan Overton and Dawn Rutledge is a drink and a feed! My thanks to both of you. My number one sounding board was my mother, Anne, a person who remains as much in love with country life now as she was when she was a girl growing up on a sheep station in western New South Wales. Mum, you're the best!

I'm also indebted to my fellow writer Ian Heads, who provided a sound ear and advice.

On a personal note, thank you to my wife Clare for continuing to put up with me. I know it ain't easy!

Most of all, I would again like to thank Milton and Cristina Jones. Because of their warmth and friendliness, I feel as though a part of me has been left in the Territory.

James Knight
June 2012

REFERENCES

Adelaide Now, June 18, 2011.
Austin, Nigel, *Kings of the Cattle Country.* Bay Books, Kensington NSW, 1986.
Bird Rose, Debra, *Hidden Histories: Black stories from Victoria River Downs, Humbert River and Wave Hill Stations.* Aboriginal Studies Press, Canberra, 1991.
Boldrewood, Rolf, *Robbery Under Arms,* [1888], New Holland, Sydney, 2008.
Buchanan, Gordon, *Packhorse and Waterhole.* Hesperian Press, Victoria Park, WA, 1997.
Bulletin, The, March 12, 1991.
Bureau of Agricultural Economics, *The Australian Brucellosis and Tuberculosis Eradication Campaign* (Occasional Paper 97), Australian Government, Canberra, 1987.
Cole, Tom, *Hell West and Crooked.* Collins/Angus & Robertson–Imprint, North Ryde, NSW, 1990.
Conservation Commission of the Northern Territory, *The Early History of The Animal Industry in the Northern Territory,* NT Government, 1985.
Coutts, Toni Tapp, *Bill Tapp: Cattle King.* Katherine, NT, 2010.
Duncan, Ross, *The Northern Territory Pastoral Industry 1863–1910.* Ross Duncan/Monash University Press, 1967.
Durack, Mary, *Kings in Grass Castles.* Corgi Books, Moorebank NSW, 1990.
Durack, Mary, *Sons in the Saddle,* Hutchinson Australia, 1984.
Flood, Josephine, *The Original Australians.* Allen & Unwin, Crows Nest, NSW, 2006.

Harney, Bill, Yidumduma with Wositzy, Jan, *Born Under the Paperbark Tree.* ABC Books, Sydney, 2008.

Hill, Ernestine, *The Territory.* Walkabout Pocket Books, Sydney, 1970.

Ingham, Anne Marie, *The Boss Drover.* Halstead Press, Rushcutters Bay, NSW, 1990.

Ingham, Anne Marie, *Wild Cattle, Wild Country,* Halstead Press, Braddon, ACT, 2007.

Johannsen, Kurt, *A Son of the Red Centre,* Published by Kurt Johannsen, Morphettville, SA, 1992.

Leichhardt, Ludwig, *Journal of an overland expedition in Australia.* 1847.

Lewiston Journal, 9 April 1986.

McCall, Luke, *Before Helicopters and Roadtrains: what was expected of a stockman.* Longreach, QLD: Australian Stockman's Hall of Fame & Outback Heritage Centre, 2000.

McLaren, Glen, *Big Mobs: The Story of Australian Cattlemen.* Fremantle Arts Centre Press, Fremantle, WA, 2000.

McLaren, Glen and Cooper, William, *Distance, Drought and Dispossession: A History of the Northern Territory Pastoral Industry.* Northern Territory University Press, Darwin, 2001.

Ogden, Pearl, *Bradshaw via Coolibah: The History of Bradshaw's Run and Coolibah Station*, Historical Society of the Northern Territory, Darwin, 1989.

Ogden, Pearl, *Chasing Last Light: Aerial Mustering 1968–1978.* Published by Pearl Ogden, Winnellie, NT, 2000.

The Oxford Companion to Australian History, Eds: Davison, Graeme, Hirst, John, Macintyre, Stuart, Oxford University Press, 2001.

Pike, Glenville, *Frontier Territory.* Cosmos Printing Press, Hong Kong, 1972.

Port Arthur News, 5 January 1986.

Powell, Alan: *Far Country: A Short History of the Northern Territory.* Charles Darwin University Press, 2009.

Queensland Country Life, 25 November 2004.

Searcy, Alfred, *By Flood and Field: Adventures ashore and afloat in northern Australia,* G. Bell & Sons, 1912.

Stevens, Frank, *Aborigines in the Northern Territory Cattle Industry.* Australian National University Press, Canberra, 1974.

The Age, 22 February 2006.

The Austin Chronicle, 22 October 1986.

The Mail, 19 December 1931.

The Mercury, 17 December 1949.

The Sydney Morning Herald, 28 January 1987.

The Sydney Morning Herald, 22 February 2006.

The Sydney Morning Herald, 17 March 2008.

The Telegraph, 8 June 2011.

SELECTED WEBSITES

Preface

http://www.naa.gov.au/collection/fact-sheets/fs176.aspx (Cyclone Tracy)
http://www.abc.net.au/nt/stories/s1255740.htm (Cyclone Tracy)
http://www.disasters.ema.gov.au/Browse%20Details/DisasterEventDetails.aspx?DisasterEventID=2174 (Cyclone Tracy)
http://www.ga.gov.au/education/geoscience-basics/landforms/longest-rivers.html (Victoria River)
http://www.enotes.com/topic/List_of_pastoral_leases_in_Western_Australia (WA pastoral leases)

Chapter One

http://www.pleasetakemeto.com/australia/outback-queensland/hydro-power-plant-9049554 (Thargomindah)
http://www.qhatlas.com.au/content/channel-country (Channel Country)
http://queenslandplaces.com.au/channel-country (Channel Country)
http://www.ridji-didj.com/Links/BillHarney.aspx (Bill Harney)

Chapter Two

http://www.accidentallyoutback.com.au/news/1408-min-min-light-festival (Min Min)
http://www.schools.nt.edu.au/ksa/ (School of the Air)

Chapter Three

http://www.nt.gov.au/d/Primary_Industry/index.cfm?Header=Portrait%20of%20the%20NT (Cattle history)
http://www.supremecourt.nt.gov.au/archive/doc/judgements/2001/0/NS000030.htm (BTEC)
http://www.daff.qld.gov.au/documents/Biosecurity_EnvironmentalPests/IPA-Water-Buffalo-Risk-Assessment.pdf (Water buffalo)
http://www.sacredland.org/mcarthur-river/ (McArthur River)

Chapter Four

http://sites.google.com/site/ntpmhsociety/our-rich-history/timeline-and-events/major-crimes-and-investigations/larry-boy-manhunt (Larry Boy manhunt)

Chapter Five

http://www.imdb.com/title/tt0090555/ (Crocodile Dundee)
http://www.mckellarangus.com/aboutus.htm (Doc McKellar)
http://www.genaust.com.au/about-us/history (Artificial insemination in cattle in Australia)

Chapter Six

http://www.dec.wa.gov.au/component/option,com_hotproperty/task,view/id,39/Itemid,755 (Bungle Bungles)
http://register.heritage.wa.gov.au/PDF_Files/O%20-%20A-D/Ord%20River%20Homestead%20(P-AD).PDF (Ord River station)
http://www.horseclipping.com.au/horse-clipping-articles/1987/2/28/the-outbacks-wild-men-take-to-the-skies/ (Stuart Skoglund)
http://www.robinson.com.au/monoartpapers/papers/mengel.htm (BTEC)

Chapter Seven

http://www.agric.wa.gov.au/PC_91764.html (Phosphorus in cattle)
http://www.abc.net.au/rural/content/2012/s3469320.htm (Ian McBean)
http://oa.anu.edu.au/obituary/bradshaw-joseph-joe-144 (Joseph Bradshaw)
http://www.nt.gov.au/d/Content/File/p/Anim_Man/771.pdf (Waybills)
http://www.securitychallenges.org.au/ArticlePDFs/vol3no4DibbandBrabinSmith.pdf (Kangaroo '89)

http://www.dpi.vic.gov.au/agriculture/farming-management/nlis/cattle (National Livestock Identification System tags)

http://www.ntca.org.au/_assets/2009_LivestockAct.pdf (Northern Territory Livestock Act)

http://www.sydneymedia.com.au/html/2280-city-of-sydney---a-snapshot.asp (Size of Sydney)

http://www.expedition360.com/australia_lessons_history/2001/10/gregory_national_park.html (Gregory National Park)

Chapter Eight

http://www.loansense.com.au/historical-rates.html (Interest rates)

Chapter Nine

http://www.mindshop.com.au/agridata2.nsf/bf72908c94ac495e4a2567ff00837a6b/d145793e214c3df0ca2568b600580901/$FILE/Crocodile%20Review%20PDF.pdf (Crocodiles)

http://www.abc.net.au/news/2011–11–15/obama-given-croc-insurance/3673476 (Crocodiles)

http://www.crocfarmsnt.com/saltwater_croc.aspx (Crocodiles)

http://en.travelnt.com/library/downloads/KidsCrocs_INTL.pdf (Crocodiles)

http://www.nretas.nt.gov.au/__data/assets/pdf_file/0018/7353/crocodile_science.pdf (Crocodiles)

http://www.abc.net.au/btn/story/s3435051.htm (Crocodiles)

http://australianmuseum.net.au/Estuarine-Crocodile (Crocodiles)

Chapter Ten

http://www.supremecourt.nt.gov.au/archive/doc/sentencing_remarks/0/93/0/NS000970.htm (Killarney Station/Tapp Family)

http://www.supremecourt.nt.gov.au/archive/doc/sentencing_remarks/0/96/0/NS000890.htm (Killarney Station/Tapp Family)

http://www.heleneyoung.com/2010/02/toni-tapp-coutts-life-in-the-top-end-and-another-copy-of-border-watch-to-win/ (Killarney Station/Tapp Family)

http://www.abc.net.au/rural/content/2010/s2966220.htm (Killarney Station/Tapp Family)

Chapter Eleven

http://www.setexasrecord.com/arguments/205579-beaumonts-main-event (Walter Umphrey)

http://www.forbes.com/forbes/2001/0514/134.html (Walter Umphrey)
http://www.provostumphrey.com/Attorneys/Thomas-W-Umphrey.shtml (Walter Umphrey)
http://www.tortreform.com/files/HidingTheirInfluence.pdf (Tobacco five)
http://northaustralianhelicopters.com.au/about/ (NAH–helicopters)

Chapter Thirteen

http://www.harryredford.com.au/about.aspx (Harry Redford)
http://adb.anu.edu.au/biography/blakeney-charles-william-3012 (Judge Blakeney)
http://www.govhouse.wa.gov.au/governors-role-link/governor%E2%80%99s-biography.html (Malcolm McCusker)
http://www.livecorp.com.au/About/Trade_History.aspx (Live exports)
http://www.abc.net.au/rural/news/content/201007/s2965256.htm (Live exports)
http://www.livecorp.com.au/About/Trade_History.aspx (Live exports)
http://adl.brs.gov.au/data/warehouse/pe_abarebrs99001344/ab07.1_live_cattle.pdf (Live exports)
http://www.environment.gov.au/biodiversity/invasive/publications/pubs/buffalo.pdf (Water buffalo)
http://buffaloaustralia.org/web/nt.html (Water buffalo)
http://aciar.gov.au/files/node/452/mn95.pdf (Indonesia beef industry)
http://www.teachers.ash.org.au/dnutting/germanaustralia/e/lchtname.htm (Snowdrop Creek)
http://ebooks.adelaide.edu.au/l/leichhardt/ludwig/l52j/chapter14.html (Leichhardt)
http://acms.sl.nsw.gov.au/_transcript/2007/D00007/a313.html#a313009 (Leichhardt)

Chapter Fourteen

http://www.abc.net.au/rural/content/2007/s2148964.htm (Katherine flood)
http://www.ourterritory.com/Katherine_NT/katherine_flood_january_1998_information.htm (Katherine flood)

Chapter Fifteen

http://qcl.farmonline.com.au/news/state/property/general/london-calling-why-we-bought-tanumbirini/2505383.aspx?storypage=2 (Sterling Buntine)

Chapter Sixteen

http://www.aaco.com.au/_upload/20070426081344122.pdf (Australian Agricultural Company)

Chapter Seventeen

http://www.atsb.gov.au/publications/safety-investigation-reports.aspx?s=1&mode=Aviation&sort=OccurrenceReleaseDate&sortAscending=descending&printAll=true&occurrenceClass=&typeOfOperation=&initialTab (Air safety)

http://www.atsb.gov.au/media/2485752/ar2011020.pdf (Air crash statistics)

http://northaustralianhelicopters.com.au/about/ (NAH and Albatross helicopters)

http://www.robinsonheli.com/rhc_r22_beta_ii.html (Robinson helicopters)

Chapter Eighteen

http://www.nretas.nt.gov.au/__data/assets/pdf_file/0016/13921/20_arafura.pdf (Arafura Swamp)

http://natgeotv.com.au/tv/outback-wrangler/matt-wright-bio.aspx (Matt Wright)

Chapter Nineteen

http://brownriggschool.co.uk/aboutus.html (Brownrigg School)

http://www.racingvictoria.net.au/p_Ron_Hutchinson.aspx (Ron Hutchinson)

http://www.racingvictoria.net.au/p_arthur_scobie_breasley.aspx (Scobie Breasley)

Chapter Twenty

http://www.abc.net.au/rural/content/2011/s3234584.htm (Live export bans)

http://www.abc.net.au/news/2011–07–06/government-lifts-live-cattle-export-ban/2784790 (Live export bans)

http://au.news.yahoo.com/thewest/a/-/wa/13801501/cattle-industry-battles-losses/ (Live export bans)

GLOSSARY

Barcoo rot	bacterial skin infection
blitz	four-wheel drive truck
bogey	a wash
bull buggy	stripped-down vehicle, usually a Toyota, used to chase and catch cattle
chaining	clearing vegetation with a heavy chain linked between bulldozers
choke down	go to sleep
cleanskins	feral cattle; unbranded
coachers	quiet cattle
donga	makeshift building
dry cattle	cattle without calves
gone flat	sprinting
horse tailer	person who looks after working horses on a station
joiner heifer	heifer sent to join the herd as a breeder

killer	a beast that is shot to provide meat for a station or stock camp
king brown	highly venomous snake
mickey	young cleanskin bull
myall	slow or stupid
nicki-nicki	tobacco
nulla-nulla	club
pink-eye	inflammation of the eyes; conjunctivitis
scruffing	forcing a beast to the ground and holding it on its side
squirt/squirter	pistol
sugarbag	native honey
tailing	use of horses to control cattle while they graze